AUTHORS AND AUTHORITY

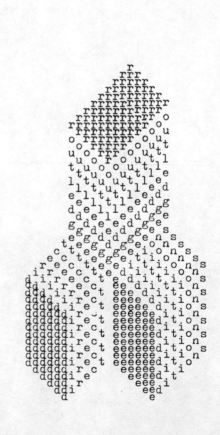

AUTHORS AND AUTHORITY
A Study of
English Literary Criticism
and its Relation to Culture
1750-1900

PATRICK PARRINDER
Department of English
University of Reading

ROUTLEDGE DIRECT EDITIONS

ROUTLEDGE & KEGAN PAUL
London, Henley and Boston

PR63
P3

First published in 1977
by Routledge & Kegan Paul Ltd
39 Store Street,
London WC1E 7DD,
Broadway House,
Newtown Road,
Henley-on-Thames,
Oxon RG9 1EN and
9 Park Street,
Boston, Mass. 02108, USA
Printed and bound in Great Britain
© Patrick Parrinder, 1977

ISBN 0 7100 8502 8

Printed by Thomson Litho Ltd., East Kilbride, Scotland.

CONTENTS

PREFACE

I began writing this book out of dissatisfaction with the view of literary criticism contained in the standard histories. They tended to view the subject either as a timeless theatre of philosophical debate or as a haphazard groping towards the 'correct' procedures enshrined in modern empirical scholarship. The close connections between criticism and the dominant form of literary culture in the past two centuries had never been systematically investigated. It was as if the prestige and influence of Arnold, Leavis and the New Critics had obscured the basic assumptions of modern critical discussion. At the same time, criticism had become institutionalized as an educational discipline. In switching from the philological to the critical study of literature, university English departments had done their best to monopolize the available notions of the function of criticism. The feeling that academic criticism may have overreached itself lies behind recent discussions of the 'decline of English'.

Among the causes of the present situation is the fact that ever since the romantic period the modern notion of 'literature' has had the force of an ideology. This book aims to review the English critical tradition in which that notion grew and developed. The method adopted is one of textual analysis, and I have tried to do as much justice as was possible within my scheme to the complexity and difficulty of writers like Coleridge and Arnold. While I hope the result will be useful for the interpretation of particular authors and texts, its overall purpose remains a revisionist one.

Material in Chapters 2 and 3 was first used in lecture-courses given at the University of Cambridge between 1969 and 1974. An earlier version of Chapters 1 and 2 was awarded the Le Bas essay prize at Cambridge in 1973. I am grateful to many former colleagues and students for their stimulus and interest, and especially to Dr Iain Wright, with whom I gave a series of seminars on twentieth-century criticism. Unfortunately, considerations of length meant that any discussion of twentieth-century critics had to be excluded from the present volume. My particular thanks are due to Chris Bristow and David Gervais, for their skill and patience in pointing out various errors and crudities in parts of the original manuscript; and to my wife for her support and forbearance throughout.

Reading, 1976   PP

NOTE ON THE TEXT

The publishers wish to point out that, in order to comply with the format of the series, roman type has been used for quoted words and titles which would customarily appear in italic type.

INTRODUCTION

He points the deathbone and the quick are still.
He lifts the lifewand and the dumb speak.
                                        James Joyce

Prophet or pedant; interpreter or judge; the critic stands, often
uncomfortably, between Joyce's two aphorisms. Criticism of literature occupies the space between our modern concepts of 'author'
and 'authority' - concepts which in the romance languages share the
same root in the Latin verb 'augeo'. There is a primal sense,
perhaps, in which the 'auctor' or creator, whether of narratives,
laws or merchandise, possessed all the 'authority' that there was
to be had. But as civilization proceeded by the progressive division of labour, one kind of authority came to be pitted against
another. The native force of the maker or originator was brought
up against the common standards of his society. Scholars find the
origins of literary criticism in scattered comments on writers and
texts; perhaps the first substantial critic is Aristophanes, who
discusses the relative merits of Aeschylus, Sophocles and
Euripides. (1) But the traces of a still earlier situation are
present in the first document of criticism which still has a living
force: the discussion of poetry and poets in Plato's 'Republic'.
Plato speaks of the 'old quarrel between philosophy and poetry'.
In Book Three, he examines poetry from the standpoint of the
interests of the state, and gives the classical exposition of the
theory of censorship. In Book Ten, as if dissatisfied with this,
he returns to the subject and discusses the intrinsic nature of art
in terms of representation. But Plato himself has traditionally
been understood as the most poetic and imaginative of philosophers.
If this is accepted, he can be seen to fulfil all three of the
possible roles of author, of spokesman for external (and ultimately
political) authority, and of critic or aesthetician occupying the
middle ground. In the latter role, he acknowledges the seductive
'natural magic' of poetry, but balances this against the demands
of the reason and concludes that poetry ought to be banned. Of
course, Plato's Republic is an imaginary city, a pattern laid up
in heaven. But in the last two hundred years literary criticism,
or the activity of rationalizing the creative practice of literature, has lost its innocence and acquired a political dimension in

1

the real world. Its modern history involves the history of culture
itself, and of the idea of culture, as well as of particular individuals, doctrines and approaches.

So far we have seen 'authority' as a property of the individual
creator or of the community to whose standards he is expected to
conform. The process of social specialization which leads to the
emergence of critical, historiographical, legal and other separate
areas of intellectual discourse endows the occupants of these
areas with a local and, as it were, delegated authority. As
classical criticism took shape, a number of modes of authority
emerged in critical discourse, which were to define the limits of
the discipline until the time of Johnson. To do justice to the
nature of traditional criticism lies outside the scope of this book.
The kinds of authority which the critics exercised may, however, be
briefly indicated by a contrast of the three major Greek and Roman
commentators on literature: Aristotle, Horace and Longinus.

Aristotle in the 'Poetics' relies on the rigorous prosecution of
an intellectual method. He is able to show poetic phenomena as
ordered and systematic by the use of a technique of logical analysis
applicable to the human world as a whole. It was because he had
already demonstrated the technique elsewhere that he could enter so
swiftly and confidently into the first principles of poetics. At the
same time, this trenchancy of method would be of little account were
it not for the empirical relevance of his distinctions and his
ability to support them with appropriate examples. But the intrinsic grounds of the appeal that he makes remain wholly intellectual,
consisting in his scientific methodology and command of his material.
The gulf between the language of his treatise and that of the
tragedies it surveys is as wide as any to be found in Greek, or any
subsequent, culture.

Horace writes as an established poet. Since his 'Art of Poetry'
takes the form of advice to beginners this alone would make his
words impressive. It is the expression in verse of a cultivated and
learned mind, full of shrewdness and good sense. His observations
draw upon his individual experience both as writer and as audience,
and the value of his criticism stands or falls by his personal
adequacy in each of these roles. Longinus, by contrast, was so
far from being a prominent intellectual that we do not know who he
was. He also presents himself as an 'intelligent reader', but
without Horace's magisterial complacency; for he is neither a
celebrity nor a pioneer. 'On the Sublime' begins with a critique of
an earlier treatment of its subject; it acknowledges itself as one
work among many in a common convention of literary discussion. The
more technical aspect of the convention derives from the discipline
of rhetoric, but this is the source of a limited rather than an
exhaustive methodology. Longinus' analytic, unlike Aristotle's,
is derivative and structures only part of his treatise. What is
outside it includes some vivid practical criticism on texts from
the established canon, as well as general observations drawn from
a shared stock of critical axioms, which the author shows a faint
embarrassment about repeating.

At the risk of being over-schematic, then, each of the three
critics assumes a different basis for his authority. Aristotle
relies on the consistency of an intellectual method and its

verifiability; Horace principally on the force of his literary
personality; and Longinus on the cogent manipulation of methods and
assumptions which are shared. In a sense it could be argued that
these three provide permanent models for literary-critical activity, so that all subsequent critics could be loosely ranged
behind one or the other of them. Coleridge, Lukács and I.A. Richards
are would-be Aristotelians. The English neoclassical critics are
for the most part content to remain as Longinian underlabourers.
The traditional strength of English criticism, however, has lain
in the Horatian mode. The major critics have all been major, or
at least important, poets: they are Sidney, Jonson, Dryden,
Dr Johnson, Wordsworth, Coleridge, Arnold and T.S. Eliot. We might
add two critic-novelists, James and Lawrence. For some of these,
poetic and critical concerns were arguably separable, but the
majority exploited their creative standing to give extra conviction to their criticism. It was Eliot who gave the best justification for this, when he wrote that 'The important critic is the
person who is absorbed in the present problems of art, and who
wishes to bring the forces of the past to bear upon the solution of
these problems.' (2)
   The 'forces' of the past, though; not its achievements or
rules-of-thumb. This word alone suggests the qualitative difference
between the traditional authority of the Horatian critic and that
assumed by his modern successors such as Wordsworth and Eliot. Since
the romantic period, the poet-critic has been conscious of a
historical role. His tone of address to the public has been at
times pontifical, exasperated or prophetic; it has rarely been
free of strain. The determination of the 'forces of the past' has
increasingly become a matter of literary and cultural politics. And
none of the various 'traditions' that have been proposed has been
more tangible or conscious than the tradition of English criticism
itself, since the major critics have invariably been closely and
jealously aware of their predecessors' work. Setting out to create
the taste by which they and their associates were to be enjoyed,
they have played a crucial part in the revolutions of modern poetic
history.
   The study of criticism, then, is an approach to the dynamics of
modern literary development, and especially the development of
poetry. At the same time, criticism exhibits the inertia of any
established intellectual discipline. The field is at once an index
of literary change and an accumulative, partially autonomous
branch of knowledge; in the broadest and least English sense, a
science. In considering the relation between the historian's view
of criticism and the ordinary critic's sense of his function at a
particular time, I believe that it is extremely useful to take
account of recent debates on the history and sociology of science.
   In 'The Structure of Scientific Revolutions' (1962), Thomas Kuhn
argued that a field of enquiry becomes a science when it possesses a
generally accepted 'paradigm'. Paradigms are defined as authoritative models of cognitive practice, such as Newton's investigation
of optics, which are capable of generating fruitful and coherent
traditions of research. Once accepted by the scientific community,
the paradigm establishes both a methodology and a delimited field
of phenomena, conceived as problems or 'puzzles', to which the

methodology may be applied. Phenomena which do not fit this field
are treated as anomalous and their scientific significance is dis-
counted. 'Normal science', in Kuhn's definition, is the activity
of filling in the gaps, or exhaustively articulating the theories
and phenomena which the paradigm identifies; and this term covers
the greater part of scientific activity. In the end, however, the
anomalies and areas of intractability can no longer be ignored, and
the science enters a crisis-period which can only be resolved by
paradigm change - the 'scientific revolution' of Kuhn's title.

In applying this set of ideas to literary criticism, we at once
meet the irony that normal science is opposed by Kuhn to 'critical
discourse'. Critical discourse is a relatively chaotic state of
enquiry in which different schools compete with one another and
there is no common body of belief. The individual worker is thus
obliged to state and defend his basic assumptions, and has very
limited scope for building on the work of others. Progress,
therefore, is fragmentary and questionable. Such a state is found
in non- or pre-scientific fields, and only reappears in science
itself at moments of imminent paradigm change. Like most philosophers of science, Kuhn looks on the transition of a field of
enquiry into a science as being desirable in itself. But not all
his colleagues share this satisfaction with the humdrum and intellectually conformist pursuit of 'normal science', and one, Paul
Feyerabend, has strongly restated the Kantian position that 'critical
discourse' is a more humane and dignified process of enquiry. (3)
If we look frankly at modern literary criticism, however, we shall
surely discover that a good deal of it has the intellectual and
sociological characteristics of a 'normal science'.

This parallel, if it is accepted, is something more than a
diagnostic convenience. It is my hope that in considering criticism
as it has been, readers will consider what it is now, and one day
should be. My own view is that it is during the revolutionary
periods in the arts, when criticism and new creation come closest
together, that criticism realizes its full potential as 'critical
discourse'. Yet the shortcomings as well as the achievements of the
romantic and modernist literary revolutions are now increasingly
manifest to us. Today it seems that a whole phase of literary
culture, in which poet and critic were masters of the 'forces of
the past', has come to an end. Some of the most influential - and,
in its time, revolutionary - twentieth-century criticism has been
a rearguard attempt to prevent our recognition of this. But so far
from being classical, traditional or identifiable with the Western
tradition as a whole, this cultural phase was of relatively recent
emergence, its great century being the nineteenth.

Chapter 1

SAMUEL JOHNSON: THE ACADEMY AND THE MARKET-PLACE

Samuel Johnson was the first Englishman to practise criticism as a major literary genre. He did so in writings that are pungent and direct, with a force of argument and a sweep of generalization that still speak to us vividly. And yet for all that his criticism is not easily understood. The voice is stentorian and unmistakable, but the words reflect not only his personality, but the age in which he felt so confidently at home. Johnson's criticism, in fact, offers a unique point of entry into the imagination of a lost literary age.

The greater part of his methods, language and assumptions as a critic were drawn from the movement that we now call neoclassicism. This term is the subject of continuing debate and confusion. In the view of an orthodox historian of criticism such as J.W.H. Atkins, neoclassicism was a narrow and vicious critical outlook imported from the Continent at the time of the Restoration. In the English setting it was characterized by the half-baked dogmatism of Rymer and Dennis, and the obsequious deference that even Dryden sometimes expressed towards second-rate French critics such as Rapin and Bossu. Gradually in the eighteenth century native empiricism and national pride (epitomized, of course, by Johnson) reawakened and struggled out from under the yoke. It is true that the early neoclassical doctrines came by way of France, where Corneille, Boileau and their followers had reduced the authority of Aristotle and Horace to a rigid system of rules. But the quite startling superficiality of Atkins's account was shown up by R.S. Crane, who argued that neoclassicism may be properly understood, not as an alien group of doctrines, but as the dominant temper of a whole century of English literary thought. Despite increasing divergences of doctrine and focus, it is possible to trace a common language and a common conceptual scheme in criticism from the Restoration to the death of Johnson. Crane defines neoclassicism as 'a large but historically distinguishable aggregate of commonplace distinctions, of a highly flexible and ambiguous kind, out of which many variant critical systems and doctrines could be constructed.' (1) Within the field of neoclassical debate we may then distinguish separate periods and separate national traditions; thus the English form looks back to Rome rather than Greece, and favours the authority of

Horace over that of Aristotle. Crane's thesis, in effect, is
that English neoclassicism is the critical language of 'Augustan'
culture as a whole. Perhaps the relative homogeneity of
eighteenth-century criticism will not seem surprising when we consider the degree of continuity in Augustan verse, from Dryden to
Goldsmith and Cowper.

Some questions are certainly begged by this; notably, the
relation between neoclassicism in literature and the other arts.
But the emphasis on neoclassicism as a language, a shared set of
ways of formulating and solving literary problems, is, I believe,
an extremely helpful one. It should not be allowed to obscure
the conflicts that do occur; the fact that Rapin and, say, Bishop
Hurd 'talked a common critical language' does not mean that they
agreed. Crane's 'structural' view of neoclassicism has a close
affinity with the account of scientific development given by Kuhn,
whose work was discussed in the Introduction. What he has done, in
effect, is to define neoclassicism in terms which suggest it may
be considered as a Kuhnian 'paradigm'. A critical literature guided
by common norms of discourse and a common range of problems is
certainly on the way to becoming a 'normal science'. And since
Augustan criticism represents the rationalization of, and the prescription for, a large part of contemporary poetic practice, the
scientific analogy might even be extended to the art of poetry
itself. This analogy shows its relevance when we consider one of
the most puzzling and even repellent features of Restoration and
Augustan literature; the writers' arrogance about their own relation
to the recent past. The eighteenth century believed that a decisive
change had recently occurred, in poetry as well as in literary
theory. English verse had just emerged from barbarity. As it
happens, an important component of this change was the emergence of
the scientific attitude as a major cultural force. Sprat's
'History of the Royal Society' (1667) was a manifesto both for
experimental science and for the rationalization of literary style.

In his book 'The Burden of the Past and the English Poet',
W.J. Bate not only calls this change a revolution, but argues that
it was the only genuine revolution in our literary history. (2)
In chronological terms it virtually coincides with the only political event in English history which is traditionally called a
revolution: the Glorious Revolution of 1688 which consecrated the
new society in which Augustanism flourished. Yet it is difficult
to conceive of a meaningful revolution in politics, art or science
without an 'ancien régime' to overthrow, and where, in the case of
neoclassicism, was that 'ancien régime'? The metaphysical poets and
Jacobean dramatists whose work was supplanted after the Restoration
hardly constituted an active opposition. The theatres had been
closed for nearly two decades, and the Civil War had put a stop to
metropolitan culture. After the hiatus Dryden did not risk unpopu-
larity when he 'modernized' the plays of Shakespeare, while the rise
of Waller's reputation as one of the poets who harmonized English
versification and 'reformed our numbers' was rapid and complete. He
was first singled out in Soames's translation of Boileau (1683); (3)
his claims as pioneer were rapidly endorsed by Rymer and Dryden,
and still held the field in Johnson's 'Lives of the Poets'. Waller
died in 1687; few minor poets can have made such an easy conquest

of posthumous fame. The 'strong lines' of the metaphysicals were
abandoned, by Dryden among others, as a vein that had been worked
out, and a new generation grew up for whom Herbert and Marvell
were hardly even names.

   We may reply to Bate, then, that the victory of neoclassicism
resembles not so much a revolution ('paradigm change') as the
creation of a 'normal science'. The Augustans were not faced with
concerted opposition in the way that the romantics were, and so
theirs was not a literary revolution on the modern pattern. In
criticism, the end of the seventeenth century saw the schematization
and rationalization of what had earlier been a far less organized
and self-conscious group of activities. The discussion of writing
was no longer confined to textbooks of rhetoric and to a largely
oral tradition. We know virtually nothing about the arguments at
the Mermaid Tavern, or between the Elizabethan dramatist and the
other members of his company of actors. Something of the
seventeenth-century poet's assumptions may be reconstructed from
isolated texts like Ben Jonson's notebooks or Carew's elegy on
Donne. But it was a very important advance that led to the proliferation of critical writing as a separate branch of intellectual
activity, and also to the convention of the critical preface in
which the writer stated his premises and defended his work. With
neoclassicism, criticism ceased to be a largely private and oral
activity and became a recognized intellectual discipline, playing
its part in the rational pursuit of knowledge. The proliferation
of critical activity in the eighteenth century is illustrated by
any bibliography of the period. (To take two popular genres:
editions of Shakespeare were compiled by Rowe (1709), Pope (1725),
Theobald (1735), Hanmer (1744), Warburton (1747), Johnson (1765),
Capell (1768), Steevens (1773) and Malone (1790). Authors of essays
on taste include Addison (1712), Hutcheson (1725), Hume (1757),
Burke (1757), Gerard (1759), Kames (1762) and Alison (1790).) It
is this development, decisively affecting the nature of literature
itself, which gives the scientific analogy for neoclassical criticism its validity.

   The change did not happen at once. The critical texts of Dryden
and Rymer do not themselves lay claim to any very high intellectual
status; that was a construction that would be put upon them
slightly later. Dryden, the first of the major English poet-
critics, is relaxed, well-informed and opportunistic; he discovered in the critical preface a new and congenial way of com-
mending his work to its readers. Rymer in 'The Tragedies of the
Last Age' (1677), with his extraordinarily crude and bumptious
manner, is still quicker to assure us that he is 'not cut out for
writing a Treatise, nor have a genius to pen anything exactly.'
Whatever their other differences, both are far removed from the
formality and self-discipline of scientific and philosophical
discourse. And yet it is clear that Rymer, Dryden and their
contemporaries thought of the new order they were introducing in
literature as rational and scientific. Their manner might be
informal, but the doctrines they were imparting to their readers
had the sanction of the ancients and the prestige of acceptance
throughout polite Europe. The practice of writing was henceforth
to be guided by rules and precedents - rules which were 'Nature

methodiz'd', as Pope was later to put it, and precedents stamped
with the authority of Aristotle, Horace and their many translators
and commentators. English versification was already being harmonized and regularized, and the history of English literature had to
be formulated and shown as a prehistory - a slow ascent from dark-
ness to the daylight of the present in which, for the first time,
the perfection of English writing could be realized.

The neoclassical paradigm, then, was drawn from the received
interpretations of Aristotle, Horace, Longinus, Quintilian and
others. Its practical embodiment was found in the various classical
literary forms, especially Greek tragedy and Roman satire, supported by the body of modern literature on strict critical principles such as French neoclassical tragedy. The elasticity of the
system was greatly augmented by the variety of the classical forms
from which precedents could be drawn. In England, however, the
attempt to rationalize the literary tradition quickly ran into
a major anomaly. It was not necessary to overthrow the foundations
of Elizabethan drama in favour of the new principles, since those
foundations had been almost entirely oral and implicit; in fact
the neoclassical critics constructed a rationale of the native drama
for the first time. Their difficulty was in making the rationale
consistent, and, above all, in determining the place of Shakespeare
within it.

Among those who adopted a rational standard was Sprat, who in
the 'History of the Royal Society' attacked allegorical and fanciful
writing as a mode of superstition. There was Thomas Rymer, who,
though impressive in his command of Greek tragedy, took it as a
universal scientific norm, the 'straight line' against which the
English dramatists were shown to have drawn woefully 'crooked'
lines. Rymer's homely imagery and truculent appeals to common
sense are notable; he follows Aristotle, but disclaims the
pretensions of a learned 'Doctor of Subtilties'. He gives the
impression of a provincial magistrate who sees the national veneration of Shakespeare and Beaumont and Fletcher as - like witchcraft
or sorcery - popular superstitions to be rooted out. His second
book, 'A Short View of Tragedy' (1692), is a good deal more
inquisitorial than 'The Tragedies of the Last Age', and contains
his notorious onslaught on 'Othello'. In the wake of the romantic
idolization of Shakespeare, Macaulay was to call Rymer 'the
worst critic that ever lived', and his whole performance was an
ignominious defeat for rationalism when applied to poetry. He
could produce any number of arguments to ridicule Shakespeare, but
was quite incapable of explaining the sources of tragic power,
even in the classical dramas he set up as models.

Rymer was the kind of pioneer who never gets his due because he
gives the whole discipline a bad name. His example reveals how
important it was for the neoclassical critics to establish a
conventional attitude to the literature of the past. Sneering
superiority was not enough, and Johnson, eighty years afterwards,
could put down Rymer simply by observing that he was a critical
bully. (4) Dryden, however, was less sure-footed in his response.
His disagreements with 'The Tragedies of the Last Age' were stated,
even in the private notes known as the Heads of an Answer to Rymer,
with a good deal of deference. It was only after 'A Short View',

fifteen years later, that he spoke out against Rymer's tone and
motivation:

> But there is another sort of Insects, more venomous than the
> former. Those who manifestly aim at the destruction of our
> Poetical Church and State. Who allow nothing to their Country-
> men, either of this or of the former Age. These attack the
> Living by raking up the Ashes of the Dead. Well knowing that
> if they can subvert their Original Title to the Stage, we who
> claim under them, must fall of course. Peace be to the Venerable
> Shades of Shakespear, and Ben Johnson: None of the Living will
> presume to have any competition with them: as they were our
> Predecessours, so they were our Masters.

Even this passage from the Dedication of 'Examen Poeticum' can
hardly be read without a suspicion of humbug; it is addressed to a
patron and is but one of the twists and turns of Dryden's career,
as he veers between reverent and debunking attitudes to his Jacobean
predecessors. Dryden himself wanted the credit for the revision
of English drama, and feared a venomous critic who might well go on
to 'attack the Living'. The relation between the Jacobeans and his
own generation was a question that worried him incessantly, and it
was he who established the convention whereby a great predecessor
is simultaneously revered and patronized, professions of love being
accompanied by an ostentatious tolerance and a careful enumeration
of faults. This is good form in English criticism down to Johnson's
'Preface to Shakespeare' (it is even unconsciously parodied in
Coleridge's criticism of Wordsworth); the result is an elegant
compromise between the rational, scientific attitude that favours
the contemporary, and the recognition of poetry as a liberal art
with an emotive basis and a duty to honour its founding fathers. (5)

Though he eventually rejected Rymer, Dryden did not reject the
rationalistic outlook that I have sketched. He was no theoretician
himself, but his mind was immensely well-stocked with the theories
of others, whose authority he assiduously invoked; he defended the
propositions of the essay 'Of Dramatick Poesie' (1668), for example,
as 'derived from the authority of Aristotle and Horace, and from
the rules and examples of Ben Jonson and Corneille'. Dryden's
attitude is very different from that of Johnson, who defended his
predecessor against charges of casuistry with the memorable remark
that 'Reason wants not Horace to support it'. For Dryden, reason
did want Horace. Submissiveness to authority, however, did not
prevent him from reflecting the explicitly scientific element in
Restoration criticism, notably in the essay 'Of Dramatick Poesie',
where he relies upon Baconian and Ptolemaic arguments at two crucial
points. The four speakers in the Essay engage in successive debates
between the ancients and the moderns, French drama and English,
and blank verse and rhyme. Crites, speaking first in defence of the
ancients, describes the intellectual context in which all these
debates take place. Natural science, he argues, has been revolu-
tionized in the past hundred years, and 'more Noble Secrets in
Opticks, Medicine, Anatomy, Astronomy, [have been] discover'd,
than in all those credulous and doting Ages from Aristotle to us.
What then should happen to literature? Crites himself raises the
scientific analogy only to deflect it; writers can best succeed
in copying Nature by copying the ancients. But Eugenius, his

opponent, does not miss his opportunity:

> for if Natural Causes be more known now than in the time of
> Aristotle, because more studied, it follows that Poesie and
> other Arts may with the same pains arrive still nearer to
> perfection ....

Later on, Lisideius argues that French drama is superior to the
English because the French writers have observed the rules, and
the rules, after all, are nature methodized. English drama, on
the other hand, bears all the marks of its lowly origins as popular
entertainment. Our stage, with its duels and battles, is 'too
like the Theaters where they fight Prizes'. The most important
rules, in the Aristotelian tradition, are those concerning the plot,
and it is here that Elizabethan drama seems most easily faulted.
Neander defends it, however, on the grounds that it is closer to
nature; and one of the arguments he uses is distinctly ingenious.
It consists of a complicated analogy in which the multiple subplots
of the English drama are compared to the Ptolemaic systems of the
universe in which 'contrary motions may be found ... to agree', and
'a Planet can go East and West at the same time'. The use of
Ptolemaic cosmology (the complexities of which are also explored by
Milton and Donne) suggests a more sophisticated notion of artistic
harmony than the straightforward Aristotelian one. If the rules
are on the side of the French, the actual study of natural science
is on the side of the English.

It is important that Dryden should have voiced such arguments;
but it is far from clear that he held them with full conviction.
There are other features of the Essay and of Dryden's criticism in
general which point in a very different direction. Dryden is a
fine example of the practitioner-critic, the first English poet to
have left us vivid discussions of versification and the poet's
craft. It was also he who turned English criticism into an
artistic genre in its own right, since whatever we may think of
the arguments of the Essay, it is rarely less than a pleasure to
read. The imaginary setting is that of a boat-trip down the
Thames to witness a naval engagement with the Dutch. Here we have
criticism as the polite conversation of gentlemen (leading not to
discord but to mutual compromise) on a patriotic social occasion.
The result is confused and unsystematic, and yet it is the nearest
that Dryden ever came to a methodical treatise. The best of his
criticism is found not in such things as the Examen of 'The Silent
Woman' - though this has been predictably cried up as the ancestor
of practical criticism (6) - but in his more relaxed and conversational writing, for example in the remarks on translation in
several of his essays which bring together his experience as a poet
and his classical learning. Dryden's intellectual opportunism
and his increasing diffuseness prevent him from being a critic of
the first rank, but his work is a unique expression of the English
literary mind becoming conscious of itself.

To become conscious of itself was to declare its independence of
natural science. A generation after Dryden, Swift satirized the
scientists of Laputa, and Pope mocked the flower-growers and
butterfly-hunters in the 'Dunciad'. Neoclassical criticism had
turned away from the intellectual purism of a Sprat or a Rymer to
define its own ideal of rationality. The result was a social as

well as a literary ideal, associating poetic excellence with a
particular understanding of 'culture' as refinement, decorum and
polish. In Dryden's prefaces to his plays, for example, we are
at once aware of the dramatist (unlike Shakespeare) professionally
seeing his work through the press, and of his self-projection as
a man of gentility and learning far superior to those of his
actors. The way was now opened for the definition of the 'standard
of taste' and the identification of literature with cultivated
enjoyment that were so widespread in the eighteenth century. The
test of pleasure, indeed, played a significant part in the essay
'Of Dramatick Poesie', where the argument between French and
English drama became a contrast of French tragedy and English
tragicomedy - the former high art, and the latter closer to mere
entertainment. Dryden's notion of tragedy was a highly secular
one, reducing it to a matter of theatrical technique with no more
powerful emotional impact than could be contained within the category of pleasure; and the result was that he discussed it on equal
terms with comedy, and favoured the latter, English, form. (Later,
under the short-lived influence of Rymer, he reverted to the
classical notion of tragic dignity.)
     Taste, as the Augustans defined it, was essentially a comparative
exercise. David Hume, in what is perhaps the classic essay on the
Standard of Taste (1742), saw it as the prerogative of 'one
accustomed to see and examine and weigh the several performances,
admired in different ages and nations'. The operation is evidently
an objective one, suggesting the availability of critical micro-
scopes, forceps and balances. In order to achieve objectivity
the critic had to free the mind of prejudice. When Hume discusses
what it is to be free of all prejudice, he not only concludes that
'few are qualified to give judgment on any work of art' but makes
out these few to be such paragons of virtue that it would seem a
tragic waste for them to devote their time to literary criticism.
The ideal Man of Taste would no doubt be Plato's philosopher-king;
but it is ludicrous to pretend that this has much to do with the
actual judging of literary works. Given the belief in a universal
standard of taste, no wonder a man of the world such as Addison
took a short cut and declared that the best works were those which
had the sanction of the ages and of the 'Politer Part of our Contemporaries'. (7) As Arnold Bennett put it rather more bluntly in
'Literary Taste' (1909), 'If you differ with a classic, it is you
who are wrong, and not the book.'
     For Addison and Pope, the equation of literature and polite
learning was quite explicit. Addison's critical papers in the
'Spectator' (1711-14) were dedicated to raising the general level
of public taste. Central to his purpose was the series of essays
which definitively established 'Paradise Lost' as a great classic.
His commentary on the poem follows an orthodox Aristotelian procedure, and its literary intention is plainly to elevate Milton
to a place beside Homer and Virgil. At the same time, Milton was
an English Christian poet, and Addison's essays, which appeared on
Saturdays, were meant as edifying literature suitable for reading
on Sundays. This result was achieved by direct hints at the poem's
devotional value, together with a liberal use of the term which
would come to express the idea of tragic and epic dignity in

Augustan writing - the adjective 'sublime'. The category of sublimity, deriving from Longinus's treatise and its translation by Boileau, helped bridge the gap between the moralistic attitude of Rymer and the hedonism of Dryden; it denotes a mode of pleasure or amazement which both edifies and exalts. Addison's stress on sublimity and the faculty of taste foreshadows the movement from objective to subjective and psychological criteria which - all observers are agreed - is the main development of eighteenth-century aesthetics. But although taste is in some sense inborn, he stresses the objective means by which it may be cultivated and improved; prominent among these are 'Conversation with Men of a Polite Genius', and reading the critics.

The air of genteel decorum is even stronger in Pope's 'Essay on Criticism' (1711). Both Addison and Pope introduced a new subject-matter, which reflects the growing volume of critical activity. They discuss the qualifications of the critic, the faults and pre-judices to which he is subject and the ideal conduct of his discipline. Pope's poem is in fact a series of versified instruc-tions to young critics, where Horace's 'Ars Poetica' consisted of instructions to young poets. As the critic's qualifications, Pope proposes Truth and Candour in addition to the conventional triad of Taste, Judgment and Learning. Above all, he should conduct him-self as a gentleman, 'Tho' learn'd, well-bred; and tho' well-bred, sincere.' The theme of good manners dominates Pope's thumbnail sketches of the 'Happy Few' who make up the history of criticism. Horace, for example,

    still charms with graceful Negligence,
  And without Method talks us into Sense,
  Will like a Friend familiarly convey
  The truest Notions in the easiest way.
Among the moderns is Roscommon, the translator of Horace's 'Art of Poetry' (1680):

    not more learn'd than good,
  With Manners gen'rous as his Noble Blood;
  To him the Wit of Greece and Rome was known,
  And ev'ry Author's Merit, but his own
- a winning combination of the classical virtues and native British modesty. Such modesty is fitting in a culture which holds that standards are already fixed and that the common sense of mankind is already enshrined in the literary tradition. Pope memorably defined wit ('What oft was thought, but ne'er so well expressed') in such a way as to virtually exclude innovation, and Addison, in his review of the 'Essay on Criticism', endorsed this: 'Wit and fine Writing doth not consist so much in advancing Things that are new, as in giving Things that are known an agreeable Turn.' Now this must mean that while current literary discourse is confined to the pursuit of ever-increasing politeness, it was not always so; and the way is open for the growth of that pervasive inferiority complex which W.J. Bate has called 'the burden of the past'. Pope writes of the modern poet who 'Glows while he reads, but trembles as he writes', and his panegyric of the ancients verges on the bardolatry of Gray and Collins:

  Hail Bards Triumphant! born in happier Days;
  Immortal Heirs of Universal Praise!

> Whose Honours with Increase of Ages grow,
> As Streams roll down, enlarging as they flow!
> Nations unborn your mighty Names shall sound,
> And Worlds applaud that must not yet be found!

The implication is that the unborn nations and undiscovered worlds
will equally respond to the classical poets who have expressed the
universal truths of human nature. In the same passage the ancients
are seen as altars to which the learned of today bring their tribute of incense. This was still, however, deliberate hyperbole;
it had not yet become an inescapable way of understanding the
literary past.

Apart from venerating the ancients, what could the neoclassical
poet do? He could cultivate new genres (the various forms of mock-
epic, topographical and descriptive verse); he could 'imitate' and
translate; and he could shoulder that sense of social responsibility for literature which is so notable in Pope and the other
Augustan poets. Dryden translated Virgil and Ovid; Pope translated
Homer and edited Shakespeare; Johnson abandoned poetry for
editorial and lexicographical tasks; Pope and Gray projected
histories of English poetry, and Johnson projected a history of
criticism. These were congenial and, at times, financially
rewarding tasks; Pope received over £5,000 for his translation of
Homer. It was unfortunate that the poets could not always fulfil
what they promised, so that the history of poetry was left to
Thomas Warton (1774-81), and that of criticism to Harris's
'Philological Enquiries' (1781). But such tasks increasingly
demanded a degree of specialized application which a major writer
could not undertake. Pope's and Johnson's editions of Shakespeare,
for example, broached problems which could only be solved by
academic textual scholarship. The idea that poets themselves
should be responsible for consolidating their art as one of the
branches of learning could not be expected to last long. But the
Augustans' zeal for this was certainly remarkable.

There were urgent reasons for it. If Dryden or Pope did not
step in to translate the classics, the job would be botched by
somebody else; it was already being botched by somebody else. It
was necessary, not only to create the series of authoritative
editions and institutional handbooks that English literature so
badly needed, but to snatch this task out of the hands of servile
pedants and unscrupulous hacks. Dryden and Pope were concerned
at once to raise the intellectual dignity of literature and to
impose conditions of fair dealing (both between authors and publishers and between authors and public) on the literary market.
The fact that these two concerns went together suggests that the
gentility and decorum of neoclassical criticism was always something of a facade. The Man of Taste reflected the ethos of the
patrons rather than of the authors themselves. To take their
doctrines only at face value would be to forget that their ultimate
source lay not so much in the Roman Empire, as in the writer's
precarious position in eighteenth-century society.

Early neoclassicism held that with the Restoration English
literature had reached a pitch of refinement which would at last
permit it to aspire to perfection. That position was maintained
for a long time - certainly by Johnson - and yet with increasing

misgivings. Wasn't something going wrong? On the one hand,
writing was seen as a gentlemanly pursuit, and the ideal Man
of Taste defined by Addison and Hume was a being to be regarded
with reverence. But then David Hume was one of many writers who
were convinced by the 1740s that cultural refinement entailed
artistic decadence; and long before this, for writers less bland
and financially secure than the Scottish philosopher, literature
had been degraded to a servile trade. The conditions of sweated
literary labour are vividly portrayed in works like Fielding's
'The Author's Farce' (1730), which contains much in the vein of
this snatch of dialogue between Grub Street authors starving in
a bookseller's attic:

Dash   I can lend you a verse, and it will do very well too ....
Blotpage It will do well enough for the middle of a poem.
Dash   Ay, ay, anything will do well enough for the middle of
          a poem. If you can but get twenty good lines to place
          at the beginning for a taste, it will sell very well.
Quibble   So that, according to you, Mr Dash, a poet acts pretty
          much on the same principles with an oyster-woman.
Dash   Pox take your simile, it has set my chaps a-watering:

There is a startling contrast between the high-flown ideology of
neoclassical criticism and economic realities such as this -
though it should be remembered that hack writing was no new phenomenon of the Augustan age. What was new, however, was the
intrusion of the concepts of writing for hire, of the author's
economic status and also of the parasitic and uncreative quality of
much literary work into almost every level of literary consciousness. It is because the 'Essay on Criticism' shuts out such
consciousness, and makes literature preternaturally respectable,
that it is such a thin work, badly needing to be complemented by a
'Dunciad'. The sociology of Augustan writing, and in particular
the vast expansion of fiction, journalism and other sub-literary
forms which sustained an author like Defoe, are of very great
relevance here. The level of economic competition promoted a new
atmosphere of mercantilism and gang-warfare in literature, comparable to the Paris of Balzac's 'Illusions Perdues' a century
later. The greatest writers of the period reflect this in the
sense of a fallen and degraded culture which is found in Pope's
'Dunciad', and in the antics of the Scriblerus Club out of which
the 'Dunciad' and 'Gulliver's Travels' emerged.

Martinus Scriblerus, according to the 'Memoirs' concocted by
Pope and Gay (1741), was the son of Cornelius, a Walter Shandy-like
figure devoted to the ancients and determined to provide the
perfect upbringing for his son. Young Martin, however, was led
astray by Crambe, his fellow-pupil, and gave himself up to the
vanities and follies of the moderns. The first evidence of this
was the treatise 'Peri Bathous', written in youth and carefully
hidden from his father. 'Peri Bathous: or, of the Art of Sinking
in Poetry', published by Pope in 1727, is in fact a satire con-
taining its own succinct assessment of the Grub-Street dilemma.
Literature is traditionally understood as a contest of excellence,
with the honours going only to the few who reach the top of
Parnassus. But what if it is now revealed in its true colours as a
trade - a woefully labour-intensive industry? Isn't it reasonable

for a trade-union attitude, demanding equal rewards for all, to
be adopted? The goal can be achieved - for all but a few surly
Parnassians - by the simple expedient of redefining the standard
of excellence as the 'Bathos'. This solution is something more
than a Tory satire on trendy mediocrity, for Pope's view of
Dulness is ultimately aimed not at individual opponents but at
the Age, and the Age will be found to include himself.

Scriblerus went on to become a great critic, as well as a great
traveller, scientist and mathematician. He is the academic rather
than the Grub Street critic, and is alleged to be the real author
of Richard Bentley's notorious commentary on 'Paradise Lost'.
Later he emerges as the protean editor, explicator, annotator and
presiding genius of the 'Dunciad', and as the theoretician of the
genre of Dunciad or 'little epic'. Now Pope, the creator of
Scriblerus, himself entertained the lifelong ambition of writing
a major epic; one of his plans for this turned upon 'civil and
ecclesiastical government'. (8) Not only are his great productions
mock-epics, but they establish a literary context in which true
epic no longer seems possible. And yet, though one cannot build a
horse in the age of the steam-engine, horse-power can be put to new
purposes. The 'Dunciad' begins by parodying the 'Aeneid', it runs
through innumerable borrowings from Virgil and Milton, and comes
to us as a Variorum already encrusted with glosses and commentaries:
the perfect synthetic ancient text. By its degraded incorporation
of the great epics it reduces them to the status of discarded com-
modities; as if after Scriblerus has taken his pickings, they are
no more than the abandoned shells of secondhand cars. The 'Dunciad'
may have exceeded Pope's intentions in its debunking of the aura
which surrounded the classical epics and was already thickening
around Milton. As for contemporary poetry, it is unnecessary to
enumerate the multitude of ways in which the 'Dunciad' reveals it
as a mug's game, a fecund anarchy of knaves and humbugs, buffoons
and sharks. Beyond Pope's attacks on his enemies we can sometimes glimpse the inexorable bathos of authorship itself:

While pensive Poets painful vigils keep,
Sleepless themselves, to give their readers sleep.

Poetry is not the expression of sublimity, heroism or good
manners, it would seem, but the musty product of bookshop and
printing-press, library and garret. Pope could pen a salute to
the 'Bards Triumphant' of ancient times like any of his contemporaries, but he reflected his age far more profoundly in his epic
of scribblers and critics. Johnson was his heir in confronting
the thinness and blandness of so much neoclassical theorizing;
with insights as pungent as Pope's, he was to write criticism that
took account of the full experience of writing in his time.

Samuel Johnson went to London to seek his fortunes in 1737, at the
age of twenty-eight. For some years he lived in extreme poverty,
producing, among other things, fictitious reports of parliamentary
debates for the printer Edward Cave. His 'Life of Mr Richard
Savage' attracted notice in 1744 (the year of Pope's death), and
a year later he published a pamphlet of 'Miscellaneous Observations
on the Tragedy of Macbeth'. Soon afterwards he began work on the

monumental 'Dictionary', not published until 1755, and although
many of his critical views were first outlined in his periodical
essays for the 'Rambler' (1750-2), he did not embark upon a
sustained literary-critical project until his edition of
Shakespeare, published in 1765. By the time he received the
commission for the 'Lives of the Poets' in 1777, he had spent
nearly forty years in literary London and had risen from Grub
Street hack to the dominant man of letters of his day.

   Johnson did not make his name by literary criticism, and he had
a low enough opinion of those who did. The scientific analogy
invoked at the start of this chapter assumed that there was a kind
of journeyman practice of neoclassical criticism analogous to
'normal science'. In fact it was Johnson, in two brief essays
in the 'Idler' (1759), who drew the most devastating portrait we
have of the critic as normal scientist. Dick Minim is an opportunist who takes advantage of the rapid development of criticism
as a profession. After working as a brewer's apprentice, he
picks up his critical knowledge orally, by listening to the talk
in coffee-houses, and supplements this with some desultory reading.
Having thus conversed with men of polite genius and read the
critics, he has acquired the qualifications of Addison's Man of
Taste, and launches himself as a critic. His reputation is made
with a few precepts cribbed from the classical authorities, and
a fine art of circumlocution and temporizing when it comes to
actually passing judgment. His success is so great that by the
end he is majestically receiving pupils:

   He is never so great, or so happy, as when a youth of promising
   parts is brought to receive his directions for the prosecution
   of his studies. He then puts on a very serious air; he
   advises the pupil to read none but the best authors, and, when
   he finds one congenial to his own mind, to study his beauties,
   but avoid his faults, and, when he sits down to write, to
   consider how his favourite author would think at the present
   time on the present occasion. He exhorts him to catch those
   moments when he finds his thoughts expanded and his genius
   exalted, but to take care lest imagination hurry him beyond the
   bounds of nature. He holds diligence the mother of success,
   yet enjoins him, with great earnestness, not to read more than he
   can digest, and not to confuse his mind by pursuing studies of
   contrary tendencies. He tells him, that every man has his
   genius, and that Cicero could never be a poet. The boy retires
   illuminated, resolves to follow his genius, and to think how
   Milton would have thought; and Minim feasts upon his own
   beneficence till another day brings another pupil.

The pupil might be imagined as a future critic or man of taste, in
which case Minim is taking good care to make his own profession
more of a closed shop than when he was a boy. But though the pupil
may turn out a critic, he seems to have gone to Minim for advice
on becoming a poet - and with this in mind, Johnson's paragraph is
one of the deadliest satires ever written on literary education.
The modern reader is not alone in being made uncomfortable by it;
scholars have pointed out that, while most of Minim's pronounce-
ments are the small change of neoclassicism, and some are
Johnson's peculiar 'bêtes noires', others express opinions of his

own. (9) Of Minim's instructions to his pupil, it might be said
that the injunction to cultivate a writer's beauties and to shun
his faults is the moral of all evaluative criticism; while the
distrust of imagination that goes 'beyond the bounds of nature'
strikes the modern reader as a particularly Johnsonian anxiety.
Something may also be deduced from the restrained and muted tone
of the essay on Minim. It is not so much that of a writer flaying
the dunces who are his political and literary enemies, as that of
a critic listening appalled to something not unlike the sound of
his own voice. 'He whom nature has made weak, and idleness keeps
ignorant, may yet support his vanity by the name of a critick': in
this we may detect the note of self-laceration that we find in
Johnson's private diaries and prayers.

While this is conjectural, there is certainly a problem about
what Minim stands for. Reynolds in a subsequent number of the
'Idler' referred to Johnson's 'ridicule of those shallow criticks,
whose judgment, tho' often right as far as it goes, yet reaches
only to inferior beauties, and who ... from thence determine the
merit of extensive works.' (10) It is true that the specimen of
Minim's textual explications that we are given is so close to
modern practical criticism that one wonders how many present-day
students have ever been told to read the essay. But Minim is more
than a finical mediocrity - he is a social and cultural phenomenon.
First of all, he is a rentier, having been set free to become a
'man of wit and humour' by a large inherited fortune - a type that
Johnson, with his Grub Street experience and lifelong class-
consciousness, (11) bitterly detested. Second, he is a would-be
academician, a middleman whose aim is to increase the pomp and
prestige of the critical Establishment so that he can shine ever
brighter in the reflected glory of the poets and sages. Johnson -
as he had made clear in the 'Life of Roscommon' (1748) - hated the
idea of an English Academy. Minim's real reason for supporting
it, he implies, is that he sees himself as its President, since
he enjoys the next best thing in his presidency of a 'critical
society elected by himself, where he is heard without contradiction.' In this society he occupies the 'chair of criticism' (it
is obvious what sort of chair he would occupy today).

Criticism, then, has become a career, and writing has entered
a new stage of institutionalization. Johnson's position, shielded
by the deadpan irony of the essays on Minim, remains a puzzling
one. As biographer, editor and lexicographer he himself was one
of the major institutionalizing forces in English literature, yet
he was also powerfully iconoclastic.

Johnson believed in cultural progress - he felt he had seen it
in his own lifetime - and the great labours of his career were
undertaken in the cause of such progress: they were the
'Dictionary' (described by his friend and biographer Arthur
Murphy as 'the MOUNT ATLAS of English literature'), the 'Rambler',
the 'Lives of the Poets' and the edition of Shakespeare. These
works made their author into a national figure and led to his
presiding over a literary circle which might well have become the
nucleus of an English Academy. Johnson's Club was founded in 1764,
and its members were such men as Reynolds, Burke, Goldsmith,
Garrick, the Wartons, Adam Smith, Fox, Sheridan and Gibbon - the

leading intellectuals of the age. The Club has far more of an
institutional air than the Scriblerus clique of Pope, Swift and
their allies, not to speak of the literary kangaroo court of Dick
Minim. The degree of unity among its members was a good deal
less than could be found in most academic communities today;
Johnson himself was not above remarking that some of his colleagues
deserved hanging for their political and religious views. (12)
The exact nature of Johnson's authority over this dining club is
hard to determine, since we rely so heavily on Boswell's glowing
accounts. There is no doubt, however, that the legend of the
Club contributed to the hardening of his reputation as a literary
dictator after his death. Boswell showed him as the victor in
innumerable exchanges, and when the neoclassical consensus had
been abandoned it became easy to caricature him, as Wordsworth did
in the Essay Supplementary, lording it over 'the little senate
to which he gave laws'. We owe a considerable amount of his reputation as a tyrant to the impressionability of Boswell and the
propaganda of the romantics.

The same causes have tended to trivialize Johnson's iconoclasm,
which came to be seen as the splenetic outbursts of an English
eccentric, lovable when he was kicking the stone, and hateful when
he did the same to 'Lycidas'. But Johnson's opposition to an
academy - his argument was that it would either fail to agree, or
to exact obedience in respect of whatever it had agreed upon -
reflects a fundamental suspicion of certain kinds of authority
that may be traced throughout his thought. In directly political
terms, he stated his position in the pamphlet on 'The Bravery of
the English Common Soldiers' (1767). Here he patriotically argued
that English soldiers were braver than the French because of the
degree of civil liberty and independence that they enjoyed.
Englishmen, thanks to their legal and economic advantages, were
naturally anarchists, but 'their insolence in peace is bravery in
war'. A cohesive society, in other words, is one that gives the
widest scope to plurality and independence, using coercion only
as a last resort. The implicit model here is evidently that of
Hanoverian constitutional monarchy as against the absolutism of
the French. Johnson's charity toward plebeian insolence did not
extend to 'surly and acrimonious' republicans such as Milton.

Johnson's letter to Lord Chesterfield (1755) dispensing with
his patronage is his own most famous display of anti-authoritarian
insolence. In fact, the manner of his rupture with Chesterfield
sums up his intellectual as well as his personal relations with the
patron who had looked to him as a 'dictator' to correct and
purify the English tongue. (13) Chesterfield was the successor of
Roscommon, Swift and others in proclaiming the need for the
stabilization of English, after the manner of the French Academy.
Johnson, however, came to see the lexicographer's task as predominantly descriptive rather than prescriptive. Without wholly
disappointing those who would look to his 'Dictionary' for
authority and direction, he sought to convey his sense of the
inherent uncertainty and fluctuation of language. The task -
conceived in accordance with the 'spirit of English liberty' -
was not to fix, but to conserve. (14) Johnson's outlook, in fact,
was that of an emergent Tory nationalism, resolutely opposing the

authoritarianism of Academies just as it opposed French absolutism
and 'popery'.

This resentment of absolutism is very strikingly found in his
attitude to the literary tradition. Johnson was full of scorn for
those who unnecessarily increased the 'burden of the past', seeing
them as part of a 'general conspiracy of human nature against
contemporary merit'. (15) His brisk reminder that 'reason wants
not Horace to support it' has already been cited; and at the core
of his opposition to most forms of literary antiquarianism and
ancestor-worship there is his awareness of the tremendous power
conferred by the 'sanction of antiquity':

> The faults of a writer of acknowledged excellence are more
> dangerous, because the influence of his example is more exten-
> sive; and the interest of learning requires that they should
> be discovered and stigmatized, before they have the sanction
> of antiquity conferred upon them, and become precedents of
> indisputable authority.
>
> ('Rambler' no. 93)

Johnson's writings contain many statements like this, and many
expressions of wariness and suspicion when he confronts a writer
of 'acknowledged excellence'. Nor does he shirk the consequence
of this, that no authority shall be indisputable in the light of
reason - in literature at least. In ethics and theology, as we
shall see, it is another matter.

In several ways, Johnson's forthright adherence to 'reason' in
critical matters (16) is linked to his adherence to 'nature'.
Both terms signalize his emphatically non-specialist approach to
literature. He constantly resolves what we might think of as
purely aesthetic problems - such as the value of tragicomedy,
the unities, or Milton's pastorals - by a down-to-earth resort to
standards of verisimilitude and common sense. Such standards do
not suggest the need for any special literary expertise, and they
reveal Johnson's steadfast opposition to those who sought to raise
the qualifications for literary judgment out of reach of the common
reader. Addison had implied that taste could be easily and
docilely acquired by cultivating the classics, but later writers
such as Hume (and eventually Wordsworth) saw its acquisition as an
arduous and exacting discipline. Johnson, however, would have
agreed with his friend Burke that 'the true standard of the arts
is in every man's power.' (17) This means that some blunt and
plain-spoken criticism must be expected; and Johnson's refusal to
allow Milton to allegorize (or, in plain language, to tell lies)
about shepherds and flocks in 'Lycidas' was a blow struck against
literary sophistication and critical gentility which continues to
reverberate. Johnson's view of the literary world in general is
that such blows ought to be struck. The individual should make his
voice heard. His own experience as self-made writer, victim of
patronage and despiser of well-heeled mediocrity lies behind the
overtly dispassionate conclusion to his discussion of academies in
the 'Life of Roscommon': 'The present manners of the nation would
deride authority, and therefore nothing is left but that every
writer should criticise himself.' The only guidelines he would
offer, where literature alone is at issue, are those of reason and
nature.

The dialectic of authority and iconoclasm in Johnson's thought led
him to seek an accommodation between individualist and institutional views of culture; and I have suggested that the model for
this lay in the idea of constitutional monarchy. What do we
actually mean, however, by these different ways of looking at
culture? The question of the Academy which exercised Johnson is
part of the problem with which we are concerned. Another part, of
which he may not have been conscious, is the meaning of the word
'literature' itself.

According to the excellent article in the 'New English Dictionary', the modern sense of 'literature' as 'literary productions
as a whole; the body of writings produced in a particular country
or period' is of very recent emergence. In Johnson's 'Dictionary'
the word is only defined in the older sense of 'learning; skill
in letters'. Johnson in fact saw 'learning', 'letters' and
'literature' as a triad of concepts to be defined in terms of one
another. 'Literature' in this sense may be either the attribute
of a learned individual (a frequent Johnsonian usage) or of a
group or nation; one of the illustrations of the 'Dictionary'
sense is Bacon's assertion that 'This kingdom hath been famous
for good Literature.' In both cases, however, the word has an
active sense, denoting a type of human attainment. During the
later eighteenth century - a period which, as Raymond Williams has
shown us, (18) saw decisive changes in the meanings of 'art',
'class', 'democracy', 'culture' and 'industry' - 'literature' came
to be used in a passive, institutional sense, to denote a body of
works already in existence. The 'N.E.D.' gives an intermediate,
active/passive sense of 'literary work or production; the activity
or profession of a man of letters; the realm of letters', first
instanced in Johnson's Life of Cowley (1779). Johnson, whether he
knew it or not, played an important part in the change of meaning,
and he was also influential in propagating the neologism 'literary'.
This word does not figure in the 'Dictionary' (1755). But in 1756
Johnson was connected with the 'Literary Magazine', and in 1779,
after the death of Garrick, his own Club was christened the
Literary Club. Johnson used 'literature' occasionally in the
'Lives of the Poets' in a sense incompatible with his 'Dictionary'
definition, and - more importantly - he had much earlier shown a
liking for the word in an elevated and patriotic context, as in
this famous sentence from the Preface to the 'Dictionary':

   The chief glory of every people arises from its authors:
   whether I shall add any thing by my own writings to the reputation of English literature, must be left to time....
Relevant, too, is the fact that the 'Dictionary' itself was the
first English literary encyclopaedia. Its range of reference and
wealth of quotation are astonishing, and between its covers 'the
body of writings produced in a particular country' seems to have
become a palpable reality for the first time. On the single page
'Listless - Litter', for example, we find quotations from Dryden,
Pope, Swift, Locke, Taylor, Addison, Hooker, Browne, Bacon, Boyle,
Milton, Shakespeare, Clarendon, Donne, Evelyn and others. The
labour of filling two thick volumes with such - semantically·
classified - quotations defies description. Johnson himself
understood that his work had a significance far beyond the bounds

of lexicography as we would now see it. The Preface to the
'Dictionary' challenges for it a central and permanent place in
the productions of the English mind. That centrality is a function
of its Englishness; Johnson implicitly connects the genius of
our language and literature to the 'spirit of English liberty'.
The emergence of the modern sense of 'literature' is indeed part
of the rise of cultural nationalism.

Looking ahead for the moment, it was only in the nineteenth
century that 'literature' came to signify fine or imaginative
writing (de Quincey's 'literature of power') in opposition to
other kinds. This usage is also a passive one, reflecting the
attitude of the consumer rather than the literary producer.
'Poetry' is the word normally used by practitioners and in revolutionary movements in writing; 'literature' comes into its own
in the ages of consolidation and categorization which succeed
such movements. The creative charge of imaginative writing is
somewhat muffled by the term 'literature'. We can speak of
'literature and society' with an air of soothing generalization,
but 'poetry and society' sounds far more tendentious and programmatic.

In Johnson's time, then, 'literature', the new nationalistic
conception, was succeeding 'learning', the international body of
knowledge founded upon the classics. Scholars and literary
historians were beginning to point out the antiquity of English
poetry, and yet for most purposes, both for the conservative
nationalist Johnson and for the public served by his edition of
the English poets, its historical span remained brief. There
were few authoritative reputations, and even fewer critical
vested interests to spring to their defence. Johnson in the
'Preface to Shakespeare' (1765) speaks of his subject as one who
has at last attained 'the dignity of an ancient', but he also
stigmatizes Shakespeare's, and later Milton's, faults with a
severity that the nineteenth century was to find intolerable. Far
from worshipping the dead, Johnson introduced his discussion of
Shakespeare's faults with the highly rationalistic assertion that
'no question can be more innocently discussed than a dead poet's
pretentions to renown.' This seems to imply both that what is at
issue - poetic merit - is something less than momentous, and that
it is in his discussion of the living that the critic is more
conspicuously on trial.

In speaking of the 'innocence' of criticism, Johnson did not
mean to deny the squabbling and spite of critical scholarship
or the tradition of the venomous footnote. What emerges from his
review of his editorial predecessors in the 'Preface to
Shakespeare' is that scholarly acrimony flourishes in inverse
proportion to the magnitude of the questions under discussion. The
general reputation of a dead poet's work can hardly be altered by
the scholar, since it is established by the repeated consent of
generations of readers largely unaffected by criticism. Johnson's
well-known criterion of literary survival exempts the reputations
of dead poets from the fluctuations of contemporary fashion, and
so drastically limits the jurisdiction of the individual critic.

It is very different when he is dealing with the living.
Johnson's essays on the subject of contemporary writing and

criticism are to be found among his periodical contributions to
the 'Rambler', the 'Adventurer' (1753-4) and the 'Idler' (1758-60):
a key text on the nature of criticism is 'Rambler' no. 93. While
the periodicals contain a number of set-piece excursions into
critical theory and analyses of classic texts (notably 'Paradise
Lost' and 'Samson Agonistes'), these essays are heavily outnum-
bered by those devoted to general problems of authorship and the
literary life. The focus is not upon 'literature' as an achieved
body of works, but upon the arduous and gruelling activity of
authorship. Johnson uses the 'life of writing' (19) as a kind of
running synecdoche for the moral struggles of life in general.
In this context, it is the psychology and motivation of the critic
that concerns him, and he implies that wrong judgments are not so
much the signs of bad taste as of laziness, envy and vanity. The
critic's verdict has far more influence when he is discussing the
living, his personal prejudices are brought into play, and - above
all - criticism of one's contemporaries is virtually a face-to-face
transaction. An author, Johnson tells us, 'may be considered as
a kind of general challenger', (20) and the contest is joined in
a small literary world in which, as we know, both personal vili-
fication and physical assault were rife (Johnson himself was
threatened by Macpherson, the forger of 'Ossian'). In such a
world, the periodical essays suggest, it is the critic's capacity
for moral behaviour that is tested, rather than his ability to
read a text.

Johnson, then, seems to consider reviewing, the discussion of
the living, as a more exacting task than the study of the dead.
But in fact the great bulk of his critical output was concerned
with a special group of writers with a foot in both camps - the
recently dead. To some extent this is the result of chance - the
commissioning of the 'Lives of the Poets' in 1777, when he was
nearly seventy - but his interest in biography was lifelong, and
he had completed the 'Lives' of Savage and Roscommon while in his
thirties. None of the subjects of the 'Lives' can be said to
have attained the 'dignity of an ancient', as Shakespeare had;
they are poised between the twin states of authorship and literature. Johnson's aim as biographer-critic is at once to recount
their careers as authors, and to pass judgment on their standing
as literature. The first of these aims is predominant in his
early critical biography, the 'Life of Mr. Richard Savage' (1744).

Richard Savage, poet, Bohemian and convicted murderer, died in
1743; the 'Life' was rushed out by his former drinking companion
in the following year. Although incorporated in the 'Lives of the
Poets' forty-five years later, this was the first of Johnson's
major works, written while he was still a starving and virtually
unknown hack. It relates the most turbulent and dissipated literary career imaginable, and yet the themes that Johnson brings
out suggest a series of affinities with those other, more resplen-
dent biographies - of Cowley, Milton, Dryden, Addison and Pope -
which are the core of the later 'Lives'.

The explicit morals that Johnson extracts from Savage's story
are these: first, that 'those are no proper Judges of his Conduct who have slumber'd away their Time on the Down of Abundance',
and second, that 'nothing will supply the Want of Prudence'. The

latter, aimed at Savage himself, was probably inserted to give an
appearance of judicious impartiality, since the 'Life', for all
its detachment and irony, is really a prolonged apology for
Savage's conduct. His story exemplifies all the misfortunes that
could be heaped upon an Augustan writer 'in extremis'. It begins
with an act of monstrous injustice, for Savage, we are told, is
disowned by his own mother, the Countess of Macclesfield, and must
suffer her persecutions continually. No sooner has be begun to
overcome this disadvantage, than his name is tarnished by a tavern
brawl in which he kills an opponent. Savage is convicted,
imprisoned and later freed by royal pardon to continue the literary
life. He is taken up by a patron and abruptly dropped. He writes
fawning dedications to men with whom he will quarrel as soon as
they are in print. He is promised places, including the Laureateship, which he will never receive. His best poem is bought by
the bookseller for a pittance, and one of its successors sells only
seventy-two copies; and his chronic poverty leads to critical
neglect and contempt. Friends organize a subscription for him,
but the amount is insufficient, and his dream of a rural retreat
proves a mirage. Finally, he is arrested on a debt of £8, and
dies in prison. Savage is a spendthrift who soon dissipates such
good fortune as comes his way, but his literary reverses are
common to any struggling writer, and it is perhaps only his natural
imprudence that prevents him from eventually winning through to
a modest prosperity. Pope, who sensibly used his publisher's
advance for the 'Iliad' to buy an annuity, is the great representative of such prosperity, and it was he who eventually became
Savage's benefactor, to the tune of £20 a year. But that prosperity, as Johnson showed it in the Life of Pope, was bought at
the price of becoming the archetypal bourgeois poet, obsessed by
money and property and the attentions of the great. Savage is the
anti-bourgeois, stigmatized from birth, outlawed and victimized,
and yet retaining to the last the 'insurmountable obstinacy of his
spirit'.

Savage's cheerfulness and conviviality, and even his fitful
brilliance as a poet, are what we should expect of such a Bohemian,
maverick hero. His obstinacy, however, is more unusual. He will
reject a gift of clothes or money if there is a hint of con-
descension or high-handedness in the way it is given; this,
surely, was the side of him which appealed to Johnson. The
contempt for those who have slumbered away on the down of abundance is Johnson's own, and throughout Savage's story we are made
to feel constant resentment against the aristocracy, 'those little
creatures whom we are pleased to call the Great.' Johnson is
much more understanding when the burgesses of Bristol find themselves unable to tolerate Savage, for these are businessmen with
work to do. What Johnson and the Bristol merchants have in common
is presumably their independence - their ability to stand on
their own feet unaided by patronage. Here Johnson reveals his
commitment to the positive values of bourgeois individualism.
Yet Savage's story is that of a writer trapped by its negative
aspect, the reduction of his relationship with his patrons to a
cash-nexus (not for him the 'liberall boord' and 'plentie of
meate' that Ben Jonson enjoyed at Penshurst). He was trapped,

but he did not give in. In later 'Lives' Johnson was to have
little mercy for Dryden's servility and flattery of his patrons,
or for Pope's spiritual bondage to snobbery and affectation. He
found as much in the life of Savage as in the lives of these men
to inspire a code of professional ethics.

The explicit themes of the 'Life' set Savage apart from writers
such as Dryden and Pope and show him, for better or worse, as a
social outcast. But it is striking to learn from Boswell that
Johnson himself may have been Savage's dupe in the matter of his
parentage; his hero had, in all probability, entered upon the
literary scene not as an outcast but as an impostor. Johnson,
however, is well aware of the theme of confidence-trickery which
runs through many other events of Savage's life, even if he does
not draw any moral from it. When his patron accuses him of
upsetting his household and stealing his books, the poet's friends
'easily credited both these Accusations', for he was one who had
'been obliged from his first Entrance into the World to subsist
upon Expedients'. His most spectacular literary expedient results
from his disappointment over the Laureateship. He decides to
publish a poem every year on the Queen's birthday entitled the
'Volunteer Laureat', and for this effrontery receives an annual
fifty guineas from the royal purse. When pay-day came round,
Johnson tells us,

> His Conduct with regard to his Pension was very particular. No
> sooner had he changed the Bill, than he vanished from the Sight
> of all his Acquaintances, and lay for some Time out of the
> Reach of the Enquiries that Friendship or Curiosity could make
> after him; at length he appeared again pennyless as before,
> but never informed even those whom he seemed to regard most,
> where he had been, nor was his Retreat ever discovered.

Savage is not only an ingenious scrounger and parasite, but an
actor consciously fostering his own public image.

Pope's 'Dunciad' was a monumental sociological satire on the life
of the writer; the 'Life of Savage' is a profound psychological
examination. Every writer is a 'Volunteer Laureat', a 'general
challenger' for social attention and approbation; every poetic
career contains some species of pretence or imposture. That is
why Savage's life, wild and crooked as it seems, is in a sense
the prototype for the major biographies in the 'Lives of the Poets'.
The biographies of Dryden, Addison and Pope in particular are full
of tales of flattery and trickery, of the poets' ingenuity of self-
advertisement and their assiduity in procuring favours. These
writers' need for self-assertion led them time and again to
'subsist upon Expedients', and their careers, when separated from
their works, come to seem as degraded as those of Pope's Dunces.
Even their works, under Johnson's scrutiny, reveal a fair amount
of imposture. Cowley wrote 'The Mistress' though he had never had
a love-affair. Pope claimed that the 'Dunciad' had a moral
design, but Johnson was 'not convinced'. And what of Dryden and
Davenant's attempt to improve upon Shakespeare's 'Tempest'?

> The effect produced by the conjunction of these two powerful
> minds was, that to Shakespeare's monster Caliban is added a
> sister-monster Sicorax; and a woman, who, in the original play,
> had never seen a man, is in this brought acquainted with a man
> that had never seen a woman.

At one level the 'Life of Savage' implies that such impostures are caused by the economic insecurity of the writer, his mercenary existence in capitalist society and his low professional status. More explicitly, Johnson related them to permanent factors of human nature, and particularly to the writer's desire for fame and his unwillingness to pay its honest price in human effort. To the moralist the lives even of major poets are a muddied spectacle of confusion and imperfection, relieved, however, by dry humour and the thought that this brings them closer to the jurisdiction of the common man. It is only with time that imposture can be detected and the true merit of a writer's works revealed. Johnson would probably have agreed with Hume, who wrote of the poetic genius that 'the longer his works endure, and the more wide they are spread, the more sincere is the admiration which he meets with.' (21) It is only when this posthumous sifting has begun that the turbulent life of an author gives place to an achieved and immutable 'literature'.

The writer, as Johnson sees him, has only a limited capacity to rise above his society. The prevalence of expedience and imposture reflects his subjugation by his environment and ultimately the fallen state of man himself. In this light, the 'Lives of the Poets' might be read as a series of cautionary tales on a text from Johnson's poem 'The Vanity of Human Wishes':
    Nor thing the Doom of Man revers'd for thee:
Johnsonian biography constantly reveals the muddle of human affairs, and the melancholy discrepancy of intention and fulfilment. It is not difficult to see how the gloom of his moral vision was linked to the anxieties and neuroses of his own life, and especially, in literary terms, to the interminable drudgery of compiling the 'Dictionary'. His sense of the tragic curve of design against performance is repeatedly expounded in essays in the 'Rambler', written in the intervals of that enormous task. Particularly memorable for their gloom are Johnson's meditations upon public libraries. Where others would see the collaborative effort of human learning and the triumph of a minority of timeless classics, Johnson's thoughts turn upon the mediocrity and destined oblivion of the vast majority of literary performances. (22) No doubt such expressions of gloom were emotionally satisfying, but they also had an important rhetorical function. The vanity of literary ambition was a recurrent topic well calculated to fill out an argument in solemn and reflective fashion, and it was by such means that, within the brief compass of the periodical essay, Johnson was able (in Boswell's words) to come forth as 'a majestick teacher of moral and religious wisdom'.
    The wisdom that he taught was a kind of Christian orthodoxy. Nor was this confined to his work as moral essayist; after all, he wrote the 'Lives of the Poets' 'in such a manner, as may tend to the promotion of Piety.' (23) Nonetheless, Johnson's religious beliefs represent something less than the boldest and most original aspects of his mind. It is as if, while so secure in his own culture, he was frightened and appalled by the infinite spaces that that culture did not touch. We miss in his writing both the

questing imagination and the cult of the immediately authentic
and personal that are found in writers less confidently at home in
their own societies. Johnson, with his masterly powers of comparison and generalization, was well fitted to

Let Observation with extensive View,
Survey Mankind, from China to Peru;

but these lines share the complacency which makes 'Rasselas',
a profoundly gloomy moral tale, seem stodgy beside the freer and
more explosive narratives of Swift and Voltaire. Johnson's
self-confinement within the world of reason and nature has important consequences for his critical outlook. He believed that
literature could offer very little in the way of religious understanding, and that on the whole it should not try. Devotional
poetry was unpleasing because it attempted to express a sacred
experience with imperfect and worldly arts:

Man admitted to implore the mercy of his Creator, and plead
the merits of his Redeemer, is already in a higher state than
poetry can confer .... Poetry loses its lustre and its power,
because it is applied to the decoration of something more
excellent than itself. All that pious verse can do is to help
the memory, and delight the ear, and for these purposes it may be
very useful; but it supplies nothing to the mind.

('Life of Waller')

Perhaps we should interpret this as a reaction to an age of
jingling Methodist hymns; but underlying it is a rejection of the
neo-Platonic argument that poetry yields a 'golden world' superior
to the world of nature. This argument, voiced by Sidney in the
'Defence of Poesie', and revived by the romantics, is quite alien
to Johnson. Poetry for him shows nature improved and regularized,
but not transcended; its province is the natural and not the
supernatural. However, he does not always condemn the material
of theology as 'too sacred for fiction', for that would mean condemning 'Paradise Lost'. Although there are times in the 'Life of
Milton' when he seems about to accuse the poet of 'lese-majesté' -
his design involves matters 'too ponderous for the wings of wit',
and 'the want of human interest is always felt' - the conclusions
that he draws are fulsome and safe. 'Paradise Lost' is the noblest
of epics, and it illustrates the 'known truths' of scripture so
effectively as to be a 'book of universal knowledge'. The key
point, however, is that Johnson, almost alone in his age, does not
concede that Milton went beyond 'known truths' - the truths of
Christian reason and nature - to those of revelation.

At its highest levels, then, poetry is still not transcendental.
Poetic truth does not take precedence over the truths of other
disciplines such as theology and philosophy. At lower levels,
Johnson views fiction as a secular and somewhat licentious activity.
Boswell tells of him refusing to take precedence over a Doctor of
Divinity, and claiming that he chose tragic poetry as his first
'métier' because he lacked the money to study law. Nonetheless, he
did consider authorship in the widest sense as the first of
professions in so far as it contributed to the 'intellectual
pre-eminence' of the nation. (24) Literary criticism was a different matter, belonging only among the 'subordinate and instrumen-
tal arts', and he doubted whether a knowledge of its technicalities

could make the lay reader 'more useful, happier or wiser'. (25)

A more general indication of the secularity of poetry may be found in Johnson's concepts of 'labour' and 'genius'. 'Genius' is defined in the Life of Cowley: 'The true Genius is a mind of large general powers, accidentally determined to some particular direction.' Thus genius is not a mission or vocation, but an endowment which may lead its possessor into any of the professions, and not merely into poetry or art. Still less is it a guarantee of success, for Johnson's view is that, like Adam and Eve after their expulsion from paradise, poets and others can only achieve this through hard and back-breaking labour. 'Labour', in fact, is one of the key words of the 'Lives of the Poets'. Johnson constantly stresses the hard craftsmanship and toil involved in literary production, and dismisses stories of inspired and instant composition as credulous fabrications. What this does is to bring poetry closer to the other skills and occupations which make up economic life. The breadth of experience that we find in the 'Lives' stems from Johnson's convictions that the conduct of a poet's life may be as instructive as his art, and that the art itself is not so mysterious that it cannot be illuminated by common observation. Like Fielding, Johnson is a master of vivid and down-to-earth analogy. There is nothing very wonderful, he assures us, in the sharp bursts in which Milton is said to have worked:

something of this inequality [of inspiration] happens to every man in every mode of exertion, manual or mental. The mechanick cannot handle his hammer at all times with equal dexterity; there are hours, he knows not why, when his hand is out.

Perhaps the iconoclasm is too abrupt in that; but one object of Johnson's investigations is to locate the ideal steady worker (the antithesis, perhaps, of himself). This ideal is most conspi- cuously found in Pope, who revised his drafts with 'indefatigable diligence'. Johnson does his best to encourage such punctilio by means of his niggling examinations of poetic craftsmanship in the final sections of the 'Lives'. He takes an almost perverse pleasure in picking out examples of faulty diction, imagery and versification. Such technical concerns might be no more than a subordinate aspect of criticism considered as a humane activity, but they were at least as important as the rules or skills of any other craft. If poetry (or 'composition' as he liked to call it) is of a piece with other crafts, this implies that the great examples of its practice are to be treated not as museum-pieces but as models to be studied and imitated by apprentice poets. The result is a practical criticism of the workbench rather than of the academy or lecture-room.

And yet, while always inclined to enjoin labour - it was part of his function as a moral teacher - Johnson reserved his highest admiration for native genius, for the gift of God rather than the contrivances of man. There is an eloquent statement of his priorities in the 'Preface to Shakespeare', couched in terms of 'design' and 'performance' rather than 'labour' and 'genius':

Every man's performances, to be rightly estimated, must be compared with the state of the age in which he lived, and with his own particular opportunities; and though to the reader a

book be not worse or better for the circumstances of the authour,
yet as there is always a silent reference of human works to
human abilities, and as the enquiry, how far man may extend
his designs, or how high he may rate his native force, is of
far greater dignity than in what rank we shall place any particular performance, curiosity is always busy to discover the
instruments, as well as to survey the workmanship, to know
how much is to be ascribed to original powers, and how much to
casual and adventitious help.

The object of Johnson's historical enquiry into the state of
Shakespeare's age - the part of the 'Preface' which this passage
introduces - is to assess the poet's 'native force'. He has
already lamented Shakespeare's carelessness of fame and moral
purpose, and his clumsiness at what required effort and study;
but he goes on to suggest that all these defects may, in one way or
another, be blamed on the age in which he lived. Even his indifference to his own dramatic texts might be attributed to a
'superiority of mind, which despises its own performances, when it
compared them with its own powers.' The purpose of editorial and
historical work on Shakespeare's texts, then, is to enable us to
glimpse the superlative powers of mind that lay behind his erratic
and critically vulnerable performances. But however great those
powers, they did not exempt Shakespeare from the doom of man -
which is to be subject to other men's criticism and censure.

In February 1767, Johnson had a conversation with George III, his
constitutional monarch, who proposed that he should undertake the
literary biography of his country. The interview, at once fascinating and richly comic, is recorded at length by Boswell. Afterwards, Johnson described the King as 'the finest gentleman I have
ever seen', and told his friends that 'I find it does a man good
to be talked to by his Sovereign' (note the passive construction).
It is hard to imagine many subsequent English critics in this
posture (Eliot, perhaps?). The King's mention of literary biography was not a prelude to royal patronage, however, and Johnson
owed his eventual commission to furnish 'Prefaces, Biographical
and Critical, to the Works of the English Poets' to a consortium
of London booksellers in 1777. Wordsworth's description in the
Essay Supplementary of the nature of the commission has not been
bettered:

    The Booksellers took upon themselves to make the collections;
    they referred probably to the most popular miscellanies, and,
    unquestionably, to their Books of accounts; and decided upon
    the claim of Authors to be admitted into a body of the most
    Eminent, from the familiarity of their names with the readers
    of that day, and by the profits, which, from the sake of his
    works, each had brought and was bringing to the Trade. The
    Editor was allowed a limited exercise of discretion, and the
    Authors whom he recommended are scarcely to be mentioned without
    a smile.

What was wanted was a standard edition of the poets most widely
read, who were almost invariably contemporaries. This must have
been the last such publishing venture without a real or feigned

educational purpose. There is no doubt that Johnson fell in easily
with the booksellers' plans, and the poets he recommended were
Thomson, Blackmore, Pomfret, Yalden and Watts.

Each of the 'Lives' is divided into three parts: a biographical
narrative, a general summary of the author's powers of mind, and
comments on his individual works. The formula is flexible, and
in general none of the three parts takes precedence over the
others. These critical and biographical prefaces were originally
to be prefixed to the works of each author in the multi-volume
edition of the poets, but as Johnson got to work they became
lengthy enough to justify publication in separate volumes. They
are arranged in a haphazard, vaguely chronological order, like
the poets in an Oxford anthology. The result - together with
Johnson's disinclination to include poets on historical rather
than commercial grounds - is a serial biography defining not a
tradition or pantheon but a loose gathering of individuals.
(Johnson had already produced a vast anthology of English writing
arranged in wholly abstract, serial order in the 'Dictionary'.)
The scale of the major 'Lives' (Cowley, Milton, Waller, Dryden,
Addison, Pope) provides some index of the eminence of their subjects, but Johnson also reprints his 'Savage' at similar length.
And there are certain moments when he sets out to rank individual
poems and to place their authors in a formal hierarchy. 'Paradise
Lost' is allowed 'with respect to design, the first place, and
with respect to performance the second' in world literature;
while Joseph Warton's question whether Pope was a poet meets the
answer that 'if the writer of the 'Iliad' were to class his
successors, he would assign a very high place to his translator,
without requiring any other evidence of Genius.' There is something faintly half-hearted about each of these judgments; the
second is only a generous testimonial. On the whole, those who
look to the final sections of the 'Lives' for penetrating appraisals
of the radical unity and uniqueness of individual works, and then
of their standing against one another in the mausoleum of Literature, will be acutely disappointed. Johnson's major interests
lie elsewhere. The General Observations on individual plays in
Johnson's edition of Shakespeare are equally terse; the main
purpose of his annotations in general is to establish the sense of
the text, and he must have felt little or no temptation to launch
into extended critical commentary.

One critical discussion in which he is totally engaged comes in
the middle section of the Life of Pope; it is a comparison of the
poetic characters of Pope and Dryden. The question at issue is
one of 'native force', and not of the ranking of particular performances. In biographical terms, Pope has been revealed as a
meticulous labourer, Dryden as a mercurial genius. Johnson
crystallizes this opposition by means of a contrast of their prose
styles, which is remarkable for its power of characterization:

> The style of Dryden is capricious and varied, that of Pope is
> cautious and uniform; Dryden obeys the motions of his own mind,
> Pope constrains his mind to his own rules of composition.
> Dryden is sometimes vehement and rapid: Pope is always smooth,
> uniform, and gentle, Dryden's page is a natural field, rising
> into inequalities, and diversified by the varied exuberance of

abundant vegetation; Pope's is a velvet lawn, shaven by the
scythe, and levelled by the roller.

Of genius, that power which constitutes a poet; that quality
without which judgment is cold and knowledge is inert; that
energy which collects, combines, amplifies, and animates; the
superiority must, with some hesitation, be allowed to Dryden.
What is it, we might wonder here, that separates neoclassical
'genius' or 'poetical vigour' from romantic imagination? The
answer is that Johnson assumes the commensurability of rival
geniuses, and in the next paragraph virtually reduces the question to the terms of a mathematical formula ('If the flights of
Dryden therefore are higher, Pope continues longer on the wing').
It is true that he also admits to 'some partial fondness for the
memory of Dryden', but this is no more than a confessional aside;
it does not interrupt the antithetical, discriminating method of
the argument.

The restraint and self-limitation that Johnson observes in
making this comparison (or 'determination', as he calls it) are
remarkable. The rules of the contest are known, there is a
strictly finite number of possible moves and the protagonists are
limited to two. Johnson makes no attempt to connect up this discussion with a total or global view of literature, even though there
are powerful implicit connections, for example in the concepts of
labour and genius. The shape of the 'Lives' in general is
episodic and aggregative rather than organic and convergent. Each
Life is a succession of separate 'determinations', concluded with
summary judgments referring outwards to general moral and aesthetic
principles which Johnson lays down 'in medias res'. In other words,
his concern is less with portraying an individual temperament or
an organic life's work, than with setting down the facts of each
biography and adjudicating upon these facts in terms of a series
of universal rules. These rules, which together make up the
framework of reason and nature, are variously derived from the
separate disciplines of ethics, theology, psychology, literary
criticism and so on. Johnson makes no attempt to overthrow the
boundaries between the disciplines or to arrive at a single,
transcendent synthesis of 'the poet'; nor does he match his poets
against a totalized 'society'; the realization of global abstractions like these was to be the critical achievement of Wordsworth.
Johnson's criticism makes use of far more empirical categories
such as the writer's career, his public image, his native force
and his style of labour, and these categories are notably deficient
in accounting for the radical uniqueness and emotional impact of
individual works on the one hand, and the institutional presence of
literature and society on the other.

What sort of public attitude to literature is presupposed by
the 'Lives of the Poets'? Their form is that of an aggregation, a
work of reference; in contemporary terms, they resemble, say, a
dictionary of British Prime Ministers rather than a 'Great
Tradition' or 'Guide to English Literature'. They help one to read
the poets but they do not provide preliminary instructions in
such reading, either in what to read or in how to read it. One
chooses the poet for oneself, and then consults the 'Life'. And
Johnson tends to evaluate the poets on strictly equal terms, as if

he were writing a reference for them or a publisher's report on
their books. That is, he treats them as colleagues working within
a general frame of assumptions which does not need to be investigated; he need only define their special concerns (pastoral,
devotional poetry and the like) and individual merits and faults.
This implied frame of assumptions is not quite life itself;
Johnson's reader will be aware not only of his general adherence
to reason and nature but of his dislike of fantasy, of republicanism, of critical sycophancy and of the aristocracy. But these are
individual traits, not those of any group that the writing defines.
Johnson does not address himself to a minority, nor does he regard
the poets he discusses as representatives of a minority. The
corollary of his belief in the common reader is that Johnson had
no idea that he was serving 'culture'. Not 'literariness' but
general literacy was the standard he set himself.

It is for these reasons that his criticism belongs to a
vanished world. His notions of writing and reading are deeply
individualistic. The reader is not a special person; if not
'homo sapiens', he is 'homo rationis capax'. The author like any
individual is held responsible for his actions and writings,
receiving praise or censure accordingly; and his choices are made
within a competitive society in which he is obliged, by one means
or another, to force himself upon public attention. We may return
to Johnson's description of the author as

> a kind of general challenger, whom every one has a right to
> attack; since he quits the common rank of life, steps forward
> beyond the lists, and offers his merit to the publick judgment
>
> ('Rambler' no. 93)

The author, that is, does not contribute to a 'culture' or social
totality, but puts himself forward in a market-place or competitive
arena. This view shares the individualism of bourgeois economics,
and is a celebration of 'equality of opportunity' within a constituted but not a corporate state. In historical terms, Johnson's
constitutionalism stands between the absolutism of two critical
systems, the early neoclassical and the romantic. His chosen method
of critical biography involves an impressive compromise between
the permanent hierarchy of the literary academy and the pure democracy of the contemporary market-place. If we are satisfied by
the academic consolidation of literary criticism since Johnson's
day, it will be the institutional side of his work that we shall
wish to emphasize. But its real value, in my view, is now the
opposite of this. He shows how criticism may be based on discri-
mination and assessment (however inadequate his criteria may
sometimes be) without congealing into closed and authoritarian
forms. And he shows its power to record the drama and confusion of
living authorship, as well as sifting and grading the deposits of
the dead.

Chapter 2

WILLIAM WORDSWORTH:
THE POET AS PROPHET

The achievement of the 'Lives of the Poets' was from one point of
view a rearguard action. Johnson was fighting off the challenge
of critical views which, mistaken or half-baked as they may have
seemed at the time, are for us loaded with historical pregnancy.
These are the - fitfully radical - views which used to be classed
as 'pre-romantic'. Among them were Joseph Warton's sceptical
question whether Pope was a poet; the theories of 'primitivists'
such as Blair and Ferguson who maintained that poetry flourished
in barbaric times and was gradually extinguished by the march of
civilization; and the cult of originality prompted by Edward
Young's 'Conjectures on Original Composition' (1759). Young
lamented the subjugation of the creative spirit by the burdensome
duty of emulating the past:

> But why are Originals so few? not because the writer's harvest
> is over, the great reapers of antiquity having left nothing to
> be gleaned after them; not because the human mind's teeming
> time is past, or because it is incapable of putting forth
> unprecedented births; but because illustrious examples engross,
> prejudice, and intimidate. They engross our attention, and so
> prevent a due inspection of ourselves; they prejudice our
> judgment in favour of their abilities, and so lessen the sense
> of our own; and they intimidate us with the splendour of their
> renown, and thus under diffidence bury our strength.

Here we have the sense of the age and exhausting fertility of
civilization, and of the contemporary writer's refusal to give
up hope. Though he lacked the mildly subversive fervour of Young,
Johnson cannot be accused of increasing the burden of the past,
and was scrupulously on guard against an attitude to the classics
that would engross or intimidate. In fact Young was an Anglican
moralist who placed Addison above Dryden and Pope, and placed
Addison's behaviour on his death-bed above the greatest of his
works; in most ways his outlook is as neoclassical and as profoundly remote from modern taste as Johnson's own. Yet he does
express a heightening of the sense of cultural power-struggle
involved in creativity that is distinctly modern. Artistic
originality involves rejection, revolt and almost superhuman
strength; Young is one of the first writers to habitually speak of

genius as 'divine'. In a revealing simile, he compares the world
of letters to 'some metropolis in flames, where a few incombustible
buildings, a fortress, temple, or tower, lift their heads, in
melancholy grandeur, amid the mighty ruin.' These incombustible
buildings are 'originals' or works of genius. Not only has a
trial of strength between works taken the place of Johnson's
economic struggle between their authors, but the victorious works
are endowed with an innate, mysterious grandeur and indestructi-
bility. It is precisely the enhancement of the grandeur and power
of literary achievements that provides the dynamic of romantic
criticism.

Johnson was not insensible to the emotive power of literature -
his aversion to the last act of 'King Lear' is sufficient proof
of this - but it is a measure of the extent of the romantic revolution in culture that his accounts of it seem so frigid and
stereotyped to us, even at the moments of his greatest critical
incisiveness. In the 'Preface to Shakespeare', for example, the
psychological arguments with which he so effectively demolishes
the doctrine of the Unities are over-intellectualized to a degree.
Johnson seems to look upon dramatic performance as an act of reci-
tation rather than a theatrical experience, and regards the
members of the audience as judicious individuals who are 'never
out of their senses', rather than as a group to some extent submitting themselves to the rhythms of the spectacle. To use
McLuhan's terms, his discussion of theatrical illusion is appropriate to a 'cool', non-involving medium, rather than a 'hot'
medium, and it is significant that when he compares the experience
of drama to that of another art, he should make the choice of
landscape painting.

No doubt this reveals the anaemia of the eighteenth-century
sensibility to tragedy, but there is a wider discrepancy, which
we might point to by contrasting the measured and public level of
Johnson's dealings with Shakespeare with Goethe's comment, as
reported by Eckermann:

> had I been born an Englishman, and had all those numerous
> masterpieces been brought before me in all their power, at my
> first dawn of youthful consciousness, they would have overpowered
> me, and I should not have known what to do. I could not have
> gone on with such fresh light-heartedness;... (1)

On the whole the romantics do not compare poetic and dramatic
power to landscape painting, but to the impact of actual landscape.
Keats likened his reading of Homer to Cortes' discovery of the
Pacific, 'Silent, upon a peak in Darien', and later Flaubert, even
more extravagantly, was to confess that

> When I have reached the crest of one of [Shakespeare's] works I
> feel that I am high on a mountain; everything disappears and
> everything appears. I am no longer a man, I am an eye; new
> horizons loom up, perspectives extend to infinity; I forget
> that I have been living like other men in the barely distinguish-
> able hovels below, that I have been drinking from those distant
> rivers that seem lesser than brooks, that I have been partici-
> pating in all the confusion of the ant-hill. (2)

For Goethe and Young, the great classics were natural obstacles
to be circumvented; but for Keats and Flaubert they were to become

locked repositories of secret and almost magical powers, available
not to the general reader but to the devotee and future poet.
Such attitudes must lead either to total subjectivism of response
or to a hermeneutic mode of criticism proclaiming the secret and
recondite properties of literary works as their artistic essence.
This facet of romantic criticism, which may be illustrated by
Blake's salutation of Milton ('he was a true Poet & of the Devil's
party without knowing it'), is totally opposed to the Johnsonian
outlook. (3) Johnson does not engage in interpretation, or the
attempt to penetrate to a hidden core of the literary work, at
all. The properties which he comments and passes judgment upon
are of the surface, and the work itself is no more than a surface.

   The growth of the sense of literary power that has been anticipated here was long drawn out. An important, though early
stage, was the eighteenth-century cult of sublimity. (4) The
term was often used merely to describe a category of poetic
excitement - the thrill of vastness, as it were - but it also
meant an ideal of elevation, both stylistic and moral. Of particular importance was the connection of sublimity and Christian
feeling. Both Miltonic and Hebrew poetry typified the sublime,
and since their sublimity expressed man's worship of nature and
its Creator, God himself came to be seen as its ultimate source.
(5) The 'primitivist' scholars located the origin of poetry in an
act of pagan nature-worship, sometimes envisaged as a communal
rite but more often as a spontaneous expression of joy and wonder
at natural phenomena. (6) The crucial jump here is that which sees
poetry as a privileged communication of transcendental experience;
not as a literary imitation of the truths of revealed religion
(Johnson's conservative view of 'Paradise Lost') but as itself the
agent of revelation. In particular, the odes of Gray and Collins
show an influential fusion of the pagan legend of the Muses with
the Christian sublime. Their presentation of Milton as the blind
seer who

                     rode sublime
     Upon the seraph-wings of Extasy,
     The secrets of th' Abyss to spy
                     (Gray, 'The Progress of Poesy')
was not entirely new; but whereas Marvell had likened him to
Tiresias in a poem which for the most part praises a fellow-
craftsman for doing a good job, Gray and Collins conjure up the
figure of Milton in a context of magical harmony and effortless
inspiration. Their poems show a curious mixture of classical
(Apollonian) and Hebraic motifs. The image of poetry as natural
harmony, symbolized by the wind-harp or Aeolian lyre, is juxtaposed with the sublime and craggy figure of the poet-prophet in
his Miltonic, Norse and Celtic manifestations. Collins' elegy on
Thomson ('In yonder grave a Druid lies') exemplifies this sort
of mixture, while the Hebraic poet-prophet is most melodramatically
realized in Gray's 'The Bard', with its shaggy and funereal hero
who prophesies the doom of the Plantagenet Kings and then flings
himself from a rock.

   The form of these poems is that of the Pindaric Ode, a lineal
predecessor of the romantic and modern lyric. The eighteenth-
century ode, as defined for example by Young in his essay 'On Lyric

Poetry' (1728), is a stiflingly literary affair, 'poetical' in
the sense of being more rhapsodic and less prosaic than any other
form.   The stylistic obscurity of Gray's odes is wholly deliberate,
and the poet helpfully provides prose summaries at the bottom of
each page. Within this form, so clearly intended to overawe the
reader, Gray and Collins expressed their own awe at the majestic
tradition of which they saw themselves as the feeble and diffident
heirs. To claim any nearer kinship to the great bards of antiquity would be little less than poetic blasphemy. And so Collins
addressed a long and obsequious poem to Sir Thomas Hanmer, the
latest editor of Shakespeare, and Gray - poised between self-pity
and democratic guilt - memorialized the 'mute inglorious Milton'
of a country churchyard.

The central myth in Gray and Collins is the history of poetry
itself. (7) Their contemporary Thomas Warton turned to academic
scholarship and wrote the first 'History of English Poetry' (1774-
81), but his unfinished achievement is of less importance than the
general availability of the potted theories of poetic history
which the romantics (beginning with Wordsworth's Appendix on
poetic diction, 1802) would take over for polemical purposes. The
spread of antiquarianism is neatly illustrated by Gray's confession
that he 'never sat down to compose poetry without reading Spenser
for a considerable time previously'. (8) Nonetheless, the activities of the poets and literary scholars who make up what has
been called the 'school of the Wartons' look bumbling and
amateurish when set beside the major theoretical investigation of
the nature of tradition in the later eighteenth century, that of
Sir Joshua Reynolds. Reynolds's 'Discourses on Art', delivered
annually from 1769 to 1790 in his capacity as first President of
the Royal Academy, were conceived as carrying on the Johnsonian
tradition, and Johnson himself regarded Reynolds as one of his
school. In fact they embody a crucial departure from Johnson,
and were to exercise their own, quite separate influence upon
literary criticism.

Johnson detested the idea of a literary academy; Reynolds
presided over an Academy of Arts. Its purpose, he decided, was
not only to provide good teachers but to act as a 'repository for
the great examples of the art', so that the student should be
exposed to 'that idea of excellence which is the result of the
accumulated experience of past ages.' The art collection, in
other words, would be there for pedagogic and not for antiquarian
reasons; thus Reynolds represents a new stage of the institutionalization of the arts, the theory of the educative function of the
museum. The students of the Academy would gain technical profi-
ciency by copying particular masterpieces, and they would acquire
reason and taste - the elements of artistic maturity - by critical
study of the whole range of the art. In the earlier 'Discourses'
Reynolds, like Johnson, emphasizes that success is proportionate
to labour; and he also advised the younger students to obey the
rules unquestioningly, and asserts that none of the great painters
was given to dissipation. All this is very much what a master
would say to his pupils. In later 'Discourses', devoted to more
advanced instruction, he concentrates upon the spiritual profit to
be drawn from the study of the great masters. The highest

veneration, he argues, should be reserved for the 'grand style'
of historical painting of noble and uplifting subjects, exemplified by the High Renaissance and the work of Michelangelo and
Raphael. The grand style is set above the 'ornamental' style of
the Venetians and the bourgeois realism of the Dutch. It
expresses not only a classical ideal but a highly literary one,
since the historical painting is an illustration of events that
have found prior expression in imaginative or historical narrative. Reynolds, indeed, considers the physical beauty and dignity
portrayed by the painter as somewhat inferior to the moral beauty
which is the province of the poet.
    The centrepiece of his discussion of the grand style lies in
his contrast of the two great masters of painting, Raphael and
Michelangelo. Reynolds argues that Raphael has the best all-round
combination of excellences, but finally prefers Michelangelo for
his greater sublimity and imaginative power. The difference
between this contrast and Johnson's contrast of Dryden and Pope
(written a few years later) is that Johnson sums up the native
endowments of two artistic lives, while Reynolds is debating the
seniority of two great monuments in the pantheon of culture. How
did this academic approach affect the students - the would-be
artists - sitting at his feet? Before the Academy was even founded,
David Hume had expressed doubts about the wisdom of setting up an
alien cultural achievement as the standard of contemporary perfection. 'So many models of Italian painting brought to England,'
he complained, 'instead of exciting our artists, is the cause of
their small progress in that noble art.' (9) While it would be
wrong to overlook the consideration that Reynolds (himself a
great portraitist) gives to forms of art less exalted than the
grand style, the ideal defined in the 'Discourses' is less that
of the creator than of the superbly cultured critic - the man who
has mastered and, above all, compared every branch of the arts.
Perhaps the best-known passage in the 'Discourses' is his cere-
monious description of that 'sovereign judge and arbiter of art',
the Man of Taste - a patrician and acquisitive figure, 'making the
universe tributary towards furnishing his mind' (and presumably
his country mansion) - a survival of Augustanism who today still
bulks large in the visual arts, if not in literature.
    Reynolds's main contribution to literary criticism lies in the
idea of the grand style, which was later taken up by Arnold. But
it is an apt symbol of the romantic revolution that the President
of the Academy was confronted by a rebellious student, who wrote
rude words all over his master's textbook. The student was Blake,
and his annotations to the 'Discourses' were made in 1808, thirty
years after he had finished his studies, and sixteen years after
Reynolds's death. The time-lag says much for the power of
Reynolds's academic teaching, and for the pre-eminence of his
reputation. How was Blake to puncture the prestige of such an
opponent? Not content with marginal interjections ('Nonsense!',
'A lie!', 'Contemptible!') and blunt statements of his own antithetical position ('All Sublimity is founded on Minute Discrimi-
nation'), Blake repeatedly denounces his enemy as a hireling and
a toady. Reynolds's admiration for his own master Michelangelo
was particularly galling: 'He praises Michel Angelo for Qualities

which Michel Angelo abhorr'd, & He blames Rafael for the only
Qualities which Rafael Valued.' Blake was in fact driven to insist
that he talked a fundamentally different language from Reynolds,
even when they seemed to agree. This is the key fact about the
annotations, even though a historian of ideas could find certain
similarities in the two men's thought. (10) Their basic disagreement is over Reynolds's conviction that the standard of
excellence can be taught. For Blake, this meant a denial of the
innate and intuitive quality of creative genius:

> Reynolds Thinks that Man Learns all that he knows. I say on
> the Contrary that Man Brings All that he has or can have Into
> the World with him. Man is Born Like a Garden ready Planted &
> Sown. This World is too poor to produce one Seed.

Hinted, but never clearly stated, in these annotations is Blake's
belief in the transcendental nature of art, as not the imitation
of the visible world but the visionary expression of eternal
reality. Reynolds, Burke, Bacon, Newton and Locke are the materialistic mockers of 'Inspiration and Vision'. In this light, it was
nonsense to talk of Raphael teaching Michelangelo, or Michelangelo
teaching Raphael, since one genius had nothing to teach another.
On the face of it this ought to demolish the eighteenth-century
problem of the 'burden of the past' altogether; the pantheon of
Old Masters could simply be ignored. But in fact the romantic
worship of transcendent genius was to bring back the problem in a
new and severer form, one manifestation of which was Blake's own
imperious self-identification with Milton and the prophets.

Nothing is more widely accepted in literary history than that the
publication of 'Lyrical Ballads' in 1798 heralded a revolution
in English poetry. Some modern scholars have attacked this reading
of history, but without much success. However the picture may be
complicated by painstaking research into the literature of the
1790s, it is enough for our purposes that the campaign of Wordsworth
and Coleridge was such a resounding publicity triumph. Their claim
to have overthrown the eighteenth-century canons of taste and to
have reconstituted the genuine tradition of English poetry came in
time to be universally recognized; and the new paradigm introduced by the romantics lasted, with modifications, throughout the
century. One important element of that paradigm was their consciousness of revolution itself. They not only produced the new
poetry but the essential commentaries upon it (notably Wordsworth's
Preface to 'Lyrical Ballads', Coleridge's 'Biographia Literaria'
and passages of Hazlitt, de Quincey and Keats). Scholars would
later learn to write history in such a way that earlier changes of
style in the arts (Renaissance, mannerism, baroque) came to be
understood as cultural revolutions; but it is European romanticism which first displays all the features of such a revolution,
and bequeaths them to such successors as realism, impressionism
and modernism. Among these features - in the English context - are
the intensely fruitful collaboration between strongly divergent
individuals (the 'Lake school'); a critical vendetta of unrelenting
hostility waged by supporters of the poetic 'ancien régime'; the
experience of discipleship with which the new writers were able to

inspire their followers and even to change their lives (the classic record of this is de Quincey's); the obsessed mixture of awe and debunking displayed by the next generation, Keats, Shelley and Byron, all so acute in their mockery of Wordsworth, and so deeply indebted to him; and finally, the change of sensibility which the innovating poets seem to personify but which is in fact so widespread as to elude causal analysis altogether. The list might be extended, but central to all these phenomena is the impact of 'Lyrical Ballads' itself, with its repudiation of the established tradition and its offer to remake society through the agency of poems of deliberate technical experiment.

Hazlitt, in his lecture On the Living Poets (1818), was the first to say that the key to the English romantics lay in their debt to the French Revolution. The relationship is complex and paradoxical. The political verse inspired by their early Jacobin sympathies, such as Wordsworth's 'Salisbury Plain', (11) is raw in the extreme, and their immediate expressions of political disillusionment, such as Coleridge's 'France: An Ode' - originally published as 'Recantation: An Ode' - are not much better. Wordsworth in 'The Prelude' tells how, after the onset of the Terror had destroyed his abstract humanitarian faith, his imagination was restored by renewed contact with nature and with the primary affections of English country people. The 'Lyrical Ballads' are full of vignettes of such people, humble and inarticulate figures who stand outside the worlds of culture and property; and Wordsworth shows a marked preference for the old, the mad, vagrants, idiots and unmarried mothers over ordinary working people. The poet's role is primarily that of memorialist and 'post facto' moralist, pointing out the general truths that are illustrated by the commonplace events of the tale. Wordsworth clearly did see the poetic description of ordinary lives as a way of promoting the democratic growth of social sympathy. He defended 'The Idiot Boy', for example, on the grounds that it was intended to promote the welfare of the mentally handicapped. But there is no question that the more successful of the 'Lyrical Ballads', such as 'Old Man Travelling'. are in a reflective, contemplative mode, and the 1798 volume ends with 'Tintern Abbey', a meditative poem whose powerful eloquence is in total contrast to the bare and mawkish diction of the more doctrinaire ballads. This dichotomy between the poetry of description, simple, unpretentious and 'levelling', and the impassioned and prophetic poetry of reflection, runs throughout Wordsworth's career. It is already present in the first of the three prefaces to 'Lyrical Ballads', the Advertisement to the edition of 1798. This is a terse and inconspicuous essay which does little more than explain why the poems in the volume may strike the reader as slightly unusual. There is a single hint of more revolutionary claims:

It is desirable that ... readers, for their own sakes, should not suffer the solitary word Poetry, a word of very disputed meaning, to stand in the way of their gratification; but that, while they are perusing this book, they should ask themselves if it contains a natural delineation of human passions, human characters, and human incidents.

The fact is that Wordsworth, who here disavows the word 'Poetry',

has already lectured his reader on the 'honourable characteristic' of the art, and goes on to intimidate him by dark references
to the authority of 'our elder writers' and to the arduousness
of critical judgment, as attested by none other than Reynolds.
Thus the reader is simultaneously urged to trust his own judgment,
and to consider an appreciation of 'Lyrical Ballads' as the
ultimate reward of a cultivated taste. If it were not prefixed to
one of the most famous volumes of poetry ever written, this would
long ago have been recognized as a grotesque example of literary
blackmail; some of Pope's Dunces were immortalized for less. The
two faces of the Advertisement, however, represent a duality
which is endemic to Wordsworth's critical thought. In Wordsworth
as in the National Assembly, revolution was to be the foster-parent
of a new authoritarianism.

Wordsworth in later life said that he 'never cared a straw
about the theory'; but the volume of criticism that he wrote
between 1798 and 1815 is substantial. There is a long-standing
problem about the relation of this criticism to his poetry.
(Compare Blake's annotation to his copy of Wordsworth's 'Poems',
written in 1826: 'I do not know who wrote these Prefaces: they
are very mischievous & direct contrary to Wordsworth's own Practise.') On the one hand, the doctrines of the 1800 Preface to
'Lyrical Ballads' do not always seem to fit the poetry; on the
other hand, it is not clear why, to supplement the poetry, a statement of doctrines should be needed. The various impulses at work
in the 1798 Advertisement suggest that the prefaces should be read
as social gestures rather than as abstract and logical contributions to literary theory - though their influence was no less
extensive for that. Wordsworth's social situation was in fact a
peculiar one. He and Coleridge did as much as anyone to define
the social status of the major nineteenth-century poet (Coleridge,
however, was a good deal less successful in enjoying this status).
Yet they began their 'Great Decade' as impoverished and isolated
Jacobins, ostracized by their country neighbours, their gentility
somewhat shabby. (12) Sales of their early work were minimal,
and an obscurity like Blake's might have faced them. Coleridge
in 'Biographia Literaria' was to advise young poets to make sure
of another profession; he himself nearly became a Unitarian
minister. He was prevented by an annuity from the Wedgwood
brothers in 1797, and Wordsworth also was supported by private
bequests - £900 from a fellow-student, Raisley Calvert, in 1795,
followed by his wife's dowry and legacies from her family - until
he secured the Stamp-Distributorship for Westmoreland and later for
part of Cumberland. A lot of this good fortune followed the
poet's public conversion to the cause of Monarchism and reaction,
though de Quincey (not necessarily a reliable witness) tells of
Wordsworth and Southey expressing republican sentiments and
joking about the royal family as late as 1807. Much has been
written about the Lake poets' religious and political recanta-
tions; less about their adoption of middle-class values and
life-style. Wordsworth became the bourgeois 'paterfamilias',
needing money to run Rydal Mount and raise his growing family.
Coleridge's theory of the 'clerisy' portrays intellectuals as a
professional élite, recognized as one of the permanent estates of

the realm. Their defiance of the public is understandable when
we remember that neither depended much upon sales for a living;
what they needed was the good opinion of philanthropic middle-class
individuals and government officials. Such patronage, bestowed
on the poet by his social equals, involved no mercenary obligations (apart, presumably, from distributing stamps, and confirmed
his self-esteem and sense of mission.

The Preface to the second edition of 'Lyrical Ballads' (1800) is
Wordsworth's most far-reaching act of self-justification. The
result is a critical document of an entirely new kind: a poetic
manifesto offering a trenchant statement of universal principles
designed to supersede all existing theory and tradition. This
plan was not fully realized until the enlarged Preface of 1802,
with its explicit warning that acceptance of the new principles
must entail a total revaluation of the reader's judgments of 'the
greatest Poets both ancient and modern'. Wordsworth did not
succeed in a total rationalization of his poetic practice, and
some of his arguments remained tortuous and muddled. Yet the gap
between the Preface and its generic predecessors, such as the
prefaces of Dryden and Fielding with their artful assimilation of
the new work to existing authority, might be compared to that
between earlier constitutions and the great documents of the revolutionary age such as the Declaration of Independence and the
Declaration of the Rights of Man. Like these, the Preface to
'Lyrical Ballads' makes a 'self-evident' statement of universal
principles valid far beyond its particular occasion. It defines
poetry and the poet in the abstract rather than by reference to
tradition and precedent, and it is written in the confident
language of eighteenth-century rationalism (whereas the critical
prose of the later romantics is far more unstable, and its relationship to rational thought increasingly problematic). The theory
of poetic language that it puts forward seems to promise a complete
emancipation of poetry from the tyranny of literature and its
conventions.

Hazlitt wrote that the Lake poets 'founded the new school on
a principle of sheer humanity, on pure nature void of art', and
that poetry for them 'grew like a mushroom out of the ground;
or was hidden in it like a truffle, which it required a particular
sagacity and industry to find out and dig up.' (13) The 1800
Preface, after announcing the need for a fundamental enquiry into
the elements of criticism, psychology and social history, puts
forward a series of radical arguments aimed at breaking down the
established distinctions of Augustan or any other centralized
literary culture. The main force of the attack is directed at
the Augustan habits of poetic diction. To say that a whole
century's poetry was vitiated by its diction was itself reduc-
tive, since diction was the lowest of the strictly poetic elements
in the Aristotelian hierarchy. Wordsworth was contemptuously
reinterpreting the 'burden of the past' which had weighed down
his predecessors as a burden of clichés, a great mass of phrases
and figures which 'from father to son have long been regarded as
the common inheritance of poets', but were now fit only to be
thrown on the scrap-heap - a verdict that he swiftly executed
upon all but five lines of a sonnet by Gray. Wordsworth justified

his attack on poetic diction with the thesis that there was
'no essential difference between the language of prose and
metrical composition': an argument which disposes of any set
of conventional distinctions that a society might use to separate
literary from other kinds of discourse. He rejected an artificial 'poetic' idiom in order to turn to nature and the twin
ideas of natural description and natural inspiration. The first,
descriptive or mimetic idea consorts with the stated aim of the
'Lyrical Ballads', which is to trace the 'primary laws of our
nature' as they are reflected in the 'incidents of common life'.
The language that he will adopt, Wordsworth says, is purified
of conventional poeticisms and of anything that does not result
from looking 'steadily at my subject'. In addition, it is to be
the language of rural life, since this is a more natural and
more permanent language than that of the city or the upper classes.
The second idea - that of natural inspiration - is also present
in 1800, although the transition from a mainly mimetic to a
mainly expressive theory of poetry is one of the principal developments that takes place between 1800 and 1802. (14) Already in
1800 we read of poetry as a 'spontaneous overflow of powerful
feelings'. Inspiration is a theme of the earliest of the 'Lyrical
Ballads', as the poet celebrates the 'impulse from a vernal wood'
that replaced any amount of moral philosophy ('The Tables Turned'),
and the 'hour of feeling' when

One moment now may give us more
Than fifty years of reason;

('Lines written at a small distance from my house ...')
Atavistic sentiments like these had a powerful attraction for
Wordsworth, and yet his theories do not bring about a total dis-
lodgment of the artificial element in poetry. His argument
surrounds natural inspiration with a network of moral and rational
channels and filters, like the purification plant of a reservoir.
Deliberate cultural intervention is needed if the sources of
feeling are to be made into a drinkable product. And we shall
find that this aspect of the theory, which contradicts some of
the bolder affirmations of the poems, is reinforced by the whole
context of discourse in the Preface itself.

A central Wordsworthian concern is with language. While there is
no doubt about the force of his opposition to stale and stilted
poetical idioms, his criterion of natural language - 'the real
language of men' - is notoriously ambiguous. It is neither a
wholly rhetorical nor a wholly sociological category. Since he
describes the language of rustics as 'a more permanent and a far
more philosophical language' than that of sophisticated poets,
Wordsworth has been seen as defining a permanent poetic rhetoric.
(15) If so, it is a rhetoric based on some strong aversions, but
without any definite rules. But the 1798 Advertisement had claimed
that the language of 'Lyrical Ballads' had a sociological basis,
being chosen from 'the language of conversation in the middle and
lower classes of society'. By 1802 Wordsworth had changed this
to 'a selection of the language really spoken by men', with the
emphasis upon the modifying influence of the selection process.

Coleridge was later to scoff at the idea of the poet 'wandering about in search of angry or jealous people in uncultivated society, in order to copy their words.' (16)   It was certainly wise to drop the word 'conversation' with its suggestions of everyday exclamations and gossip.   Wordsworth had probably meant to indicate the language of folk-tale, reminiscence and popular narrative - 'the real language of men in a state of vivid sensation' (the phrase is common to the texts of 1800 and 1802).   The implications of this are ethical rather than sociological;   real language is language which expresses the feelings with directness and sincerity, as men are supposed to do in the 'natural state' of rustic life.   The adequacy of the language can then be established pragmatically, by examining particular poems and their power to move us, so that the Wordsworthian theory of rustic life is technically a side-issue.   For at this point he shifts the focus of the argument from the poem as end-product to the process of composition.   If the method of writing can be shown to be 'natural', then the language will be so too.

Whatever he means by 'real language', it is the mainstay of his attack on the poetic tradition.   In the Appendix on poetic diction (1802), Wordsworth's target is not simply Augustan diction, but any inherited poetical rhetoric.   Borrowing heavily from the primitivist theorists such as Ferguson and Blair, he argues that the earliest poets expressed themselves in figurative language as the natural vehicle of passionate feeling.   Later poets lacking in genuine feeling tended to repeat the same rhetorical devices to obtain a heightened emotional effect.   The tradition-conscious poet, in other words, is a kind of commercial entertainer well versed in the tricks of his trade.   His opposite, the true poet, must cut loose from this 'motley masquerade', and struggle for recognition in the face of a corrupt public taste.   If he is to find his poetic identity, he must totally ignore his predecessors.   This seems - and for a time it was - a wholly revolutionary position, like Blake's.

How, in fact, was poetry written?   Wordsworth's radicalism went furthest in part of the expanded Preface of 1802, where he decided to strengthen his argument about poetic language by taking the difficult case of dramatic verse.   Clearly dramatic speech should sound real and plausible, but how could its origins be anything but willed and artificial?   Wordsworth admitted that the poet's task was 'in some degree mechanical, compared with the freedom and power of real and substantial action and suffering'.   We might concede this to be true, while feeling that real action and suffering is often unrealized because inarticulate.   But Wordsworth assumed that command of language was innate in everyone.   All that the poet needed to do, therefore, was to put himself in the situation of his characters, and

even confound and identify his own feelings with theirs;
modifying only the language which is thus suggested to him,
by a consideration that he describes for a particular purpose,
that of giving pleasure.

The final qualification is larger than it seems at first sight; but it does not alter the striking assertion that once the right state of feeling is attained, the proper language will come

automatically. Wordsworth describes another technique for the
simulation of feeling in the famous passage where the poet, now
apparently an author of meditative lyrics, seeks to recreate the
emotion that he has 'recollected in tranquility'. In each case,
the spontaneity of poetry is the outcome of a deliberate induced
emotional state.

It is not only the poet's feelings that are deliberately
induced. In the 1800 version, Wordsworth went straight on from his
denunciation of poetic diction to 'answer an obvious question,
namely why, professing these opinions have I written in verse?'
His answer was not wholly satisfactory, but the main point is
clear: metre must be added to 'natural' language for the purpose of giving pleasure. But why should metre be exempted from
the objections he brings against poetic diction? If we compare
his theoretical accounts of the two elements which distinguish
poetry from prose, there can be no question about his discrimina-
tion in favour of metre. Metre tends to 'divest language ... of
its reality', and therefore to make descriptions of harrowing
events more palatable (hence Shakespearean tragedy is preferable
to 'Clarissa'); but poetic diction is condemned precisely because
it obscures reality. Metre is said to be regular and uniform,
where poetic diction is arbitrary and capricious; but the advocates of poetic diction, such as Johnson in the Life of Dryden,
had stressed its regularizing and controlling function. Wordsworth
views metre as a mechanical adornment, and adds that part of the
charm is caused by association with the pleasure received from
previous metrical works. But when poetic diction aspires to the
charm of imitation, he condemns it as false and artificial. (We
might add that an insistent metric is the main sign of the 'poetic'
status of the experimental poems of 'Lyrical Ballads'.) Wordsworth, in effect, treats metre as the positive sign of tradition,
where poetic diction is the negative sign. The basic problem is
that he is deeply attached to metre, and recognizes its primitive
emotional power; but at the same time, fearing to leave a gaping
anomaly in his system, he denies it an intrinsic creative role.
He describes it as ornamental, and then makes the startling observation that, given comparable passages in verse and prose, 'the
verse will be read a hundred times where the prose is read once.'
Perhaps the reason for all this confusion (and for Coleridge's
exhaustive attempts in 'Biographia Literaria' to clear it up) is
that metre occupies a crucial position in the dialectic of the
natural and the cultural idea of poetry. Metre for the modern
poet is a social skill, an aspect of the laborious and visible
poetic craftsmanship which Johnson scrutinized in the 'Lives of
the Poets'. And this is why Wordsworth can only grudgingly admit
it to poetics, as a mere process of arrangement, a necessary
constraint upon the poet's inspiration. Yet Wordsworth also knew
that metre has innate psychological functions. Did he perhaps
obscurely sense that metre is a primordial attribute of poetry,
which could not be rationalized away however hard he tried;
that metre is at once a mechanical skill and the product of
organic, instinctive perception, so that its ambivalence is that
of poetry itself?

Nothing could be further from Wordsworth's outlook than Johnson's
vision of the drudgery of authorship as an allegorical drama of
the human condition. The poet whom Wordsworth envisages does not
toil over his work, for the crucial operations occur in his mind
and not on the manuscript page. This devaluation of literary
labour belongs in the general category of romantic idealism. It
is associated with the cult of originality and genius, going back
to Young, (17) and also with the remarkable semantic shift undergone by the word 'poetry' in later romantic writing; 'poetry'
came to be habitually used to mean an essence or spirit, where
it had formerly signified a genre. Romantic idealism is not
merely a philosophical position, however, and at the same time as
the creation of poetry comes to be seen as an internal and invis-
ible affair, the poet himself is elevated to a level far above
that of the humble craftsman. The author (a word which Wordsworth
tends to avoid, preferring 'Poet' with a capital 'P') has become
the quintessential 'authority'.

In Wordsworth's theory, as we have seen, the poet's authority
does not derive from his command of language. But while poetry
is the natural expression of the ordinary and basic emotions of
life, this does not mean that poetic success is open to all. The
poet is a man of exceptional gifts, who has rigorously cultivated his mind through a discipline of meditation. Having done
this, he can boast, as Wordsworth does, that each of his poems
has a 'worthy purpose'. The poetry may have its source in the
springs of inspiration, but it has been duly filtered through the
poet's conscience and moral sensibility. It is notable what a
solitary and internalized picture this gives of poetic creation.
The key determinants - the author's mental endowments, his
experiences of observation and habits of meditation, and finally
the inspiration itself - are all held within the self. Thus the
poet is not, as Johnson had said, a 'general challenger' who
'offers his merit to the publick judgment'. There is no challenge
or submission or reward; only the eventual recognition of his
intrinsic and inalienable merits. I have suggested that Wordsworth's peculiar class position helped him to take this attitude,
the results of which are seen in his lofty eloquence and poetic
pride.

It was not only by writing Odes to Liberty that the romantics
participated in the revolutionary 'spirit of the age'. Though
the changes in social structure seemed to threaten the very existence of poets and poetry, men such as the later Wordsworth,
Browning and Tennyson emerged in the Victorian period as revered
and leading members of the bourgeoisie. The early deaths of
Byron, Shelley and Keats left unanswered the question of what
other role - apart from that of Bohemian exile - the major
nineteenth-century poet could adopt. All of these poets, however,
claimed to be the incarnation of higher and more permanent values
than those which the contemporary social world acknowledged. They
were much more than just the spokesmen of these values.
Wordsworth's prefaces had pioneered the claim that to accept
the authority of a new volume of poems was to accept a particular
social ideology.

There is a distinction to be made between the proud individualism

of Wordsworth, his determination to stand on his own feet unaided
by tradition, and his eventual acknowledgment of a spiritual
kinship with his fellow-poets which differs from his feelings
towards ordinary men. 'Resolution and Independence' illustrates
all three kinds of feeling: it is a powerfully egotistical poem,
it presents a famous symbol of fellow-man in the Leech-gatherer,
and it also, through the recollections of Chatterton and Burns,
invokes a kind of freemasonry among poets:

We Poets in our youth begin in gladness;
But thereof come in the end despondency and madness.
The poets' existence here manifests the kind of seriality that is
attributed to humanity as a whole in Arnold's 'To Marguerite':
there are Wordsworth, Chatterton and Burns, spiritual beacons
flashing at one another, and between them stretches the 'unplumb'd,
salt, estranging sea'. Among other things, Wordsworth as a critic
attempts to portray a better condition, in which the poet, while
retaining his profound individuality, would no longer be encircled
by a sea of despondency. This is only partly accounted for when we
say that the prefaces are an attempt to create an audience for his
poetry.

Wordsworth is determined to attribute his loneliness as a poet
to external causes. So much depends on the poet's own efforts -
'By our own spirits are we deified' - because he has been robbed of
an established tradition. He can no longer write directly and
sincerely in the Augustan mode, but that mode is only the expression
of a frivolous and corrupted society. In order to justify his
poetry it is necessary to remind his readers what the foundations
of 'real society' are. When he did this, Wordsworth was using his
poetry as a base from which to launch one of the many competing
ideologies of the revolutionary age. As an abstract and total
account of social relations, the theory of poetry he put forward
invites comparison with the other new ideologies such as utilitarianism, republicanism and Burkeian conservatism. Naturally it
shares some elements with its rivals: the rationalistic frame of
the 1800 Preface is taken from republicanism, while the lofty and
dignified role that he assigns to 'pleasure' would align Wordsworth
with the utilitarians. But it would be a mistake to reduce his
theory to its political constituents and to call it conservative,
utilitarian or democratic. The romantic theory of poetry is a
distinct ideology, in conflict with those around it. Conceived by
Wordsworth and Coleridge as a substitute for their shattered
beliefs in republicanism and pantisocracy, it would later become a
powerful weapon against the assumptions of utilitarians and
nineteenth-century liberals. (18)

Wordsworth's claim for the poet's authority is implicit in the
very language of the Preface - a stately and orotund prose that
is totally at variance with the 'natural' ideal that it is employed
to convey. For genuinely 'natural' and spontaneous prose in the
romantic period we may go to the marginalia and graffiti of Blake
or to the notebooks of Coleridge, but certainly not to Wordsworth.
Within the Preface, however, there is strictly speaking not one
style, but two. The first, which dominates the text of 1800, is
the style of egotistical self-defence. Its lofty and occasionally
provocative arrogance resembles the 1798 Advertisement, but the

manner is now that of a credo, a first-person affirmation. In the
1802 text, however, Wordsworth added a more stately and impersonal
section, presenting an abstract sketch of the nature of the poet
and his function in society. Here he presents his 'sublime notion
of Poetry' in extravagant terms:

> The Man of Science seeks truth as a remote and unknown bene-
> factor; he cherishes and loves it in his solitude: the Poet,
> singing a song in which all human beings join with him,
> rejoices in the presence of truth as our visible friend and
> hourly companion. Poetry is the breath and finer spirit of
> all knowledge; it is the impassioned expression which is in
> the countenance of all Science. Emphatically may it be said
> of the Poet, as Shakespeare hath said of man, 'that he looks
> before and after.' He is the rock of defence of human nature;
> an upholder and preserver, carrying everywhere with him
> relationship and love. In spite of difference of soil and
> climate, of language and manners, of laws and customs: in
> spite of things gone silently out of mind, and things violently
> destroyed; the Poet binds together by passion and knowledge the
> vast empire of human society, as it is spread over the whole
> earth, and over all time.

The noble idealism of this is only equalled by its abstraction from
any tangible social reality. What we respond to is chiefly the
religious fervour; it is the prose equivalent of the Miltonic
and visionary verse of much of 'The Prelude'. To speak of the poet
in 'ideal perfection' is to instil a belief in the miracle of
incarnation. The realm of permanent values can be made flesh in
history; if we can envision the 'vast empire of human society',
and feel relationship and love towards it, Wordsworth's work has
begun to bear fruit. The religious terms in which he couches his
new ideology make him the first of the nineteenth-century literary
prophets. His 'vast empire' is a secularized Kingdom of Heaven,
in which the poet can assume his full stature as priest and even
as god.

The messianic vision came to dominate Wordsworth's verse as he
planned his 'great philosophical poem' and began work on 'The
Prelude'. The opening lines record an occasion when

> poetic numbers came
> Spontaneously, and cloth'd in priestly robe
> My spirit, thus singled out, as it might seem,
> For holy services:

Imagination is the 'vision and the faculty divine', and the poet is
its priest. At his loftiest he may aspire to

> breathe in worlds
> To which the heaven of heavens is but a veil (19)

- but at the same time he is fated not to fulfil his designs, and
to feel a continuing guilt about his own inadequacy:

> Thus from day to day
> I live, a mockery of the brotherhood
> Of vice and virtue, with no skill to part
> Vague longing that is bred by want of power
> From paramount impulse not to be withstood,
> A timorous capacity from prudence;
> From circumspection, infinite delay.

('The Prelude', Book 1)

There are many varieties of romantic despondency, but Wordsworth's usually has the appearance of a saving ritual, a kind of humility that is the reverse of unproductive. His membership of the 'brotherhood/Of vice and virtue' obliges him to bear witness as a critic in this world as well as aspiring to a higher, and to bring his readers down to the level of common humanity as well as up to the realm of absolute values. Mankind, he wrote in the Essay Supplementary, must be 'humbled and humanized, in order that they may be purified and exalted'.

Thus Wordsworth is both the possessor and even apostle of the 'vision and the faculty divine', and the critical revolutionary bringing plain, down-to-earth remedies for the ills of literature and society, confident in his direct grasp of the principles of universal nature. Coleridge would later attack the authority of Wordsworthian natural reason in the name of literary experience and tradition, just as Burke had attacked the French revolutionaries and their doctrines of the Rights of Man. But Wordsworth's assumption of this authority was an essential part of his legacy to literary criticism. Criticism, he suggests, has a task of social hygiene before it, which should be the common pursuit of the right-minded:

> reflecting upon the magnitude of the general evil, I should be
> oppressed with no dishonourable melancholy, had I not a deep
> impression of certain inherent and indestructible qualities
> of the human mind, and likewise of certain powers in the great
> and permanent objects that act upon it which are equally
> inherent and indestructible; and did I not further add to this
> impression a belief that the time is approaching when the evil
> will be systematically opposed by men of greater powers and
> with far more distinguished success.

Here was a programme for such successors as Arnold, Eliot and Leavis: critics of culture who share his propagandist instincts, as well as his contempt for frivolities such as 'frantic novels' German tragedies and a taste for sherry. In these lines the defence of a volume of poems gives rise not merely to an ideology but to a crusade.

> High is our calling, Friend!   Creative Art ...
> Demands the service of a mind and heart,
> Though sensitive, yet, in their weakest part,
> Heroically fashioned....
>   ('To B.R. Haydon')

One of the remarkable aspects of Wordsworth's later years was his concern for the architecture of his collected works. He began to consider the classification of his shorter poems in 1809, (20) and by 1815 he had devised the complex scheme that is still perpetuated by the Oxford editors. At the same time, he planned what was to have been his greatest poem, 'The Recluse', and in the Preface to 'The Excursion' (1814) he wrote of his life's work as a vast Gothic cathedral of which 'The Prelude' and the minor poems were subsidiary chapels. The nave, in the event, remained uncompleted, but this remarkable simile is enough to show how profoundly his attitude to poetry had changed since he and Coleridge had launched

their revolution with a handful of experimental ballads. Much of
his later criticism, like the sonnet to Haydon, is concerned with
the heroic nature of the artist's vocation. He steadily abandons
the mimetic and anti-literary doctrines of 1800 ('I have at all
times endeavoured to look steadily at my subject') in favour of a
more exalted and mystified version of 'poetic truth'. In the
first of the three 'Essays upon Epitaphs' (1810), he stipulates
that an epitaph should not be too precise or analytical, but should
view the deceased 'through a tender haze or a luminous mist'. The
result would not be falsehood, as might be expected, but a higher
order of truth - 'truth hallowed by love - the joint offspring of
the worth of the Dead and the affections of the Living!' 'Truth
hallowed by love', of course, reflects the orthodox Christianity
which Wordsworth had now embraced; poetic truth, he argues,
was that which produced right feeling in the reader, and could
only be achieved by the possessor of a 'devout heart'.

This higher order of truth is what both he and Coleridge would
soon be calling 'imaginative' truth. The term 'imagination' is
twice used in the Preface to 'Lyrical Ballads', once in a positive
and once in a negative context, but its precise significance
remains obscure. In the Preface of 1815, however, Wordsworth
rejected the definition of imagination in terms of mimesis (ascribed
to a contemporary lexicographer, William Taylor of Norwich) in
favour of one reflecting his new sense of the dignity of poetry:

Imagination, in the sense of the word as giving title to a Class
of the following Poems, has no reference to images that are
merely a faithful copy, existing in the mind, of absent external
objects; but is a word of higher import, denoting operations
of the mind upon those objects, and processes of creation or of
composition, governed by certain fixed laws.

We have come a long way from the ambition of transcribing
natural emotions and common incidents expressed in the Advertisement
of 1798. The movement, however, had been anticipated in Wordsworth's poetry. 'The Prelude', for example, begins with a passive
invocation of the muse of nature ('Oh there is blessing in this
gentle breeze'), and ends with natural objects transformed into
the emblems or outward manifestations of mind. The poet climbs
Mount Snowdon and interprets the panorama from the summit as 'the
type of a majestic intellect'; and he finally closes the poem
with an eulogy of the human mind, 'A thousand times more beautiful
than the earth/On which he dwells'. The critical counterpart of
this movement is the 1815 Preface, written to explain the classification of his shorter poems. Wordsworth's system of classification
was a psychological one, avoiding the traditional hierarchy of
genres which he had rejected in 1800. Instead, a new and idiosyncratic hierarchy was set up. The main part of the Preface
consists of the distinction of fancy and imagination, and then of
a review of the 'grand store-house' of lofty imagination present
in great literature. Examples are given from the Bible, Milton,
Spenser and Shakespeare - to which list, anticipating the judgment
of posterity and defying 'these unfavourable times', Wordsworth
unashamedly adds himself. He was now relying on a new understanding
of the poetic tradition, rather than the principles of abstract
reason, to legitimize his authority.

The 1815 Preface was followed by the supplementary Essay which
constitutes his most embattled piece of literary propaganda. Here
at last he let fly at Jeffrey of the 'Edinburgh Review' and at the
other critics whose hostility had galled him for years. In the
first paragraph, dropped from subsequent editions, little is left
of his normally imperturbable stance:

> By what fatality the orb of my genius (for genius none of them
> seem to deny me) acts upon these men like the moon upon a
> certain description of patients, it would be irksome to inquire;
> nor would it consist with the respect which I owe myself to take
> further notice of opponents whom I internally despise.

What Wordsworth did feel he owed himself was an imposing piece of
self-justification. The Essay, however, is a complex document,
partly a discussion of the act of reading, partly a history of
English poetry and partly a rehearsal of his own claims to greatness. The latter aspect may be disposed of first. Wordsworth
begins by discussing the qualifications for critical judgment.
He asserts that the qualified critic must have devoted the best
part of his understanding to literary study (significantly, he
has no trust in the common or naive reader). But he then turns
furiously on the majority of cultivated readers with their 'palsied
imaginations and indurated hearts'. The true critic is distinguished by his reverence for original genius; no doubt, as in the
1798 Advertisement, there is a strictly contemporary yardstick
that he has in mind. He proceeds to give a history of English
public taste, angled to prove that genuinely original poets have
always been neglected - an important example of the post-
revolutionary rewriting of history. Finally he pronounces himself
satisfied with his own hostile reception; it is proof that he has
not worked in vain. A poet's allegiance, he says, is owed not to
the literary public but to the 'People, philosophically characterized' and the 'embodied spirit of their knowledge'.

Maybe such allegiance is easily sworn; and the spectacle of a
poet publicly awarding himself the crown of survival is a little
undignified. However, we have here the faith which kept Wordsworth
going as a poet, and saved him from the defeatism of the late
Augustans. The conspicuous satisfactions which he managed to draw
from initial public rejection were far from discouraging to later
poets. And the Essay has a classic status, not merely on account
of the eloquence that genius can bring to the task of self-
vindication, but because of its analysis of the concept of taste.
Though he stresses the rarity of taste (which may, therefore, be
considered the possession of an élite), he also redefines it in such
a way as to assert the reality of literary revolutions. Taste,
Wordsworth points out, is not a passive response to literary consumption, but the product of 'intellectual acts and operations'.
Here he introduces an idea which is of crucial importance throughout
romantic theory - the idea of poetic power.

'Every author, as far as he is great and at the same time
original, has had the task of creating the taste by which he is to
be enjoyed.' The great author, on this view, does not stand at
the bar of public opinion; he has the task of forming that opinion,
and need make no concessions to it until he has done so. The act
of reading poetry is not one of acquiring knowledge, but involves

'the exertion of a co-operating power' in the reader's mind. This power is a latent sympathy or source of psychic energy. Once the poet has overcome the reader's resistance or inertia and awakened it, it makes a permanent extension of consciousness - 'widening the sphere of human sensibility, for the delight, honour, and benefit of human nature.' Genius - the ability to communicate and excite such power - then appears as an arduous moral and educational responsibility, and the poet as a shaper of civilization. Wordsworth's discussion presents a curious mixture of psychological analysis and submerged political implications. There is something Napoleonic about the great poet, seen as a wielder of 'power':

> If every great poet with whose writings men are familiar, in
> the highest exercise of his genius, before he can be thoroughly
> enjoyed, has to call forth and to communicate power, this
> service, in a still greater degree, falls upon an original
> writer, at his first appearance in the world. Of genius in the
> fine arts, the only infallible sign is the widening the sphere
> of human sensibility, for the delight, honour, and benefit of
> human nature. Genius is the introduction of a new element
> into the intellectual universe: or, if that be not allowed,
> it is the application of powers to objects on which they had
> not before been exercised, or the employment of them in such
> a manner as to produce effects hitherto unknown. What is all
> this but an advance, or a conquest, made by the soul of the
> poet?

Political metaphors are never far from the surface of romantic criticism. No doubt this reflects the disappointment of their youthful revolutionary hopes, but the evidence in Wordsworth's writings is that his political energies were thoroughly sublimated. By 'power' he means an emotional charge which takes possession of the reader and moves him to vital and passionate response; an elemental aspect of literary experience which had previously been muffled by such traditional formulae as those of 'sublimity' or 'pity and terror'.

'Power' became a jargon-word among romantic critics and reviewers. It was found particularly useful when dealing with the uneven and unpolished works of Byron, Shelley and Keats. Thus Lamb wrote of Byron that 'I never can make out his great power, which his admirers talk of.' (21) Coleridge offered to demonstrate the 'specific symptoms of poetic power' in Chapter Fifteen of 'Biographia Literaria', and concluded that 'In Shakespeare's poems, the creative power and the intellectual energy wrestle as in a war embrace.' Shelley spoke of the 'electric life' burning in the words of modern poets, while de Quincey wrote unforgettably of the conflict of 'power' and self-repression that he saw in Dorothy Wordsworth's face. (22) It was de Quincey, also, who did his best to preserve the term for serious criticism with his famous distinction of the 'literature of knowledge' and the 'literature of power' - essentially a popularization of Wordsworth's argument in the Essay Supplementary. De Quincey's 'literature of power' means simply imaginative literature, or literature considered as one of the fine arts, and the communication of power is the awakening of latent emotions and feelings in the reader. In fact, though he speaks of a 'literature of

knowledge', de Quincey also suggests that this is not really
literature at all: 'All that is literature seeks to communicate
power; all that is not literature, to communicate knowledge.' (23)
Since this is a crucial moment in the evolution of the term 'literature' as the permanent, imaginative heritage of a people, it is
significant that it emerges not only in opposition to eighteenth-
century aesthetics, but in opposition to the utilitarian emphasis
on useful knowledge. (24) It was de Quincey, a lifelong critic
of Benthamism and political economy, who forged the idea of a
'literature of power' as a weapon of Victorian debate.

De Quincey was one of the many writers in whom Wordsworth's
seminal influence took effect. That influence, indeed, may be
pursued throughout later romantic criticism. Given Wordsworth's
combination of profound originality and extreme self-assurance,
it is not surprising that he himself should show divided aims,
so that very different emphases could be drawn from his work; he
could be seen as revolutionary or authoritarian, as nature-
worshipper or cultural dictator, as enemy of literature or apostle
of the imagination. It remains to be recorded that, in a personal
and idiosyncratic way, Wordsworth himself was able to reconcile
many of these conflicts. After all, the original source of 'power'
for him lay not in the arts but in nature itself. All other sources
of the experience of power in his work are eventually compared to
the forces of nature. This is true of the experience of the
Metropolis in Book Eight of 'The Prelude' and of the books that the
poet read as a boy in Book Five. It is also true of poetry,
including Wordsworth's own, so that our exploration of his poetics
must finally go full circle, from nature to art and back to nature
again.

A simple example is the genre of the epitaph, to which Wordsworth devoted three consecutive essays in 1810. These neglected
essays are the most mature expression of the Wordsworth who
revolved against the literary Establishment of 1800. The
epitaph as he describes it is a genuine mode of folk-poetry,
expressing common feelings in the ordinary language of men. It
has a very tangible social function, and yet one which tran-
scends the world of human society, since it is an expression of
man's belief in immortality. If for a moment we can be persuaded
to think of the epitaph as a central poetic genre, it will not be
hard to accept Wordsworth's feeling for the elementality and
permanence of rustic life centred upon the village churchyard.
Still better, the epitaph is not 'a proud Writing shut up for the
studious', but an outdoor object, and part of the permanent landscape: 'it is concerning all, and for all: - in the Church-yard
it is open to the day; the sun looks down upon the stone, and
the rains of Heaven beat against it.'

The Essays upon Epitaphs, then, present an idyllic and somewhat
feudal vision. It is no more than an idyll, of course, because
whatever their merits epitaphs cannot be great art, and Wordsworth
does not claim that they are. They may epitomize wisdom and
common humanity, but not the energy of 'power'. And yet in his
poetry Wordsworth aspired to a vision in which even the most
grandiose and heroic of artistic works might appear as natural
objects. The aspiration is stated at the beginning of one of the

great visionary passages in 'The Prelude':

>   forgive me, Friend,
> If I, the meanest of this Band, had hope
> That unto me had also been vouchsafed
> An influx, that in some sort I possess'd
> A privilege, and that a work of mine,
> Proceeding from the depth of untaught things,
> Enduring and creative, might become
> A power like one of Nature's.
>   (Book 12)

Wordsworth goes on to recall the summer of 1793 when he roamed
over Salisbury Plain. Amid the prehistoric monuments of the
plain, he 'had a reverie and saw the past': lurid visions of
battle, of human sacrifice, and then, in calmer moments as he came
across the great megaliths of the plain, the worship of the Druids.
The 'lines, circles, mounts' left by the Druids are a perfect
image of the work of art which has arisen out of culture to merge
with the natural landscape. These monuments were 'imitative forms',
designed to represent the plan of the heavens. In Wordsworth's
imaginative vision, the Druids who made them become unmistakable
archetypes of the tribe of the Bard:

>   gently was I charmed
> Into a waking dream, a reverie
> That, with believing eyes, where'er I turned,
> Beheld long-bearded teachers, with white wands
> Uplifted, pointing to the starry sky,
> Alternately, and plain below, while breath
> Of music swayed their motions, and the waste
> Rejoiced with them and me in those sweet sounds.

(The 1850 version is quoted here; the slight revisions have the
effect of increasing the rapt and visionary quality.) The long-
bearded Druids are set over against a bloodthirsty society, with
no taint of that society's guilt or toil, though they are its
'teachers'. We see them performing ritual gestures to the sounds
of a wind-borne music - a community of poets worshipping in tune
with the 'gentle breeze' of natural inspiration. It is an atavistic, arcadian vision, located in a society far removed in time,
though continuous with us in its occupation of natural space.
Wordsworth's evocation of Stonehenge to exemplify his view of
art as a 'natural' power - the poem as megalith - closes the
penultimate Book of 'The Prelude', and it is counterbalanced in
the final lines of the poem by a Utopian exhortation to the poets
of the future. They too will be exempted from the general human
condition, and set in authority over men as the prophets and
teachers of a Christian revelation. The source of this vision,
however, lies not in religious orthodoxy but in the romantic
exaltation of the poet and the world of literature:

> Prophets of Nature, we to them will speak
> A lasting inspiration, sanctified
> By reason and by truth; what we have loved,
> Others will love; and we may teach them how;
> Instruct them how the mind of man becomes
> A thousand times more beautiful than the earth
> On which he dwells, above this Frame of things

> (Which, 'mid all revolutions in the hopes
> And fears of men, doth still remain unchanged)
> In beauty exalted, as it is itself
> Of substance and of fabric more divine.

The perfection that the poet reveals is at two removes from the
world in which we live our lives, and make and suffer 'revolutions'. Beyond society and untouched by it lies the 'Frame'
of nature, and above that the realm of mind. It is to such an
ideal, Platonic world that the romantic poet would conduct us,
offering us reason and truth in the form of a sanctified symbol.
The symbol is realized in literature. Wordsworth's criticism
must be read alternately as symbol and as interpretation of the
symbol; that is to say, as the expression of a creative vision
seeking to awaken a co-operative 'power' within us, and as a far-
reaching but misleading and contradictory poetic theory. No
other poet-critic has left so much for his heirs to fight over.

Chapter 3

THE ROMANTIC CRITICS

1 REVIEWERS AND BOOKMEN

'The language of poetry naturally falls in with the language of power.' So Hazlitt, in his essay on 'Coriolanus', underlined the political analogy which is implied by much of romantic criticism. The poetic imagination aggrandizes and dominates; its possessor commands and holds sway over the emotions of his readers. The analogy is double-edged. Though intended as a ringing affirmation of the poet's authority, it frequently expresses his underlying impotence. Coleridge, for example, sounds slightly peevish as he manipulates the concept of power in the following remarks:

All men in power are jealous of the pre-eminence of men of letters; they feel, as towards them, conscious of inferior power, and a sort of misgiving that they are, indirectly, and against their own will, mere instruments and agents of higher intellects.... So entirely was Mr. Pitt aware of this, that he would never allow of any intercourse with literary men of eminence; fearing, doubtless, that the charm which spell-bound his political adherents would, at least for the time, fail of its effect. (1)

It is not only Pitt's political adherents who might have felt that the boot was on the other foot. Once Wordsworth, Coleridge and Southey had renounced their revolutionary beliefs, they succumbed all too easily to the charms of the men in power. Moreover, their retreat to the Lake District did not protect them from an unparalleled degree of political animosity. There was in fact no position of dignified 'eminence' from which the romantics could escape unscathed. Wordsworth in the Preface to 'The Excursion' might challenge comparison with Milton for his high purpose, but, as Byron savagely reminded his readers, Milton was no renegade from the republican cause:

Would he adore a Sultan? He obey
The intellectual eunuch Castlereagh?

Wordsworth appears in the notes to 'Don Juan' as 'this poetical charlatan and political parasite [who] licks up the crumbs with a hardened alacrity' at the table of Lord Lonsdale (to whom 'The Excursion' was dedicated). (2) Such bitterness ran high in the years of the Peninsular War, of Waterloo and the Peterloo Massacre - the years, too, in which Wordsworth's greatness, or at least his influence, came grudgingly to be admitted. While the better critics tried to hold the balance between their aesthetic and political inclinations, much that was written was as crude as a cartoon by Rowlandson. The atmosphere was not improved - though neither, in all probability, was it made any worse - by the emergence of the great reviews. With the founding of the 'Edinburgh' in 1802, and the 'Quarterly' as its Tory competitor in 1809, literary criticism became more a matter of party lines than at any time since Pope and Swift. The quarterlies were far from indifferent to the major developments in poetry, and Wordsworth at least found that it was far better to be bated than to be ignored.

The quarterlies were a product of the Scottish enlightenment, and played a significant part in the nineteenth-century broadening of culture. The 'Edinburgh Review' was founded to promote political and social reform. Hazlitt, writing in 1825, saw it as a great organ of democratization, spreading the example of informed, rational comment on public and intellectual issues to a wide readership (its rival, by the same token, was dedicated to leading multitudes by the nose). (3) Though articles in the 'Edinburgh' and 'Quarterly' were by far the longest and best paid, these two journals were not alone in their field. John O. Hayden records that the number of periodicals carrying regular reviews doubled between 1800 and 1810, and reached a peak of at least thirty-one in the early 1820s. (4) This explosion of literary reviewing must be considered as a social phenomenon in its own right.

Probably all of the early reviews were run by small cliques. For breadth of outlook and the sense of the columns being open to all-comers we must wait until the mid-Victorian period. Jeffrey's inveterate habit of rewriting his contributors' copy is symptomatic; the 'Edinburgh' and 'Quarterly' in their early days were closed shops. Nonetheless, Hazlitt's enthusiasm was not entirely misplaced, and his claims would have been fully justified had they been made on behalf of the institution of reviewing as a whole, and not just in defence of one particular editor. To have a periodical composed entirely of book reviews presupposes a constant stream of new books demanding attention, and a literary or cultivated class anxious to be informed about them. Their anxiety to be informed stems from a consciousness of social change - to consider oneself enlightened one must keep up with events - so that it is no accident that the first of the great reviews was on the side of the Whigs. The stream of new books is felt as at once a promise and a threat. There is the promise of intellectual progress and cultural improvement; one is bound to widen one's sensibility (in Wordsworth's phrase) by keeping up with the new. But there is also the threat of losing one's bearings, of being carried along in the cultural torrent with no sense of fixed standards or priorities which can be taken for granted. Any review, therefore, is bound to combine up-to-dateness with a sense of stability, providing a source of judgment on which the reader can rely. That the early 'Edinburgh' and 'Quarterly' have achieved such a bad reputation is partly due to venality and corruption, but more to their over-emphasis on this stabilizing function. Thus Jeffrey began his

review of Southey's 'Thalaba' (the first of his onslaughts on the
Lake Poets) in volume one of the 'Edinburgh' with the following
stultifying credo:

> Poetry has this much, at least, in common with religion, that
> its standards were fixed long ago by certain inspired writers
> whose authority it is no longer lawful to call in question;
> and that many profess to be entirely devoted to it who have no
> good works to produce in support of their pretensions.

Jeffrey was completely sincere in suggesting that Wordsworth and
Southey were propounding a dangerous, Rousseauistic heresy, but
the very existence of a review casts doubt on this notion of incon-
testable authority.

Behind the early reviews lay the ideal of Hume's Man of Taste,
serenely applying the comparative method to each new book and
trying it by the standard of everything that already existed. The
critic's stance was judicial and informative, his style was pellucid
and his points were lavishly illustrated by quotation. Jeffrey
came closest to this ideal, though outside his notorious attacks
on the Lake School his lawyer-like displays of trenchant platitudes
are often rather dull. Jeffrey was no orthodox neoclassic, and
though he detested Wordsworth he admired various romantic traits in
Scott, Crabbe, Byron and Burns. Where he seems to take up the
burden of Addison and Pope is in striving to defend a literary
decorum plainly based on class. The standard of politeness and
gentility is fixed, but writers seem increasingly unwilling to
conform to it; hence the critic's patience is easily tried, and
contempt and ridicule come to his aid. The challenge of simplicity and 'vulgarity' in literature was the main thing that had to
be met. Besides the attacks on Wordsworth, Jeffrey's essay on
Burns was given over to fine discriminations of what was, and was
not, acceptable to a gentleman, while he found Scott's ability to
please both informed judges and the general public to be the most
provocative feature of 'The Lady of the Lake'. But if the democratic impulse in poetry had to be viewed with intense suspicion,
neither was patrician hauteur any more acceptable; hence, perhaps,
Brougham's savaging of Byron's 'Hours of Idleness' in the
'Edinburgh Review' for January 1808: 'The poesy of this young
lord belongs to the class which neither gods nor man are said to
permit.' The politeness and gentility of the 'Edinburgh' was
essentially middle-class.

But this, perhaps, is to look at the matter too impersonally.
Keats was not alone in being praised by the 'Edinburgh' because he
was damned by the 'Quarterly'. In Balzac's 'Illusions Perdues',
concerned with the Parisian 'petits-journaux' of the same period,
the hero is appalled by a journalist's demonstration of critical
denigration to order: 'But what you are saying is full of reason
and truth!' To which the reply is 'Of course - how else does one
attack a book?' In England too the judicial rhetoric of periodical
reviewing was often only a facade. It is nice to see Hazlitt
gracefully extricating himself at a tricky moment in 'The Spirit
of the Age': 'We had written thus far when news came of the death
of Lord Byron, and put an end at once to a strain of somewhat
peevish invective, which was intended to meet his eye, not to
insult his memory.' ('Phew! I nearly had to tear that up and

start all over again.')   All too often reviewing was intended to
meet somebody's eye.   Poets who had smarted under the lash were
inclined, like Coleridge, to sneer at the whole business as a
despotism of eunuchs, with broad hints of their own superior
potency. (5)   The quarterlies had succeeded in demonstrating the
existence of a new public eager for literary instruction.   In the
Victorian period the reviews were destined to reach a level of
integrity and seriousness which made them the central organs of
literary culture;   but that time was not yet.   How could the public
be offered a less partial and opportunistic version of critical
reason and truth?

One answer lay in the literary survey and lecture.   In 1804 the
Royal Institution in London began to offer public lectures on non-
technical subjects, and four years later Coleridge gave there the
first of his lecture-courses, and the first important series of
public lectures on literature in England.   Coleridge's motives for
lecturing were mainly financial, and despite his personal magnetism
his success was very variable.   Sometimes we hear of him holding
forth to a fashionable London audience of six or seven hundred, and
attracting droppers-in like Byron and Rogers.   At other times he
disconsolately faced a dozen or so in a hotel at Clifton.   In all,
he gave ten courses of lectures between 1808 and 1819, and the
results must have awakened the rivalry of Hazlitt, whose three
courses began in 1818.   Hazlitt and Coleridge between them covered
the development of English literature from Chaucer onwards;   a new
mode of criticism had arisen to fulfil a new demand.   Coleridge's
prospectus for his 1818 course exhibits rather nakedly the lecturer's rueful sense of his audience, earnest for literary
instruction so long as they could feel it was useful, not too
arduous, and productive of small-talk in the presence of ladies.
But here he was selling himself short.   When the lectures succeeded
it was because they were an intellectual event, not a useful social
diversion.   The young men present were scribbling down their notes
for posterity.

The intellectual origin of the romantic lecture-courses lay in
Germany.   Hazlitt made his acknowledgments to A.W. Schlegel's
'Vorlesungen über dramatische Kunst und Litteratur' (1809-11)
in the Preface to 'The Characters of Shakespeare's Plays'.   In
his erratic 1811-12 course, the first of which we have detailed
records, Coleridge suddenly pulled himself together in the ninth
lecture when (perhaps not for the first time) he had managed to
procure a copy of Schlegel. (6)   In 1813 we find him writing from
Bristol to his London hosts, the Morgans, asking them to send his
copy of the 'Vorlesungen' together with two thick memorandum-books
inscribed 'Vorlesungen: Schlegel' which he had taken to his
earlier lectures at the Surrey Institution. (7)   There is no
question that a good proportion of the material in his lecture-
courses was plagiarized;   scholars argue over whether there is
sufficient original material to support his enormous reputation as
a Shakespeare critic.   Coleridge tended to claim that his
thoughts coincided with the Germans, rather than being overwhelm-
ingly influenced by them.   Whether or not this can be proved, it
can hardly affect our recognition of the greatness and originality
of the German romantic critics whose words he liked to borrow.

Basically, their achievement was to view literature as an international cultural heritage to be understood in the light of a philosophy of history. Literary history, that is, if properly interpreted, reflects or embodies the essential history of civilization. The primitivist literary historians of eighteenth-century England had put forward a simple version of this essential history: poetry, they argued, flourishes in a rude and barbarous state of society, and recedes as rationality and decorum advance. This argument was so widely disseminated that few romantic critics could refrain from outlining a potted history of culture. Although the primitivist theory regularly had an anti-Enlightenment thrust, since it focused on the shortcomings of 'rational' civilization, its crudity was typical of Enlightenment historiography. To the German critics influenced by Kant and Herder, history appeared a more complex process and one that demanded more systematic study. Culture was interpreted in terms of dialectical oppositions such as Schiller's naive and sentimental, and Schlegel's classical and romantic; the nostalgia inherent in the primitivist case was acknowledged, even though its licence was extended. Since different kinds of artistic excellence could be achieved at different times, criticism became a subtle blend of normative and relativistic tendencies.

It was the elder Schlegel who applied the new approach to a methodical survey of European drama from Aeschylus down to Goethe and Schiller. He was disparaged for his professorial approach both in Germany and England, but the 'Lectures on Dramatic Art and Literature', translated into English in 1815, now appear as one of the foundation stones of modern humanistic criticism. Schlegel has the epic sweep, if not quite the depth, of an Auerbach or a Lukács, and his is the first Grand Tour of the European literary museum. Much depends on his ability to get the tone right - to bring a sense of rational, urbane and yet personal appraisal to every work that he studies. English readers were particularly attracted by his treatment of Shakespeare, a majestic expression of the Shakespearean vogue in Germany which had begun with Lessing and Herder. Schlegel's emphasis on fair-minded appreciation might seem thoroughly neoclassical - the ideal expression of Hume's doctrine of universal taste - were it not for his emancipation from the historical parochialism of the Enlightenment (Shakespeare is no longer the 'child of nature'), and his confident recognition of the irrational. For Schlegel was able both to endorse the new values of poetic power and creativity, and to contain them within a framework of rationalistic history. His doctrine of organic form, which was immediately borrowed by Coleridge, is a clear example of such containment. Schlegel was able to write with warmth of the romantic 'expression of the secret attraction to a chaos which lies concealed in the very bosom of the ordered universe' (8) precisely because he felt able to explain it. He is a modern humanist, however, because his rationalism seems something less than inevitable; it is only one of the possible ways of responding to the challenge of the human condition that he expounds (Wordsworth, Coleridge, Hazlitt are among those who represent other ways) and this gives it a willed and precarious quality. Schlegel among the romantic critics is

the professor who always has an explanation for things. He never
acknowledges that reason and creativity might be incompatible or
exert strange influences on one another. The criticism of the
other romantics is more far-reaching, but its relation to rationality is much more problematic than his.

One irrational aspect of literature is its connection with
national pride. The English response to the fulsome reception of
their national poet in Germany was necessarily ambivalent.
Coleridge and Hazlitt rushed to supply an 'English' Shakespeare,
purloining the best features of Schlegel while going one better
and ticking him off for his lapses. The detachment of Schlegel's
comparatist outlook, however, owed much to his German nationality.
The European dramatic heritage appeared to him as a sequence of
foreign literatures; he could survey these impartially (allowing
for some bias against the French) while proclaiming that the present
and future belonged to his own country. But patriotism was an
issue that divided English critics. De Quincey became a champion
of the international character of great literature; he saw that
poets belong not to the nation-state but to the 'vast empire of
human society'. Hazlitt, likewise, wrote of those capable of
appreciating the writers of Shakespeare's age as 'true cosmo-
polites'. (9) But the attitude which has often been uppermost in
English studies is the reverse of this - the conservative nationalism represented by Coleridge. Coleridge speaks of 'mock
cosmopolitism', (10) and when lecturing on English literature
his heart often swells with patriotic pride. At best, he shows
that grasp of the inner nature of national institutions to which
John Stuart Mill was to pay tribute; but at his worst - as on
King Alfred - he gives us Kiplingesque school-history. Nonetheless, Coleridge has an unprecedented intimacy with the historical
tradition of literature, above all in his fascination with the
seventeenth century. Lamb's influential 'Specimens of English
Dramatic Poets Who Lived About the Time of Shakespeare' (1808) are
precisely what their name implies - specimens gathered on aesthetic
grounds by a good antiquarian. Hazlitt's 'Lectures on the Age of
Elizabeth' are reputed to have been mugged up in six weeks,
presumably to satisfy a public demand. Coleridge stands alone in
the depth with which he took the imprint of seventeenth-century
language and its ways of thought.

Although Hazlitt and Coleridge both attempted the genre of the
critical survey, neither embraced it wholeheartedly as Schlegel
had done. They only went through the motions of systematizing
literary history. As had happened a century earlier, a mode of
rationalistic criticism imported from the continent was transmuted
into a more English form, in which the social attitude conveyed
by the critic seems at least as important as his facts and arguments.
The study of English literary history in the nineteenth century
became the preserve of those whom we may call the 'bookmen' - the
cosy, antiquarian bibliophiles whose outlook was defined by Lamb
and Hazlitt, the essayists of the 1820s. John Gross has shown that
the bookish ethos emerged with the 'London Magazine' (1820-9) to
which Lamb, Hazlitt, de Quincey and Landor all contributed. This
was at once a metropolitan phenomenon ('It was less like a magazine
than a club', Gross comments) (11) and an attempt to insulate the

critic from all those considerations of standards and party
politics which ruled in Edinburgh reviewing.

The bookishness of the essayists may be approached by way of
the new attitude to drama that was emerging. Johnson's discussion of the Unities of Place and Time in the 'Preface to
Shakespeare' had dislodged the neoclassical rules, without putting
anything very satisfactory in their place. All the romantics
felt that his blunt assertion that 'the spectators are always in
their senses' was derogatory to art, and several accepted the
challenge to produce a new theory of dramatic illusion. Schlegel
and Coleridge both argued that drama makes its appeal to the
imaginative faculty, and our experience of it is a kind of voluntary dreaming. Hence, Coleridge says, there is neither complete
delusion nor complete detachment, but 'a sort of temporary half-
faith' or, in his most famous phrase, a 'willing suspension of
disbelief'. (12) This is a psychological account which applies
to drama and to the 'perusal of a deeply interesting novel'; (13)
that is, it will do as well for solitary reading as for the
theatre. Schlegel, by contrast, goes on to discuss what he calls
the 'theatrical effect' - the communal effect of drama, based on
the traditional comparison of drama and oratory. The poet in the
theatre, he argues, can 'transport his hearers out of themselves'
by evoking the 'power of a visible communion of numbers'; the
result is the intensification and expression of normally hidden
emotions, and the breaking down of conventional barriers. (14)
Schlegel reminds his readers of the dangers of mass emotion, and
hence of the necessity for censorship and state regulation of
theatres. This is all very orthodox and Platonic. Coleridge,
however, disregards the effect of the communal audience as completely as Johnson had done. The English romantic critics in
general have lost the sense of the essentially public character
of drama. Coleridge, Hazlitt and Lamb all express the feeling that
Shakespeare's plays are far better when read than on the stage. The
case is argued most fully and interestingly in Charles Lamb's
essay On the Tragedies of Shakespeare, Considered with Reference
to their Fitness for Stage Representation (1811). Lamb does
recognize a 'theatrical effect', but he attributes it entirely to
the actor rather than the dramatist, and goes so far as to suggest
that 'Hamlet', rewritten without the poetry, the intellectual
content and the profundity of characterization, would retain the
same degree of theatrical impact. This essay is something of a
'jeu d'esprit' - an argument that actors since Garrick have been
getting too big for their boots. But it is also an important
expression of changing taste. Lamb was not alone in his revolt
against the crudely spectacular and melodramatic appeal of theatre
in his own day, but the conclusions that he drew show a profound
distrust of theatrical performance, which he sees as an inevitable
vulgarization of the written text. (He did not, however, abstain
from theatregoing.) The nineteenth century in general came to
emphasize those aspects of Shakespeare which seemed to deny performance. It turned his dramas into novels.

Lamb points out that dramatic speech is, like the novel in
letters, a non-realistic convention - and in good drama the
purpose of the convention is to give us knowledge of the 'inner

structure and workings of mind in a character'. But the inner
structure of a literary character can only be truly savoured by
the solitary reader:

> These profound sorrows, these light-and-noise-abhorring rumi-
> nations, which the tongue scarce dares utter to deaf walls
> and chambers, how can they be represented by a gesticulating
> actor, who comes and mouths them out before an audience, making
> four hundred people his confidants at once?

How indeed: the argument is unanswerable, given Lamb's confidence
that his own way of responding to Shakespeare is more sensitive
and more truly imaginative than anyone else's. Hamlet, inevitably
enough, is the character referred to, and it seems obvious that
Lamb is making him into a private 'alter ego', rather than a
tragic hero and Prince of Denmark. Lamb is explicit in his belief
that Shakespearean characters need 'that vantage-ground of
abstraction which reading possesses over seeing', and are properly
'the objects of meditation rather than of interest and curiosity as
to their actions'.

'Meditation': the term is Wordsworthian, but it takes on an
un-Wordsworthian literariness here. For Lamb is defining a
literary or poetic element in drama which can only be profaned
in the theatre. The ideal reader of Shakespearean drama, he
implies, is the connoisseur savouring his appreciation in the
solitude of a book-lined study. The cultivation of older English
literature in the nineteenth century can hardly be separated from
this image of the bookish life, with its frequentation of forgotten
authors and rare editions and its mellow storehouse of anecdotes
and 'characters'. Lamb and Hazlitt savour the atmosphere rather
than the substance of reading; they delight in melancholy
reminiscences, in out-of-the-way quotations, and in confessions of
personal likes and dislikes; their world is the world as seen
from a comfortable armchair. Yet the leisured bookman of the
'Essays of Elia' and Hazlitt's essays was necessarily only a persona, a fiction created by harassed professional men (Hazlitt was
a journalist and lecturer, Lamb a civil servant). The bookman
represented a spare-time ideal of which all men might become
amateurs. As the century continued, the notion of romantic withdrawal to the world of the study became increasingly trivialized.
At best, 'fin-de-siècle' bookmanship might be represented by a
figure such as Saintsbury, relaxed, agreeable and (to the modern
reader) intolerably mannered, but nonetheless a formidable professional scholar. Equally representative, however, was the commercial approach of the 'Bookman' magazine (founded in 1891)
with its gossip about publishers' autumn lists and its portraits
of best-selling lady novelists.

Lamb's essay on Shakespeare argued that the essentially poetic
element in drama lay in characterization. This may suggest that
there are broad connections between the rise of bookmanship and
the rise of the Victorian novel - both of them reflecting the trend
toward the cultivation of private experience. Lamb's essays themselves are indebted to Fielding and Sterne, and look forward to
Thackeray and Dickens; the ruminative voice of Elia is not so far
from that of the more clubbable Victorian novelists. Both
novelists and bookmen may be seen as offering ideals of gentility

and spiritual culture to the new middle- and lower-middle-class
reading public. Yet the bookish ideal was certainly a meagre
one, which insulated its adherent from the pressures of social
reality while eliciting none of the ethical and imaginative zeal
tapped by the more robust gospels of Dickens, Ruskin or Carlyle.

The Victorian novelist of lower-class origins first had to learn
to adopt the social tone of gentility; one can see this in
Dickens, and later in the young H.G. Wells. Similarly, the bookman had to pretend to a leisure he did not possess. A title such
as Leslie Stephen's 'Hours in a Library' suggests, surely, the
fruits of idle browsing, not the industry of a prolific historian,
intellectual and 'D.N.B.' editor (let alone that of a Karl Marx).
And for all the candour of the self-portrayal of the Regency
essayists, what is missing from their work is any sense of themselves as writers. The essayists did not tell the full truth
about their reading experiences, since reading for them was part
of the work of earning a living. The bookman with time on his
hands is made to seem the antithesis of the reviewer and contributor to the 'London Magazine'. (A clear illustration of the
gulf between 'bookman' and reviewer is provided by the state of
Jeffrey's library when it was auctioned off after his death: 'a
very poor collection, made up largely of law books and review
copies'. (15) Jeffrey was much more interested in his wine
cellar, one of the finest in Scotland.) While the reviewer is
a metropolitan creature, the bookman often flourishes best in a
country home or cottage. Early examples are Southey, who protested
that letting Wordsworth into his library at Keswick was 'like
letting a bear into a tulip garden'; and de Quincey, who never
forgave the same poet for cutting open the pages of a new volume
of Burke with the Dove Cottage butter-knife. (16) Hazlitt was
proud of his country retreat, Winterslow Hut in Wiltshire, and
in 1839 his son published the first selection of his so-called
'Winterslow Essays'. Though a coaching inn, Winterslow Hut
directly anticipates the writer's cottage of later in the century -
peaceful, rustic, but not too far from the railway station - see,
for example, Gissing's 'Private Papers of Henry Ryecroft' (1903),
one of the key celebrations of bookmanship. But Winterslow was
also the place where Hazlitt mugged up the 'Lectures on the Age
of Elizabeth' from borrowed volumes in six weeks - a glimpse of
the reality underlying the ideal.

If Hazlitt stops short of total candour, the strain of living
up to the bookish ideal manifests itself in his outbursts of
self-pity. There is his notorious confession that 'Books have in
a great measure lost their power over me', and his dejected
response to Keats's 'Endymion':

> I know how I should have felt at one time in reading such
> passages; and that is all. The sharp luscious flavour, the
> fine aroma is fled, and nothing but the stalk, the bran, the
> husk of literature is left.

(On Reading Old Books, 1821)

This is romantic 'Weltschmerz', and somewhat embarrassing. But one
might read 'literature' here as the subject of Hazlitt's professional attentions as writer and journalist, while what he aims at and
cannot manage is the pure appreciation due to 'poetry'. This is

the 'fine aroma' which he, like so many of his successors, saw it
as the critic's duty to try to convey. The desultory and
impressionistic nature of his and Lamb's criticism is an attempt
to realize such a poetic essence of the literature with which they
deal. Lamb's preface to his 'Extracts from the Garrick Plays'
(1827), for example, after dwelling fondly on the 'luxury' of
reading through the collection of old plays at Montagu House,
outlines his editorial method in these terms:

> You must be content with sometimes a scene, sometimes a song;
> a speech, or passage, or a poetical image, as they happen to
> strike me. I read without order of time; I am a poor hand at
> dates; and for any biography of the Dramatists, I must refer to
> writers who are more skilful in such matters. My business is
> with their poetry only.

The critic as bookman soaks himself in an atmosphere of passive
literariness, and finally draws out of it a single elixir, poetry
alone. This is the decadence of the romantic sense of poetic
power - its containment within a cosy and ruminative sphere of the
private consciousness which augurs no harm to anyone and can be
held up as a spiritual ideal to the new middle classes. But in the
best criticism of Hazlitt, as well as of Coleridge, Keats and
Shelley, the sense of power which inspired and frustrated the
romantics has far more heroic manifestations than this.

2   SAMUEL TAYLOR COLERIDGE

Three generations of scholars have hailed Coleridge as the greatest
English critic. The claim was first made by George Saintsbury, and
was taken up by I.A. Richards, whose 'Coleridge on Imagination'
(1934) effectively claimed its subject as the founding father of
the New Criticism and of Richards's own pet discipline of semasi-
ology. Though long criticized as a meretricious book, cavalier in
its interpretation of Coleridge's texts and tendentious in its
insistence on a scientific basis for criticism, 'Coleridge on
Imagination' did inspire a whole generation of scholars, (17) and
sanctioned the enraptured tone in which they have tended to
announce their findings. When the distinction between fancy and
imagination fully entered our intellectual tradition, Richards
announced, the 'order of our universes [would] have been changed'.
(18) George Watson rounded off the introduction to his Everyman
edition of 'Biographia Literaria' in 1956 with a more modest, but
equally vulnerable forecast:

> To set out from the 'Biographia' and go straight on in the same
> inquiring spirit could give the criticism of to-morrow a pro-
> fundity and a certainty we lack to-day.

In fact there is endless uncertainty about what the key passages in
Coleridge's book really mean. In recent years Coleridge's
defenders have become somewhat more troubled and have been forced
to admit that the 'inquiring spirit' of the 'Biographia' was also
the perpetrator of the plagiarisms, postures, cant and unfulfilled
promises abounding in that book. The recent publication of Norman
Fruman's 'Coleridge: The Damaged Archangel' made it clear that
scepticism about Coleridge's achievement is far from being merely

residual. The strongest part of Fruman's controversial case is
his attack on Coleridge's reputation as critic and metaphysician.
'Biographia Literaria' (1817) is central to this reputation, and a
detailed analysis of this book will be needed to evaluate
Coleridge's position in criticism. Some of his warmest champions,
notably Richards and Herbert Read, have been quite explicit in
praising him for anticipating their own concerns, or in other words
for being on the right side. But is he on the right side? And
granting that the 'Biographia' is a many-sided, fascinating book,
and hence a classic, isn't it partly a classic of the genus of
'Tristram Shandy', entertaining us by its barefaced audacity at
least as much as it instructs us in critical wisdom?

 'The Poet is dead in me', Coleridge told Godwin in 1801. His
criticism grew out of that death, at least in the sense that it
signals the end of the random plundering of old books and fabrica-
tion of archaic forms that had been responsible for 'The Ancient
Mariner', 'Christabel' and 'Kubla Khan'. In a letter to Sir
George and Lady Beaumont in 1804, Coleridge announced that he was
now turning to a far more disciplined and methodical form of
literary study:

> Each scene of each play I read as if it were the whole of
> Shakspere's works - the sole thing extant. I ask myself what
> are the characteristics, the diction, the cadences, and metre,
> the character, the passion, the moral or metaphysical inheren-
> cies and fitness for theatric effect, and in what sort of
> theatres. All these I write down with great care and precision
> of thought and language (and when I have gone through the whole,
> I then shall collect my papers, and observe how often such and
> such expressions recur), and thus shall not only know what the
> characteristics of Shakspere's plays are, but likewise what
> proportion they bear to each other.

The voice of the virtuous literary scientist would often be heard in
the years leading up to 'Biographia Literaria'. The bark of this
particular excursion into pedantry was much more formidable than its
bite, though a handful of brilliant analyses of scenes from
Shakespeare were to emerge. The origins of Coleridge's leaning to
systematic literary analysis around 1804 might be found in his visit
to Germany (1798) and his acquaintance with the trend of German
criticism; more immediate considerations, however, were his need
to earn money by writing and lecturing, and to distract himself
from his personal miseries. Two other main strands led to his
emergence as a critic. The first was his discovery that he could
use literary theory as a form of disguised self-expression. In
October 1800 he had written to Humphry Davy of his plan for an
'Essay on the Elements of Poetry' which would be 'in reality a
disguised system of morals and politics'. His political interests
at this time were intense; he was discovering a new basis for his
beliefs after his repudiation of the republican cause, and was
contributing leaders and even parliamentary reports to the 'Morning
Post'. (19) As he had rejected democracy and the doctrine of
abstract rights, it is tempting to suggest that the 'disguised
system of morals and politics' was to have been a Burkeian riposte
to the arguments from natural reason in the contemporaneous Preface
to 'Lyrical Ballads'. But we do not know, and Coleridge did not

openly dissociate himself from Wordsworth's doctrines until 1802.
Three years later, personal confession had become a more urgent
necessity than working out a political creed. A new scheme went
down in his notebook:

> Seem to have made up my mind to write my metaphysical works as
> my Life, and in my Life - intermixed with all the other events
> or history of the mind and fortunes of S.T. Coleridge. (20)

This was possibly the crucial moment in the evolution of the form
of the 'Biographia'. In adopting the autobiographical form,
Coleridge seems to have been making things easier for himself,
much as Wordsworth did in writing a 'Prelude' to his 'great philosophical poem'. Coleridge continued to dream of a metaphysical
Treatise on the 'Logos', though not of an objectively structured
treatise on poetry. But the majority of his published prose consists of systems of morals and politics: witness 'The Friend',
'The Statesman's Manual', 'Aids to Reflection' and the 'Constitution
of Church and State'. Criticism was to prove a vital but not a
lasting interest of his.

The other strand leading to the 'Biographia' is that of disagreement with Wordsworth. This was brought into the open by the
revised Preface of 1802. Coleridge responded both by claiming
his share in the original conception of 1800 ('Wordsworth's
Preface is half a child of my own brain') (21) and by taking a
very cool look at the revised version, complaining of its obscurity
and over-elaborate diction. Two letters of July 1802 suggest that
the Preface had been the occasion of a mild quarrel with Wordsworth, in which he was enlisting his friends' support: 'we have
had lately some little controversy on the subject, and we begin to
suspect that there is somewhere or other a radical difference in
our opinions.' The difference of opinion was over the key question
of the nature of poetic diction. Disagreement with Wordsworth was
both now and later the most important factor which goaded Coleridge
into ordering his thoughts about poetry and getting them down on
paper. The main critical chapters of 'Biographia Literaria' were
eventually written in the summer of 1815, when he had received a
further prod from Wordsworth's Preface and Essay Supplementary,
which had come out in March. (22) Coleridge had sketched out his
distinction between fancy and imagination long before, but it was
only after Wordsworth's discussion of 1815 that it took its final
shape. Yet the disagreement was not a matter of friendly correction
of Wordsworth's statements, despite the show of courtesy in the
'Biographia'. In writing his critique, Coleridge was announcing
his disaffiliation from the poetic revolution that Wordsworth had
advocated and led. Already in 1802, while 'The Ancient Mariner'
was still included in the new edition of 'Lyrical Ballads', he had
told Southey of his intention of 'acting the arbitrator between the
old school and the new school.' Southey must have found this air of
detachment surprising, to say the least.

What kind of book is the 'Biographia'? In the struggle to make
sense of it, readers have turned to the programmatic statement at
the end of Chapter Four, where Coleridge promises to

> present an intelligible statement of my poetic creed; not as
> my opinions, which weigh for nothing, but as deductions from
> established premises conveyed in such a form as is calculated

either to effect a fundamental conviction or to receive a
fundamental confutation.
The image of Coleridge as the great rationalist among critics sur-
vives, although there are few who feel either fundamentally
convinced by his deductive arguments, or capable of fundamentally
confuting them. In order to achieve either result, we have to
reconstruct the arguments, to complete what Coleridge himself
left fragmentary and implicit. Theoretical his procedure may
have been, but impeccably rational it certainly was not. And in
any case, the immediate purpose of the above passage is, characteristically enough, to forestall complaints of obscurity.
Moreover, it comes in a book that he was not ashamed to subtitle
'Biographical Sketches of My Literary Life and Opinions'. Considered as literary criticism, the biographical framework is the
source of some of its strengths and of most of its weaknesses.
'Biographia Literaria' might be seen as the albatross of what
Fredric Jameson has called 'dialectical criticism', or criticism
which is based on a constant strategy of self-awareness and self-
commentary. Coleridge's acute self-consciousness gives even his
most daring paragraphs an air of caluclation or controlled
exhibitionism; yet his impulse to show off is as often checked by
that impulse to hide behind turgid qualifications, empty elabora-
tions and professions of good faith which gives to his prose its
garrulous, cobwebby quality. Far from being a rational treatise,
the 'Biographia' is a remarkable product of romantic egotism, in
which thought constantly reflecting on itself merges into thought
transparently attempting to conceal its own nature. Plagiarism,
almost inevitably, is one of the forms which this takes.

Fortunately, the book falls into two halves, and the Shandean -
and Pecksniffian - aspects are mainly apparent in the first half.
The first three chapters are a tedious parade of self-defence
against real and imagined enemies. Between digressions, Coleridge
tells of his early literary education and tastes, ending with a
remarkably fulsome tribute to Southey. Then, in Chapter Four, he
recounts the climax of his early development - his meeting with
Wordsworth - and at last rises to his subject, passing from
garrulousness to one of the finest expressions of the critic's
experience in English literature.

There is just one intermediate stage in the transition, for the
theme which opens Chapter Four is Coleridge's attempt to dispel
'this fiction of a new school of poetry' and the 'clamors against
its supposed founders'. He begins to emerge as the kind of revolutionary who aims to consolidate the change of power by denying
that it ever took place. He suggests that the hostility which
greeted 'Lyrical Ballads' was largely accidental, since the omission
of less than a hundred lines would have precluded nine-tenths of
the criticism. Moreover, the 1800 Preface was chiefly to blame,
as it unnecessarily put people's backs up; the 'Lyrical Ballads',
Coleridge feels, should have come into the world more quietly.
Despite the venomous attacks on Jeffrey elsewhere in the 'Biographia', this line of argument prepares us for the lengths to
which Coleridge was prepared to go in conceding his opponents'
case in order to discredit the Preface and Wordsworth's own account
of his poetic strengths.

In the Essay Supplementary, Wordsworth had written that the
great poet must create the taste by which he is to be enjoyed -
thus defending his decision to produce a manifesto. Coleridge
was now disputing this. His argument makes the reception of a
poet not a public and sociological phenomenon, as it was for
Wordsworth, but a private and psychological one. Poetry speaks
for itself, regardless of the general state of culture, as long as
the poet does not needlessly irritate the reader - that is what he
seems to be saying. The proof lies in his own experience:

> During the last year of my residence at Cambridge I became
> acquainted with Mr. Wordsworth's first publication, entitled
> 'Descriptive Sketches'; and seldom, if ever, was the emergence
> of an original poetic genius above the literary horizon more
> evidently announced.

Coleridge proceeds to summarize the essential impact that
Wordsworth's poetry made upon him:

> It was the union of deep feeling with profound thought; the
> fine balance of truth in observing with the imaginative faculty
> in modifying the objects observed; and above all the original
> gift of spreading the tone, the atmosphere and with it the
> depth and height of the ideal world, around forms, incidents
> and situations of which, for the common view, custom had
> bedimmed all the lustre, had dried up the sparkle and the dew-
> drops.

This famous passage draws on the language of poetic 'power' which
we have already seen in Wordsworth and de Quincey: consider the
adjectives 'deep', 'profound', 'imaginative', 'original'. The
poet's power is that of seeing the world in its ideal wonder and
novelty, and of communicating his vision to others. Coleridge is
concerned with the psychological and ontological status of this
power. He 'no sooner felt' Wordsworth's genius, he tells us,
than he 'sought to understand' it. He felt that it involved the
interrelationship of feeling and thought, of observation and the
'imaginative faculty', and of the ideal world and the world of
common experience. These were the antinomies from which he would
construct his theory of imagination. And a theory of imagination,
he believed, was a philosopher's stone which would not only
'furnish a torch of guidance to the philosophical critic', but
would make the production of great poetry easier and less sporadic
than in the past; for 'in energetic minds truth soon changes by
domestication into power'.

By the end of Chapter Four, then, we have been made to antici-
pate something far more ambitious than just 'Biographical Sketches'.
But equally Coleridge can claim that the theoretical programme he
is now announcing contains the inner meaning of his literary life.
For the skeleton of argument in the book follows the pattern of a
'circuitous journey', which M.H. Abrams has shown to be common to
many other romantic confessional works: (23) Quite possibly
Coleridge was half-consciously imitating one of these, Wordsworth's
'Prelude' (Wordsworth had read the poem to him in 1807). The
'circuitous journey' of romantic autobiography is inaugurated by a
natural or instinctive experience of insight into reality; it
proceeds by a process of investigation and interrogation of
accumulating experiences until the final point is reached at which

the initial experience is maturely comprehended in the light of
universal reason. In 'The Prelude' this path is traversed by the
poet who comes to a mature religious understanding of the glimpses
of man's connection with nature that he experienced as a child
in Book One. In the 'Biographia', the primal experience is that of
Coleridge's critical response to the 'union of deep feeling with
profound thought'. His task then is to deduce the nature of the
imagination in ontological terms, and to apply the result to the
psychology of the creative act, to the aesthetic definition of the
work of art and finally to the purposes of poetic analysis, culminating in the examination of Wordsworth's achievements in the
hope of a full understanding of his imaginative genius. Such, at
least, is the foundation on which Coleridge based his reputation
as a philosophical critic. Like the vast majority of his literary
schemes, he did not fulfil it, though he made a moderately concerted attempt to do so. The 'Biographia' does have a skeleton of
argument such as I have described, but the amount of flesh on the
bones is uneven, and some of the bones are cracked or missing. The
important themes of the book are the nature of imagination, the
correction of Wordsworth's poetic theories and the celebration of
his achievement as a poet. But when we reach the final chapter
with its set evaluation of Wordsworth's poetry, we are a good deal
less enlightened by the discoveries of the long journey than we
might have hoped.

The structural parallel between the 'Biographia' and 'The
Prelude' should not, of course, be allowed to obscure the vast
contrast between the mode of discourse of the 'Biographia' and any
work of Wordsworth's. In political terms, Coleridge's discussion
of the imagination and of diction in the context of philosophical
and literary tradition is a Burkeian reply to the Tom Paine manner
of the 1800 Preface. Yet the gossipy and anecdotal parade of
learning in the 'Biographia' owes nothing to Burke and is a
deliberate rejection of eighteenth-century clarity. Coleridge's
thinking proceeds not through rational and deductive statement, but
through ratiocinative commentary. His feverish sense of intellectual complexity is conveyed by a chaotic mixture of styles:
seventeenth-century prolixity jostles with German cloudiness,
romantic precision and evocativeness with proto-Victorian humbug.
The contents of the first volume (Chapters One to Thirteen) are
equally varied, with chapters of exhortations and anecdotes sand-
wiched amid the philosophy.

Coleridge starts out from Chapter Four with a heavily derivative
account of philosophical history. Eventually we reach the transcendental system enumerated in the Ten Theses of Chapter Twelve,
translated without acknowledgment from Schelling. Among the inter-
missions are those in which Coleridge speaks of truth as the
'divine ventriloquist', and accuses Hume (on nebulous grounds) of
plagiarizing Aquinas. Yet this section of the 'Biographia' has
considerable historical importance for the part it played in dis-
seminating the Kantian revolution in England. Coleridge tells how
he rejected the mechanical account of the operations of mind put
forward by the British empiricists. He traces the theory of
association down to the eighteenth century, and attacks the tenets
of the prevailing Hartleian philosophy. He objects to Hartley's

theory on two grounds: first, that it is implicitly materialist
and thus anti-Christian; second, that it denies the active and
voluntary nature of consciousness. What the materialistic philosophers have discovered, Coleridge argues, are not the determining
laws of mind itself but simply some of the conditions of mental
activity. The individual is logically prior to such conditions and
is able to mould them to his own use rather than merely obeying
them passively. The acts of perception and consciousness are not
determined but voluntary; it is only on this view of mental
activity that we can comprehend the creative quality of art and
thought. Coleridge's sense of the mind's creative activity is
illustrated by the example of jumping (in which we initially resist
the external force of gravity in order to make use of it) and by
the beautiful analogy of the water-insect in Chapter Seven:

> Most of my readers will have observed a small water-insect on
> the surface of rivulets which throws a cinque-spotted shadow
> fringed with prismatic colours on the sunny bottom of the brook;
> and will have noticed how the little animal wins its way up
> against the stream, by alternate pulses of active and passive
> motion, now resisting the current, and now yielding to it in
> order to gather strength and a momentary fulcrum for a further
> propulsion. This is no unapt emblem of the mind's self-
> experience in the act of thinking. There are evidently two
> powers at work which relatively to each other are active and
> passive; and this is not possible without an intermediate
> faculty, which is at once both active and passive. (In philo-
> sophical language we must denominate this intermediate faculty
> in all its degrees and determinations the imagination. But
> in common language, and especially on the subject of poetry,
> we appropriate the name to a superior degree of the faculty,
> joined to a superior voluntary controul over it.)

The mind here is both the stream and the insect - the experience of
the self and the self that experiences. The 'intermediate faculty'
of mental motion which provides the field of operation for both the
active and passive powers of mind is what Coleridge names the
imagination; while 'a superior degree of the faculty, joined to
a superior voluntary controul over it' constitutes the imagination
that is operative in art. Thus the passage is a direct anticipation
of the distinction of primary and secondary imagination in Chapter
Thirteen, and foreshadows its essential ambiguity. For what
precise differences does Coleridge envisage between the act of
imagination in general, and that act in respect of poetry, and the
'act of thinking' of which he examines the 'mind's self-experience'
here? These questions can only be answered, if at all, from within
the cloudy terrain of Coleridgian metaphysics.

Coleridge, who was willing to speak of a 'revolution in philosophy' (24) if not in poetry, found in Kant and the post-Kantians
a more adequate correspondence to his own intuitions about the
nature of mind as both active and passive. The need was now to
adopt a philosophical system which would clarify the distinctions
which the water-insect analogy leaves begging. But it was one
thing to endorse the Kantian critique of rationalism and empiricism, and quite another to follow the German philosophers in their
subsequent quest for the definition of the Noumenon or Absolute

Idea. The religious objections that Coleridge had brought against
Hartley raised themselves again; a philosophy which found its
starting-point in the creative powers of mind was as likely as one
which started from the laws of nature to lead to atheism or
pantheism. Coleridge himself had left behind the heterodoxy of
the 1790s, and was now a staunch Christian apologist. In his new
position he could do without Hartley, but not without the Germans,
and he chose to base his aesthetics on the transcendental idealism
of F.W.J. von Schelling, even though Schelling's system, expounded
in Chapter Twelve of the 'Biographia', is implicitly pantheistic.
(25)

The question of the relations of Coleridge's theory of imagination to the aesthetics and metaphysics of Kant, Fichte and
Schelling has been exhaustively discussed in recent years, and this
is not the place to enter such a discussion. I suspect that too
much has been made of the whole problem, and the prestige of the
Coleridgian Holy of Holies has been bolstered up by the fascination
of an obscure and tortuous conundrum in the history of ideas. Too
often the scholars add further mystifications to the matter they are
trying to elucidate. What are we to make, for example, of Thomas
McFarland's claim that Coleridge, who plagiarized large chunks of
Schelling, in fact possessed a 'massive, coherent, and reticulated
opposition' to Schellingian pantheism? (26) If we refuse to take
such paradoxes in our stride we are likely to be accused of precisely the simple-minded empiricism which Coleridge rejected. So
be it; it seems better to admit the ramshackle quality of
Coleridge's thinking in its higher metaphysical reaches. His
defenders are fond of quoting the visionary passage on the transcendental philosopher as explorer of a realm above and beyond the
'scanty vale of human life' in Chapter Twelve of the 'Biographia'.
This is a palpable translation of the language of faith in the
existence of a spiritual world into rationalistic terms; and
there is no doubt that Coleridge had such faith. Yet his actual
performance in the role of transcendental philosopher was abysmal.

His theory of imagination offers a metaphysical basis for the
fancy-imagination distinction empirically arrived at in Chapter
Four. Whereas fancy is an arbitrary rearrangement of conscious
material, poetic or secondary imagination is a willed creative
act in which the poet moulds and reshapes his experience of the
external world to produce an artistic form 'sui generis'; an act
analogous to the primary imaginative act by which we constitute and
perceive reality itself. Such is the distinction that Coleridge
seems to intend, and while we might argue that it is only one of
degree, he insists that it is one of kind. Besides the task of
establishing that there is such a generic difference between imagination and fancy, Coleridge faces at least two other problems. The
first is whether the act of primary imagination by which the mind
reshapes external reality is to be understood as an everyday psychological phenomenon (that is, as present in ordinary perception)
or as a mode of perception of ultimate truth (and so as partaking of
religious and philosophical insight). J.R. Jackson has recently
argued, in the face of the prevailing opinion, that the latter
alternative was what Coleridge meant. (27) This emphasis, of
course, lends support to the philosophical dignity of poetry, since

the secondary imagination 'echoes' the primary. But if primary
imagination is part of ordinary sense-perception, then the chief
characteristics of its 'echo' in poetic creation must be naturalness and spontaneity.

The reason for this ambiguity may be that in Schelling's 'System
des Transcendental Idealismus' Coleridge had found a way of
deriving the imagination from a First Cause secure in the mystified
realm of pure logic. The imagination in Schelling was a metaphysical entity serving as the medium of human participation in the
creation of the world. (28) Coleridge hoped that such a theory
could underpin his own more concrete concerns. But when - having
completed his logical argument with the Ten Theses establishing
Schelling's 'I AM' principle as basic in Chapter Twelve, and the
further argument about the product of the interaction of two
forces in Chapter Thirteen - he was faced with the necessity of
applying merely logical principles in the realm of psychology, he
panicked. The result was the notorious break in the argument, with
its spurious letter from a 'friend' advising the postponement
of any full discussion until it could take its proper place in the
Treatise on the 'Logos', which Coleridge happily never completed.
After these excuses, he offered no more than a page of hasty and
cryptic definitions.

The second problem arises from the first one. For regardless of
the purely logical tangles in which he found himself, it would seem
that Coleridge at the time of the 'Biographia' had not made his
mind up about the ultimate nature of poetry. In his later prose
works, he invariably draws a distinction between the faculties of
(mechanical) 'Understanding', and of the (philosophical) 'Reason'.
Reason, in 'The Statesman's Manual' (1816), 'The Friend' (1818)
and elsewhere, is presented as the highest of human faculties. If
the secondary imagination of the 'Biographia' is to be understood
as a mode of perceiving ultimate truth, then it is hard to see how
it is distinguishable from the Reason. This would make Coleridge's
theory one concerned with the psychology of being a good Christian,
rather than having anything necessarily to do with art. But if,
as has usually been understood, the secondary imagination is a
special case of ordinary perception, then it is a specifically
poetic faculty indeed, but the relation of that faculty to the
philosophical Reason remains forever obscure. Coleridge tells us
that a great poet is a 'profound philosopher', but refuses to be
more specific. (29) After 1818, however, he gave up writing
literary criticism while remaining a Christian apologist, which may
well suggest some doctrinal embarrassment. The theory of imagination, then, may be read as his failed attempt to translate his
intuitions into the nature of mental activity, as represented by
the water-insect analogy, into the language of metaphysics. The
cryptic definitions at the end of Chapter Thirteen represent a
blurred though impressive affirmation of the creative nature of the
mind; but the metaphysics which he has so ceremoniously summoned
to his aid in defining the 'imagination, or esemplastic power'
give us no clear indications about poetry at all.

At this point, the first volume of the 'Biographia' ended. The
second volume represents a complete break, taking us back at once
to the meeting with Wordsworth, the planning of 'Lyrical Ballads'
and the shortcomings of the 1800 Preface. Coleridge is now pre-
paring for the long-promised statement of his 'poetic creed',
and he launches the discussion by defining his notions 'first, of
a poem; and secondly, of poetry itself, in kind and in essence'.
These definitions are the main business of Chapter Fourteen. The
definition of 'poetry', Coleridge tells us at the end, has been
anticipated by the preceding discussion of fancy and imagination:
this claim is the only evidence of a logical link between the metaphysics of the 'Biographia' and the literary criticism. In terms
of the rationalistic criteria by which Coleridge has consistently
asked to be judged, it is very weak evidence. For the question
'What is poetry?', he says, is virtually the same as the question
'What is a Poet?', and there follows a famous description of the
poet 'in ideal perfection' as one who 'brings the whole soul of
man into activity', fusing together its various faculties by means
of 'that synthetic and magical power to which we have exclusively
appropriated the name of imagination'. The prophetic and symbolic
quality of the prose invites direct comparison with Wordsworth's
'What is a Poet?' passage of 1802. But we may say of it, as
Coleridge himself said of the Wordsworth passage, that it is 'very
grand, and of a sort of Verulamian power and majesty, but it is,
in parts ... obscure beyond any necessity'. (30) This is
Coleridge's tribute, not only to the power of imagination, but to
its magic. Yet, just as the poet in him was half-dead, the mode
of revelation had been superseded in the 'Biographia' by that of
commentary. As a whole, the book presupposes the efforts of
previous writers and thinkers, the accumulation of traditions of
usage and all those other matters which Coleridge refers to as the
'obligations of intellect' as a kind of screen between the author
and the reality (whether metaphysical or textual) to be investigated. The final paragraphs of Chapter Fourteen make an incongruous
conclusion to one of his more convincing performances in the role
of literary scientist. For the description of the poet succeeds
his definition of 'a poem', a definition which is comparatively
drab, and equally obscure, but in the long run a good deal more
important.

  Coleridge had worked at his definitions in notes and in lectures
for several years, but in 'Biographia Literaria' he was distinguishing between the ideas of 'poetry' and 'a poem' for the first
time. He even says that 'a poem of any length neither can be, nor
ought to be, all poetry'. 'Poetry,' that is, is original creation,
the product of the secondary imagination in man. Coleridge cannot
explain it except in prophetic and magical terms. 'A poem',
however, is an artificial construction serving a limited cultural
purpose. It is

> that species of composition which is opposed to works of science
> by proposing for its immediate object pleasure, not truth; and
> from all other species (having this object in common with it) it
> is discriminated by proposing to itself such delight from the
> whole as is compatible with a distinct gratification from each
> component part.

The definition falls into two parts. The first refers us to the
neoclassical formula for the poet's purpose (to instruct by
pleasing) and to Wordsworth's opposition of poetry and science.   The
second tells us what kind of pleasure is peculiar to poems, and
combines a doctrine of poetic form with a doctrine of the psychology of aesthetic response, both of which Coleridge proceeds,
somewhat cryptically, to elaborate. It will be seen how neatly he
has separated off the area of purely aesthetic concerns from that
of the 'truth' of poetry which may have been proving an embarrassment to him.

Coleridge's formal doctrine is that the criterion of a genuine
poem is unity; the parts must cohere to form a whole. This is
compatible with, though not the same as, the doctrine of 'organic
form' which he expounded in his Shakespeare lectures in words pur-
loined from Schlegel. Organic form, when it goes beyond the level
of explicit analogy, becomes an expression of romantic nature-
mysticism, in which birds can be described as lyrical composers,
and poets affirm that their art is as natural to man as humming to
bees, twittering to swallows or mourning to small gnats. Schelling,
the most rhapsodic of the German post-Kantian philosophers,
seriously expounded a mysticism which corresponds to the licensed
assertions of the romantic nature lyric. (31) But the notion of
organic form which Coleridge took from Schlegel is simply an
attractive way of distinguishing internal and intuitive from rigid
and external structuring. Organic form appears later in the
'Biographia', but the formal doctrine of Chapter Fourteen is
couched in the more traditional aesthetic terms of 'harmony' and
'proportion':

if the definition sought for be that of a legitimate poem, I
answer it must be one the parts of which mutually support and
explain each other; all in their proportion harmonizing with,
and supporting the purpose and known influences of metrical
arrangement.

The principle of harmony, it is clear from this, decisively affects
the question of metre. Metre can only be successfully 'superadded', in Wordsworth's phrase, if all other parts or elements of
the poem are made consonant with it; and so metre alone is
sufficient ground for the distinction between prose and poetry
which Wordsworth had rejected. Thus Coleridge's definition of a
poem directly anticipates his commentary on the 1800 Preface.

The other aspect of Coleridge's definition is his doctrine of the
psychology of aesthetic response. The presence of metre, he argues,
tends to promote the kind of pleasure which is peculiar to poetry.
This specifically poetic pleasure is the result of heightened
attention. The importance of metre is that it stimulates our
attention to every facet of linguistic communication, producing
not a generalized, blurred sense of meaning or message, but 'a
distinct gratification from each component part'. Coleridge's
concept of aesthetic attention effectively solves the hopeless
muddle in which Wordsworth had found himself when he denied that
metre made any generic difference to poetry, while admitting that
a piece of verse would be read a hundred times where its prose
equivalent was read once. The solution is contained in the following
statements:

If metre be superadded, all other parts must be made consonant
with it. They must be such as to justify the perpetual and
distinct attention to each part which an exact correspondent
recurrence of accent and sound are calculated to excite.
     The philosophic critics of all ages coincide with the
ultimate judgment of all countries in equally denying the
praises of a just poem on the one hand to a series of striking
lines or distichs, each of which absorbing the whole attention
of the reader to itself disjoins it from its context and makes
it a separate whole, instead of a harmonizing part; and on the
other hand, to an unsustained composition, from which the
reader collects rapidly the general result unattracted by the
component parts. The reader should be carried forward, not
merely or chiefly by the mechanical impulse of curiosity, or by
a restless desire to arrive at the final solution; but by the
pleasurable activity of mind excited by the attractions of the
journey itself.
Not least among the 'attractions of the journey itself', it may
be suggested, were the pleasures of sound. Coleridge and Wordsworth
were noted for the chanting intonation with which they read verse
aloud. The concern with pleasure and the perfection of form in
these passages foreshadows the musical qualities of later romantic
and symbolist poetry; the same qualities were enthusiastically
advocated by Hazlitt in his 'Lectures on the English Poets'. When
we think of poetry as harmonious and pleasurable we are very likely
to see it as a kind of music. But Coleridge's concept of aesthetic
attention leaves something to be accounted for - the sense of
poetic power. This is the quality that thrills through his own
response to Wordsworth's 'Prelude' (1807):
                    An Orphic song indeed,
     A song divine of high and passionate thoughts
     To their own music chaunted!

                              ('To William Wordsworth').
Coleridge's definition of a poem is a formalist definition, and what
it does is to give a more dynamic and analytic understanding of the
poem as aesthetic object. To see the poem in terms of power,
however, is to see it as the product of a creative activity of mind
in the poet - of 'high and passionate thoughts' - and as capable
of exciting a similar creativity in the mind of the reader. Though
it was this discovery, prompted by Wordsworth's poetry, that had
inaugurated his 'circuitous journey' in Chapter Four, he was unable
to bring it wholly within the province of rationalized aesthetics.
That is why he adopted the expedient of distinguishing 'poetry'
from 'a poem', and why when it came to defining 'poetry' - where
power was involved - he launched into the rhapsody on the 'poet,
described in ideal perfection', with which Chapter Fourteen ends.
     If aesthetics could not cope rationally with the power of
poetry, what about practical criticism? It was to this that he
turned in the next chapter, claiming to elucidate the 'specific
symptoms of poetic power' in an analysis of 'Venus and Adonis'.
Though he discussed the use of imagery in some particular passages
of the poem, these discussions are rather desultory, and follow
what Wordsworth had done in the 1815 Preface. Coleridge's main
concern is not with the linguistic energy of the poem, but the

moral energy and 'genial and productive nature' of the mind that
produced it. (33) Coleridge lists four main symptoms of power in
Shakespeare's poems - sweetness of versification, powers of
dramatic creation, handling of imagery and 'depth and energy of
thought' - and the chapter culminates with a brilliant but very
general appreciation of the 'protean' quality of Shakespeare's
genius. Shakespeare, who 'darts himself forth, and passes into
all the forms of human character and passion', is contrasted with
Milton who draws all things to himself, 'into the unity of his own
ideal'. Shakespeare and Milton are seated upon 'the two glory-
smitten summits of the poetic mountain'; the question from here on
is whether there is to be a third summit, occupied by Wordsworth.
But first, a good deal of the critical view is still blocked by a
jerry-built edifice called the Preface to 'Lyrical Ballads'.

Coleridge's reply to Wordsworth is one of the most dramatic documents of English criticism. Here, in the clash of two strongly
idiosyncratic minds, is a telling realization of that conflict
between author and critical authority which is implicit throughout
literary history. The fact that Coleridge was Wordsworth's friend
and admirer should not disguise the magnitude of the conflict.
Wordsworth's sense of mission and his sternly egotistic genius
stand, even today, as awkward obstacles to our sense of English
poetry as a continuous tradition. Coleridge's purpose was to
show how the best of Wordsworth could and must be assimilated within
that corporate tradition. The price of such assimilation was high,
since not only Wordsworth's theories but the whole idea of a
poetic language - and, by extension, of creative genius - independent of literary education and cultural precedent was at stake.
Coleridge won the argument, but his was in part a victory of the
intellectual or one-man academy over the unsophisticated, visionary
poet. His detached and judicial air is particularly notable when
he exposes Wordsworth's weaknesses in expounding his own point of
view. The issue is, of course, greatly complicated by the personal relationship between the two men. Their close association
during the writing of the 1800 Preface makes some of Coleridge's
later misunderstandings seem wilful and perverse. At the same
time, he is still Wordsworth's warmest advocate, though the 'GENUINE
PHILOSOPHIC POEM' that he envisages as the poet's crowning achievement is partly a product of his own over-intellectual expectations
of genius. If he read between the lines of the 'Biographia',
Wordsworth could hardly have found its argument welcome. Coleridge
claims, it is true, that the excision of the Preface and a few
dozen lines of 'Lyrical Ballads' would be enough to satisfy the
poet's most stringent critic; but the damage his arguments seem
calculated to cause is more far-reaching than this. What they do,
in effect, is to cut the poet off from what he believed were his
external sources of creativity, undermining that sense of confident oneness with the world of nature which irradiates the
'Lyrical Ballads' and the 1805 'Prelude'. Where Wordsworth himself felt cut off from the Platonic essence of nature (as we know
from the 'Immortality Ode'). Coleridge suggested that his grasp
of what was left behind, the human and material world, was

imperfect and idiosyncratic. Poetic powers like his rested
wholly on inner resources and intuitions. In inviting his friend
to look still more into himself, and to cultivate his solipsistic
bent, Coleridge was condemning some of the best things (as well as
the worst things) Wordsworth had written by the standards of
poetry that he was still expected to write. The demise of the
'genuine philosophic poem' shows how misguided these expectations
were.

'Language', Coleridge wrote, 'is the armoury of the human mind;
and at once contains the trophies of its past, and the weapons of
its future conquests.' (34) Wordsworth's criticism was the work
of a poet who saw his responsibility as necessarily extending to
questions of culture; but Coleridge in the 'Biographia' speaks
with the voice of a philologist, not of a poet of nature. Such a
voice can command the past and the future but may feel threatened
by a poet who writes as if in an eternal present. In fact, Coleridge
launched a two-pronged attack on the Preface, aiming to save
Wordsworth's poetry as literature while countering its cultural
effects. The underlying motive of Wordsworth's theory of diction
seems a very simple one: it was to expose the sterility of
Augustan verse and to state the case for a revolutionary plainness
of style and subject-matter as trenchantly as possible. But the
argument had implications which Coleridge recognized and fought
against for all he was worth. That is why he attacks the Preface
as a philologist, linguist, sociologist, aesthetician and philosopher, but never as a fellow-poet. The author of 'Frost at
Midnight', 'The Ancient Mariner' and 'This Lime-Tree Bower My
Prison' - poems as radical and as free of intellectualism as any
of Wordsworth's - has given way to a brilliant dialectician
exposing the absurdity of the left-wing views he had held in his
own youth. He is not interested in Wordsworth's immediate objects,
only in the conformity of his views with tradition and precedent;
thus there is 'no poet whose writings would safelier stand the
test of Mr. Wordsworth's theory than Spenser.' (35) He plays down
the revolutionary aspects of Wordsworth's poetry, and he pronounces
the experiments of 'Lyrical Ballads' an unmitigated failure. (36)
Some of his arguments, as Hazlitt and others noticed, were taken
from Wordsworth's bitterest opponents; and the 'Biographia' was
seen as an act of apostasy by the 'Monthly Review', which rated
Wordsworth as a 'very moderate writer', but greeted his critic as
an 'unintentional defender of good taste and good sense in
poetry'. (37)

The argument commences with a diversion: Chapter Sixteen, a
charming little essay on the Renaissance lyric. The key to it
is perhaps found in a footnote referring to Sir Joshua Reynolds
and his belief that good taste is acquired from 'submissive study
of the best models'. Similar references had appeared in the 1798
Advertisement and the 1800 Preface. Coleridge asserts that the
fifteenth- and sixteenth-century lyrics and madrigals are among
the best models, but the simplicity and purity of diction which he
admires in them are the reverse of Wordsworthian simplicity.
Their writers used a highly polished diction, and 'placed the
essence of poetry in the art', or, as we should say, in perfection
of form. This is a tacit rebuke to Wordsworth, and establishes

the context of philology and literary history within which the
Preface is to be discussed. Coleridge admits that there is a
more ambitious kind of poetry than this, and from here on he tends
to divide good poetry into two sorts: first, a simple (though
preferably polished and musical) mode written not in the 'real
language of men' but in a purified and public traditional style
which he christens the 'lingua communis'; and second, a more
impassioned and imaginative mode in which style becomes more
personal and idiosyncratic. The first is found in the madrigalists
and in Chaucer and Herbert, and is opposed to the false simplicity
or 'matter-of-factness' of the experimental 'Lyrical Ballads'.
The second is Miltonic, and also Wordsworthian. Coleridge looks
to a combination of the two modes for the perfection of English
poetry; it seems a prophecy less of what Wordsworth would do than
of the 'musical' imagination of Keats and Tennyson.

     In Chapter Seventeen he at last reaches the discussion of the
Preface, and outlines an alternative theory of language. Language
is not the natural expression of man, but the bearer of culture
and civilization; it is what the human race laboriously creates,
and each individual has to learn. Wordsworth had stressed the
spontaneity of the individual's use of language, finding in rustics
the virtues that we would now find in children. Coleridge replies
that a language is created and sustained by the educated classes
of a society; its best parts are the products of philosophers and
not of shepherds. The sociological bearing of his defence of the
values of education leads to the theory of the clerisy or intellectual class that he was to develop in 'Church and State' (1830).
In relation to poetry, it leads to concurrence with Johnson's and
Reynolds's view of literary language. The headnote 'Poetry
essentially ideal and generic' could have been written by either
of them, and his substitution of the literary concept of a 'lingua
communis' for Wordsworth's 'real language of men' clearly har-
monizes with Johnson's ideas about poetic diction. But in
Coleridge's case, the neoclassical ideas are underwritten by Kantian
transcendentalism, in the shape of his commitment to the 'Science
of Method'.

     Coleridge's essays on Method dominate the otherwise haphazard
material of 'The Friend' (1818). Like his metaphysics, his
interest in method is logically prior to literary criticism, though
he turns to criticism for its application and illustration.
Essentially these essays are an analysis of the operations of the
perfect or 'philosophic' mind; they elaborate Coleridge's ideal
of intellectuality. The truly educated man, Coleridge writes,
is accustomed to contemplate, not things on their own, but the
relations between things. He possesses a 'prospectiveness of
mind' or 'surview' which enables him to express his thoughts with
the maximum of discipline and organization. It may well be
argued that poets work through quite other faculties than the
methodical intellect; and perhaps this was why Coleridge became
half-ashamed of 'The Ancient Mariner' and 'Kubla Khan'. Nonetheless, the 'Biographia' is based on the assumption that the
principles of Method must be applied in the sphere of poetry.

     The language of rustics is lacking in Method on two counts. The
rustic is poor in linguistic resources; Coleridge does not share

Wordsworth's faith in the natural articulateness of men under the stress of passion. Moreover, being uneducated, he has nothing to express save 'insulated facts'; he has not learned to contemplate the relations between things. In arguing this, Coleridge not only seems blind to any non-intellectual mode of human awareness, but rejects the particularism of detail which is the essence of much romantic poetry and poetic theory. He is quite clear in preferring philosophical to poetic perception:

> For facts are valuable to a wise man chiefly as they lead to the discovery of the indwelling law which is the true being of things, the sole solution of their modes of existence and in the knowledge of which consists our dignity and our power. (38)

Coleridge clearly does not value the sheer pleasure which facts can give; the 'wise man' of this passage would no doubt prefer the versified philosophy of Erasmus Darwin, for example, to the naked observations of John Clare. Coleridge seems prepared to concede the autonomy of poetry only in the matter of expression and not of substance. He is far more pertinent when he comes to the formal aspect of the choice of diction and metre. When Wordsworth spoke of selecting from the real language of men, what he mainly had in mind was a selection of its vocabulary. But Coleridge points out that the essence of style lies in 'ordonnance', or the syntax and arrangement of thought. Thus in order to adopt the 'language of a class', we must imitate not merely its vocabulary, but its word-order as well. This argument leaves Wordsworth in a cleft stick. The 'Lyrical Ballads' use the word-order appropriate to verse rather than prose; hence they are not in the real language of men. Since the presence of metre forces the poet to use a different word-order, poetic diction, defined as the form of linguistic ordonnance appropriate to metre, is something that he cannot avoid. A choice of different styles or 'languages' is inevitable in any culture which can distinguish between verse, prose and conversational forms.

Presumably, there is no logical necessity for these alternative styles to form a hierarchy; but Coleridge evidently believes that this is and ought to be the case. Verse, he argues, ought to command a heightened style; this follows both from the principles of harmony and aesthetic attention introduced in Chapter Fourteen, and from the authority of the poetic tradition. The final objection he deals with is Wordsworth's argument that once the 'arbitrariness' of poetic diction was allowed, no limits could be set to it. On the contrary, Coleridge replies, the limits are set by 'the principles of grammar, logic, psychology!' These would not have sufficed as revolutionary slogans in 1800, but then neither could Wordsworth have written, as Coleridge does, of Gray's sonnet that 'That the "Phoebus" is hackneyed, and a schoolboy image, is an accidental fault, dependent on the age in which the author wrote and not deduced from the nature of the thing.' The abuses of Augustan style which bulked so large in 1800 are now shrugged off as a trifling matter and do nothing to disturb Coleridge's sense of literary precedent broadening down from age to age. And though he is famous for his emphasis that the principles of logic and grammar must be organically and intuitively applied by the poet, this is balanced by his

insistence on their objective, canonical status. Thus Wordsworth's theory of diction is incapable of
> furnishing either rule, guidance or precaution that might not,
> more easily and more safely, as well as more naturally, have
> been deduced in the author's own mind from considerations of
> grammar, logic and the truth and nature of things, confirmed
> by the authority of words whose fame is not of one country nor
> of one age.

In these closing words of Chapter Eighteen, the 'author' is
firmly put down by the consensus of literary authority. The time
is now ripe for Coleridge to examine Wordsworth's claims as a poet
to enter the pantheon of literature.

The formal balance-sheet is presented in Chapter Twenty-Two,
but Coleridge has long before this made some damaging points about
the 'Lyrical Ballads'. Most importantly, he uncovers a failure
of realism, a failure on Wordsworth's part to disclose the world
as it really is. We may go back to Chapter Fifteen, where he
praised Shakespeare's prodigious dramatic powers and unerring
treatment of 'subjects very remote from the private interests and
circumstances of the writer himself.' It is precisely this power
that, in Coleridge's view, Wordsworth lacks. We might, indeed,
wonder whether a poet whose gift was so fundamentally solipsistic
would be well equipped to become the 'profound philosopher' of
whom Coleridge speaks. Yet Coleridge was no empiricist, and saw
no contradiction in boosting Wordsworth's philosophic powers at
the very same time as he denigrated his grip on reality. The
principal example here is 'The Thorn'; Coleridge ridicules the
device of the sea-captain as narrator, pointing out that the poem
veers uncertainly between the dullness and garrulity attributed
to the captain, and a degree of imaginative intensity which
appears to belong to the poet's own character, and cannot be
taken from the 'language of ordinary men'. This might seem a
trivial failure, but Coleridge brings the same objection against
'The Excursion', a far graver matter. 'Is there one word, for
instance, attributed to the pedlar in the "Excursion" characteristic of a pedlar?' (39) This is a very harsh exposure of the
solipsistic tendency of Wordsworth's imagination. Wrapped in his
own life, Coleridge seems to be saying, Wordsworth understands
neither society, nor rustics, nor the 'language of men' that he
professes to write. He struggles to cover this up with 'matter-
of-factness', 'a laborious minuteness and fidelity' in the
representation of objects, together with the 'insertion of
accidental circumstances' such as those of the Wanderer and the
sea-captain. (40) Coleridge's strictures on 'The Thorn' thus
turn out to be aimed at much more than a single, mawkish ballad.
They are but pallidly counteracted by a page or so of praise for
Wordsworth's 'truth of nature', mainly in his nature-lyrics. The
social realism of Wordsworth's poetry is something to which
Coleridge does no justice at all. 'Michael' and 'The Old
Cumberland Beggar', for instance, are not even mentioned.

In Chapters Nineteen and Twenty he distinguishes between the
legitimate mode of poetic simplicity - here the 'neutral style'
of Chaucer and Herbert, based on a literary 'lingua communis' or
purified diction - and the style ordained for the higher and more

philosophical powers of Wordsworth. The advocate of the real
language of men is revealed as 'a poet whose diction, next to
that of Shakespeare and Milton, appears to me of all others the
most individualized and characteristic.' Coleridge relies largely
on quotations to convey his sense of this idiosyncrasy; so much
so that, in the final chapters of the 'Biographia', the deductive, rationalistic ideal of criticism he had aspired to earlier
seems to give way to a new and more empirical procedure like
that which was later to be championed by Matthew Arnold. Arnold
quotes in order to avoid abstract definitions which he feels
inappropriate to poetry; but Coleridge's use of extensive quotation to redress the balance of his critique and reveal the
'positive' side of Wordsworth suggests that he has run out of
steam. Nonetheless, these last chapters are a decisive rejection
of the 'simple Wordsworth' in favour of the lofty and Miltonic
poet-prophet, whose strengths, Coleridge argues, come from his
internal powers of meditation and imagination rather than from
a direct grasp of the real world. The Preface to 'Lyrical Ballads'
had expressed Wordsworth's strong conviction that his poetry was
the spontaneous vehicle of natural emotions and of natural responses to external objects. In the 1815 Preface, despite his
stress on the modifying role of imagination, he had not altogether
abandoned this conviction. Coleridge, however, argues that his
diction depends for its success on 'striking passages' that come
from within - passages which belong quintessentially to poetry
rather than to prose and which reflect the full idiosyncrasy of
his genius. The faults which he assiduously notes down in Chapter
Twenty-Two are of two main kinds: the matter-of-factness and
abuse of the dramatic form which result from Wordsworth's mistaken
attempts to write on subjects remote from his private interests,
and, as the converse of this, a self-indulgent idiosyncrasy of
style which fails to 'satisfy a cultivated taste'. All of which
emphasizes the solipsism of Wordsworth's imagination. When he
moves from the poet's defects to the beauties, Coleridge in
effect lists those qualities of mind which make such solipsism
heroic: Wordsworth's precision of language, the weightiness of
his thoughts, his 'meditative pathos', and finally, the 'gift
of imagination in the highest and strictest sense of the word'.
These are the qualities which distinguish Wordsworth and qualify
him for that 'FIRST GENUINE PHILOSOPHIC POEM' which Coleridge
believes may be the summit of his work. The implication is that
it is precisely by following the ideal of the self-reflecting
philosopher which Coleridge had inherited from the post-Kantians
that Wordsworth would achieve this. (Contrast Ruskin's much
cooler view of the side of Wordsworth which Coleridge tended to
idolize: 'Wordsworth ... understands how to be happy, but yet
cannot altogether rid himself of the sense that he is a philosopher, and ought always to be saying something wise. He has
also a vague notion that Nature would not be able to get on well
without Wordsworth; and finds a considerable part of his pleasure
in looking at himself as well as at her.' (Of Modern Landscape,
in 'Modern Painters', vol. 3, 1856).) For Wordsworth, and
perhaps for any other romantic poet, the ideal of self-
consciousness growing out of critical scepticism that Coleridge

put forward must have meant creative emasculation. It is at
variance both with the prophetic confidence and the humble fidelity
with which the poet alternately approaches the world of nature.

Though their background is Kantian, Coleridge's list of
Wordsworth's virtues seems on the face of it rather academic. The
issues raised by the 'Biographia' strike deep, but the depth does
not extend to establishing the 'strictest sense of the word'
imagination. His final tribute to Wordsworth's imaginative
power is paid by means of quotations, and, characteristically,
Coleridge reserves the full articulation of his meaning for a
further work:

> I shall select a few examples as most obviously manifesting
> this faculty; but if I should ever be fortunate enough to
> render my analysis of imagination, its origin and characters,
> thoroughly intelligible to the reader, he will scarcely open
> on a page of this poet's works without recognizing, more or
> less, the presence and the influences of this faculty.

It is with a declaration of faith rather than a 'quod erat
demonstrandum' that the long critique ends.

The 'Biographia' is a product of the revolution it condemns;
so much must be obvious. It is a work of intellectual commentary,
creating a field of brilliantly ingenious discussion and hard-
hitting debate, out-flanking the positive, abstract rationalism
of the Preface and all but overwhelming it. Coleridge's critical
performance is almost impossible to sum up, magnificently far-
sighted as he is in some directions, and unable to see what is in
front of his nose in others. If we subtract that part of the
book which grew out of Wordsworth's poetic impact and the outspoken
radicalism of his prefaces, we are left with little but a
Shandean facade, some desultory reminiscences, and some borrowed
metaphysics. For if the apotheosis of the poetic imagination
seems to be prompted by Wordsworth, so is Coleridge's theory of
language and his doctrine of aesthetic attention. The second
half of the 'Biographia' is dominated by his obsession with contradicting Wordsworth, correcting his views and stating the terms on
which he may be accepted as a great writer. What kind of personal
and creative symbiosis had gone on between Wordsworth and
Coleridge, we can only guess; but judged simply as a book, the
'Biographia' more than any other critical classic invites the
strict biological sense of the word 'parasitic'. Whatever view
we take of the outcome, there could be no more graphic demonstration of the clash of interests in criticism and the power-
struggle that ensues when poet and critic meet, to use
Coleridge's phrase, 'in a war embrace'.

Apart from the 'Biographia', Coleridge's criticism consists
almost entirely of scattered lecture-notes and marginalia, and of
reports of his lectures and conversation. Very high claims have
been made for this material. T.M. Raysor introduced his edition
of the Shakespeare criticism in 1930 with the statement that 'In
the history of English literary criticism there is no work which
surpasses in interest Coleridge's lectures upon Shakespeare.' Yet
the lectures do not really live up to their reputation, especially

when one is familiar with the works of Schlegel and Schiller
from which many of their most famous ideas are drawn. Coleridge,
in general, inherits the comparative and historicist outlook of
German thought, adding to it a more detailed interest in poetic
texture and an explicitly patriotic concern with the English
literary heritage. To his Shakespeare lectures Coleridge brought
a genuine sense of mission, feeling that he was the first English
critic capable of appreciating the Bard's true powers. The
eighteenth-century critics, he complained, were in the habit of
treating him like an errant schoolboy; he devoted two lectures
(now lost) in the 1811-12 course to a savage analysis of
Johnson's 'Preface'. Coleridge was the first major English critic
to idolize Shakespeare, (41) and he saw in him not only a great
genius, but a genius of diametrically opposite type to Wordsworth.
It seems almost commonplace to describe Shakespeare's as a
Protean imagination, darting forth and passing into all the forms
of human character and passion, and it was in any case what
Schlegel had said. But Coleridge's characterization of Shakespeare's genius both contrasts with and complements his description
of Wordsworth. Both the great extrovert genius and the great
solipsist owe their pre-eminence, he suggests, to their intellectual and meditative powers. Shakespeare was not a child of
nature but a philosophical poet whose greatness was the result of
reflection and of 'knowledge become habitual and intuitive'. (42)
And it was not in knowledge of the world so much as in knowledge
of himself - but of his 'representative' self - that he excelled.
It is in this way that Coleridge adapts his post-Kantian view of
genius to fit the case of the great dramatic poet, and we need
not be surprised that as a practical critic he stresses the novel-
istic, at the expense of the theatrical, side of his achievement.
Coleridge's favourite role as a Shakespeare critic is precisely
that which Johnson, in his 'Preface' and notes on the plays,
refused to fill. It is the role of omniscient narrator, explaining
and commenting on the action in such a way that nothing is lost
and verisimilitude is enhanced to the utmost degree. The narrator
of a nineteenth-century novel has privileged access to the secret
motives of his characters; so it is with Coleridge and
Shakespeare's heroes. His interpretation of 'Hamlet' is the
classic example. When Hamlet refuses to kill Claudius at prayer,
Johnson exclaims in horror at the callousness of a revenge which
would condemn its victim to eternal damnation. Coleridge,
however, knows the 'germ' of the character, his inner secret; so
he explains that Hamlet's speech is a device of procrastination.
(43) His imagination responds most strongly to the enigmas of
character in the plays, and to the creation of realism and
'atmosphere' in Shakespeare's opening scenes. His analysis of
the beginning of 'Hamlet' is unforgettably evocative, but it is
the fruit of lavish concentration on speeches and actions which
the theatrical audience must take in very quickly. Opening scenes
in novels tend to be far more amply presented than in Shakespeare,
even where the material is 'dramatic' - consider 'Middlemarch' -
and though Coleridge's discussion will enrich the experience of
anyone who has studied the text of 'Hamlet', we are often discon-
certed by the relentless pace at which productions of plays we

have studied (and still more, dramatizations of novels) seem to
get under way.

A good example of Coleridge's procedure in discussing Shakespeare is his commentary on the opening of 'The Tempest', in the
ninth lecture of 1811-12. This is the first lecture in which
Schlegel's influence is acknowledged and beyond dispute, and
Coleridge approaches 'The Tempest' by way of Schlegel's distinction
between mechanical and organic form. He then illustrates this by
analysing the altercation between Gonzalo and the Boatswain in the
brief scene of the storm. As he tries frantically to organize the
crew, the Boatswain forgets the deference due to rank and rudely
challenges Gonzalo either to silence the elements with his
authority, since he is a Counsellor, or to get out of the way.
Gonzalo fails to answer the taunt directly, however:

> An ordinary dramatist would, after this speech, have represented
> Gonzalo as moralizing, or saying something connected with the
> Boatswain's language; for ordinary dramatists are not men of
> genius: they combine their ideas by association, or by logical
> affinity; but the vital writer, who makes men on the stage what
> they are in nature, in a moment transports himself into the
> very being of each personage, and, instead of cutting out arti-
> ficial puppets, he brings before us the men themselves.
> Therefore, Gonzalo soliloquises, - 'I have great comfort
> from this fellow: methinks, he hath no drowning mark upon him;
> his complexion is perfect gallows. (44)

The fact is that this is not a soliloquy. The whole royal party
are on stage when it is spoken, and it is obviously meant to cheer
them up. Coleridge's 'ordinary dramatist' is a short-sighted
theatrical technician for whom each speech must be a response to
the one before. Gonzalo's speech is certainly different in that
it emerges from a whole imaginative conception, but its function,
surely, is to reassure the audience by a momentary nonchalance
hinting that the bangs and rumbles in the wings are not to be
taken seriously. It does not give us insight into the unique
individuality of Gonzalo, which is the last thing we want in the
middle of a storm. Coleridge's concern, however, is to show the
rounded conception of Shakespeare's characters and the philosophical powers revealed in his mastery of an inexhaustible range
of mental types.

The theme of Coleridge's Shakespeare criticism is that of
'Shakespeare's Judgment Equal to his Genius'. His analyses are
punctuated by exclamations ('But observe the matchless judgment
of Shakespeare!'), and the tone is almost invariably hagiographic.
One of his marginalia records his bafflement over a passage in
'Coriolanus' (IV.vii.28-): 'I cherish the hope that I am
mistaken and, becoming wiser, shall discover some profound
excellence in what I now appear to myself to detect an imperfection. S.T.C.' (45) Coleridge might have written 'I wish I
understood this', but he didn't, and there seems little doubt to
which area of human experience his sentiments properly belong.
He affirmed that criticism of Shakespeare should be 'reverential',
and we might say that in his hands it becomes a kind of spilt
natural theology. Paley sought for evidences of design in the
natural universe, arguing back from the watch to the watch-maker.

The belief that the hand of God was discoverable in every aspect of Nature sanctioned the minutest study of natural history in the eighteenth century; this was the heyday of the botanizing and birdwatching parson. Criticism of Shakespeare, too, could produce proofs of design and Authorship where careless eyes had seen nothing but accident: such was the justification to be advanced by de Quincey for his essay On the Knocking at the Gate in 'Macbeth' (1823), and it is implicit in Coleridge's attempts to make the smallest details of the texts yield evidence of Shakespeare's conscious control, and hence of his creative omnipotence. Like a parson examining the geological vestiges of the Flood, he feels vaguely threatened when something in the text proves recalcitrant.

Coleridge on Shakespeare, then, is a commentator who tends to translate drama into fiction at the behest of a quasi-theological piety. It is not surprising that his reverence should sometimes seem personal or ideological rather than purely aesthetic. If he confessed to having a smack of Hamlet himself, he also compared Macbeth to Napoleon and Caliban to the Jacobins, and praised Shakespeare for his patriotism, his conservatism and his habit of 'never introducing a professional character, as such, otherwise than as respectable.' (46) Shakespeare's political and patriotic merits, however, were subordinate to his highest excellence as a manifestation of 'divine' genius. We have traced Coleridge's concern with judgment and genius as a theme of his criticism, but it led him in the end to abandon criticism for Christian apologetics. As early as 'The Statesman's Manual' (1816) he described the reason, the organ of the immediate spiritual consciousness of God, as a higher faculty than the imagination. (47) When criticism comes to be recognized as a mediated form of theology, its scope must be very limited. Coleridge finally came to such a recognition; so much is clear from his marginal note on a volume of Milton (c. 1823?):

Of criticism we may perhaps say, that those divine poets, Homer, Eschylus, and the two compeers, Dante, Shakespeare, Spenser, Milton, who deserve to have Critics, $\kappa\rho\iota\tau\alpha\acute{\iota}$, are placed above criticism in the vulgar sense, and move in the sphere of religion, while those who are not such scarcely deserve criticism in any sense. (48)

Before reaching this slough of critical Despond, he had a last fling at aesthetic theory in the lecture On Poesy or Art (1818). Though a fine source for rapt Coleridgian utterances, this lecture is little more than a translation of Schelling, and in any case it offers a theory of the visual arts rather than of literature. His later years produced only some desultory critical table-talk, and some hints about the place of literature in society. In 'The Friend' (1818), he somewhat economically divided human social activity into the 'two main directions' of Trade and Literature - forces which both sustain the national identity of a society, and seek to transcend it. (49) But what is the social function of the imaginative element in Literature? We would naturally look for an answer to this in 'On the Constitution of the Church and State' (1830), where Coleridge outlines his theory of the national culture. Here he argues for the recognition of the 'clerisy' -

the class of intellectuals and educators - as one of the permanent
estates of the realm. The task of the clerisy is to exercise the
faculty of Vision (that is, imagination), as well as those of
Reason and Understanding. Yet apart from a dutiful quotation or
two from Wordsworth, the figure of the poet plays no part in
Coleridge's description of the clerisy, whose culture consists of
the traditional hierarchy of 'literae humaniores', crowned by
theology. There is no Coleridgian equivalent to Wordsworth's
'rock of defence for human nature', or to Shelley's 'unacknowledged
legislator'. 'Church and State' really confirms the academic and
intellectualizing tendencies that were present throughout his
earlier career in literary criticism. It leaves us, however,
with the baffling paradox of Coleridge, a brilliantly intelligent
literary critic by any standards, and for many the undisputed
master of the discipline in England, yet who fails so many of the
tests we put to critics, including in the end the test of commitment to the creative spirit itself. Coleridge, it seems, can
admit of poetic genius only as a means to more intellectual and
spiritual ends. Whatever the personal struggles that marked his
thought, there is a logical link between his criticism of
Shakespeare and Wordsworth, and the later years in which the
evidence of his disillusionment with criticism and even with
literature is so strong.

3   SHELLEY, HAZLITT AND KEATS

In his famous dictum about 'negative capability', Keats chooses
Coleridge as his example of the non-poet irritably reaching after
fact and reason. Coleridge had managed to convince himself that
the poetic spirit, while deeply hostile to British empirical
philosophy, could be subsumed under the higher reason of Kantian
transcendentalism. Others did not agree. Nonetheless, the theme
of opposition to utilitarian doctrine is very widespread in the
period, from Coleridge's 'Church and State' to de Quincey,
Hazlitt, and Shelley's 'Defence of Poetry'. The ancient quarrel
between philosophy and poetry took on an urgency quite unknown
in Johnson's time, for the ideological upheavals of the 'age of
revolutions' had shaken customary beliefs about the nature and
demarcations of culture. The metaphysics of Coleridge and the
literary witch-hunting of the quarterlies suggest the variety of
possible conservative responses to this situation. The revolution
in literary values instigated by Wordsworth was, however, carried
on by Keats, Shelley and their circle. Like many of their
predecessors, they show signs of a deep frustration and insecurity
about the position of the poet, but for them the frustration is
a source of energy and a guarantee that they can only benefit
from living in a revolutionary age. They respond with militant
assertions of the ideals of literary culture, and with poetry
fervently embodying those ideals. Shelley, in particular, is a
prophet of humanism denouncing the tyranny of aristocratic
government and bourgeois materialism. We have to distinguish here
between the broad humanism of the romantics and the effect of
their beliefs within the narrower sphere of poetry and criticism.

After his death Shelley came to personify the charisma and magic of poethood for generations of Victorians who had no time for his political views. Though he failed in his revolutionary aims, the attitude of poetic absolutism which he asserted against Peacock's rational and 'enlightened' view of history found a much wider echo. It was symptomatic of the romantic revolt that the language of criticism became unpredictable, and its relation to rational thought problematic.

One of the ways in which romantic militancy and the breakdown of the eighteenth-century cultural consensus are reflected in language is in the redefinition of the word 'poetry'. 'Literature', as we have seen, was redefined concurrently as an existing tradition or heritage of imaginative works, and this sense was established as normal. The mutations undergone by the word 'poetry' were more exotic and temporary. Essentially what took place was a species of linguistic imperialism, which was able to claim the sanction of Plato since a passage in the 'Symposium' describes poetry as originally a generic term for the processes of creation and invention. Wordsworth declared that the philosophical opposite of poetry was 'Matter of Fact, or Science', and Coleridge stipulated that 'All the fine arts are different species of poetry.' (50) Elsewhere he suggested 'poesy' as the generic term and 'poetry' for the metrical art alone, but this distinction failed to stick. Once poetry came to denote a common quality of all the arts, a new importance was given in literary criticism to the problems of the relationship between the arts, and of the place of the poetic faculty in human nature as a whole. Hazlitt memorably tackles the former question, and Shelley the latter. The poets, in the meantime, found that the words 'poetry' and 'poesy' could be used with an easy evocativeness that was unprecedented. Hence the title 'Sleep and Poetry'; lines like 'Perhaps on wing of Poesy upsoar', and 'Framed in the silent poesy of form'; the kiss in Keats's 'Isabella', where Lorenzo's lips 'poesied with hers in dewy rhyme'; and, at rock-bottom, Coleridge's grisly lines to his future daughter-in-law:

My Derwent hath found realiz'd in thee, ...
The fair fulfilment of his poesy,
When his young heart first yearn'd for sympathy!

('To Mary Pridham', 1827)

'Poesy' seems to have been the more 'poetical' form and rapidly became trivialized to mean fantasy, yearning or love-play. Apart from its wilder excesses, however, the extended definition of poetry implied a heightened sense of the poet's responsibility and mission. This in turn led to the romantic instability; messianic conviction alternated with failure and despondency.

Keats, for example, can sound very down-to-earth when it is a question of what he is actually writing: 'I must make 4000 Lines of one bare circumstance and fill them with Poetry', he says of 'Endymion'. Yet a sentence earlier he writes that 'the high Idea I have of poetical fame makes me think I see it towering to [sic?] high above me.' (51) The classic statements in his letters are meditations on what it is to be a poet (the 'poetical Character') rather than on poetic technique. Keats was both ambitious and fearful of becoming a poet; in his description of the poet as 'the

most unpoetical of any thing in existence' and in the initiation
scene of 'The Fall of Hyperion' he seems alarmed by the prospect
of losing his identity and submitting to an alien power. He often
had to tell himself to keep his head, even if that meant renouncing
poetic aspirations. 'There is no greater Sin after the 7 deadly
than to flatter oneself into an idea of being a great Poet - ...
how comfortable a feel it is that such a Crime must bring its
heavy Penalty?' he wrote priggishly of Leigh Hunt. (52) This is
a reminder that the intensely literary pretensions to which Keats
gives classic expression were almost commonplace among his fellow-
writers. It was necessary to be a great poet; simply to be a
poet was not enough. In a letter to Haydon, another artistic
pretender, Keats announced his choice of Shakespeare as his
presiding genius in 1817. Shakespeare came to seem his special
good fairy in the struggle between his reverence for the literary
past and his search for authentic self-expression. As a romantic
literary poet, Keats felt his relation to his predecessors not as
a public but as a peculiarly private relation. When he announced
his rejection of the Miltonic mode of the first 'Hyperion'
('Miltonic verse can not be written but in an artful or rather
artist's humour'), he said bluntly that 'I wish to give myself up
to other sensations.' (53)

The contradiction between the poet's sense of high calling and
public responsibility and the private and unique character of his
struggle to develop, is surely what accounts for the difficulties
the romantics experienced in handling the traditional literary
genres. Wordsworth, despite the influence of Milton, created new
models for the long poem in 'The Excursion' and (far more
radically) in 'The Prelude'. But Keats and Shelley sought poetic
fame in forms far closer to traditional tragedy and epic, though
their real concerns lay elsewhere. Shelley's Preface to
'Prometheus Unbound' expresses the literary alienation that is
central to their work:

> This Poem was chiefly written upon the mountainous ruins of the
> Baths of Caracalla, among the flowery glades, and thickets of
> odoriferous blossoming trees, which are extended in ever
> winding labyrinths upon its immense platforms and dizzy arches
> suspended in the air. The bright blue sky of Rome, and the
> effect of the vigorous awakening spring in that divinest
> climate, and the new life with which it drenches the spirits
> even to intoxication, were the inspiration of this drama.

In traditional terms the inspiration should have produced an ode,
not an epic verse drama. 'Prometheus Unbound' strives after a
consciously revolutionary, symbolic form to accommodate its
author's visionary humanism. Keats's 'Fall of Hyperion' seems to
me a more successful poem, though Keats was less aware of the
problem of generic alienation and so left the poem unfinished and,
surely, unfinishable. The personal inspiration which he brought
to the classical fable seems exhausted by the scene with Moneta,
and in telling the story of Apollo he would simply be covering
the theme of poetic initiation twice over. Both poems are
expressions of their authors' belief in the public and monumental
status of great literature. Yet in the lyrics of Keats and
Shelley, and in some of the criticism of their contemporaries, a

new evaluation of the poetic art quite independent of the public, classical genres was emerging.

Shelley's 'Defence of Poetry' (1821) is the most outspoken of the romantic assertions of the public function of poetry. It was written, so he told Peacock, in a 'sacred rage' to vindicate the 'insulted Muses' against his friend's challenge in 'The Four Ages of Poetry' (1820). (54) Peacock's essay is a satire on his contemporaries (Wordsworth, Coleridge, Southey, Scott, Byron, Moore and Campbell are all named targets) written in the form of a pastiche of Enlightenment historiography. He sees poetry as a product of man's earliest civilizations and posits an iron age followed by a golden age (the classical flowering of tragedy and epic) followed by a silver age and, finally, an age of brass. There is little in his outline of cultural history that was not anticipated by the Scottish primitivists of the eighteenth century. But Peacock presents it with great verve and dash, and adds an extra turn of cynicism, as when he attributes the rise of poetry entirely to the savage's need to flatter his chieftain. His attack on the modern age is a 'reductio ad absurdum' of arguments that had already been brought against Wordsworth and Coleridge. Wordsworth's return to nature, he asserts, is the second childhood of the art, a hopeless and puerile raking over of the past which serves as a prelude to poetry's final extinction. The backward-looking, semi-barbarous modern poet has been left stranded by the progress of the mechanical and social sciences, and has nothing to contribute to social utility: 'The march of his intellect is like that of a crab, backward.' Even the pleasure that he gives is not enough to ensure his survival, since there are enough good poems already, and anything still to be produced must be worse than what already exists.

Peacock is in no doubt about who are the real revolutionaries of contemporary poetry, but he writes off their movement as a predestined failure. The shallow determinism of the position he adopts can only really be refuted by an unanswerable demonstration of the power and creativeness of the present generation. This explains Shelley's anxiety to destroy his friend's position, and the impotence of mere arguments to do so. Moreover, Peacock's espousal of utilitarian values - however much this has a merely debunking intention - challenges his antagonist to declare his own attitude to utilitarianism. Shelley, as poet and political revolutionary, mounts his defence from the left, and argues that poetry belongs in the van and not in the rearguard of social progress; hence his arguments do not ultimately conflict with a rational and enlightened utilitarian standpoint. (55) What these arguments lack he tries to make up with the rapt and imperious utterance of a 'sacred rage'.

The 'Defence' opens with the contrast of reason and imagination. Peacock had said that poetry, once the 'all-in-all of intellectual progression', had been left behind by the development of reason and science. Shelley replies that as the 'expression of the imagination', poetry is 'connate with the origin of man'. Its origins are found in the pleasure we take in imitation, whether in dancing, singing or creating a language. Thus Shelley replaces Peacock's debunking historical account of poetry's genesis with an

anthropological explanation grounded in the universal nature of
man. If he is right, either poetry must retain its original centrality in modern society, or we have ceased to be fully men.
For Peacock, such centrality belonged to 'semi-civilized society',
whereas Shelley summons all his faith, ingenuity and power of
persuasion to the task of asserting that it still persists and
that poets are the 'unacknowledged legislators'. He does so by
adopting the extended neoplatonic definition of poetry and writing
a panegyric on human creativity throughout history, giving all
the credit to poets as they come highest in the hierarchy of
creative spirits. The difficulties in the way of such an argument
are airily disposed of. Shelley asserts, for example, that the
superiority of poetry in the restricted sense over other modes of
social activity is proved by the fame of the poets, which is only
exceeded by that of 'legislators and founders of religion, so
long as their institutions last'. The latter, however, are arti-
ficially bolstered up by the flattery of the vulgar, and by the
fame which is rightfully theirs 'in their higher character of
poets'! Very soon, in fact, the distinction between reason and
imagination becomes of use only as a weapon against 'mere
reasoners'; Shelley describes Shakespeare, Dante and Milton as
'philosophers of the very loftiest power', and claims that poets
excel all others in political, social, ethical and religious
insight. Reason and imagination are certainly merged in the
'Defence' itself, which opens with a parade of distinctions and
definitions, but ends in pages of impressionistic rant. Poets,
we discover, may be not only the rulers of society but autocrats
who justifiably present a watered-down version of the truth for
popular consumption ('Few poets of the highest class have chosen
to exhibit the beauty of their conceptions in its naked truth
and splendour'). And Shelley himself is a super-autocrat who can
award or withhold the title of poet at will (Rousseau was one,
but Locke, Hume, Gibbon and Voltaire were 'mere reasoners'). If
we read it, as we must, as special pleading, the 'Defence' is
unconvincing and somewhat repellent.
   There is more to be said than this, however, for Shelley's
glibness cannot disguise the fact that he has a case against
Peacock, and an important one. Where 'The Four Ages of Poetry'
is vulgarly deterministic, the 'Defence' at best - as in the
section on Milton - is an eloquent affirmation of human freedom.
Peacock sees poets as slaves to history, and Shelley reacts by
airlifting them into the permanent world of the human spirit.
The historical narrative in the 'Defence' is devoted to showing
that poetry is immanent in history without ever being fundamentally corrupted by it. The poets unveil the essential morality
of their societies, rather than having to abide by that morality
as the Augustans thought. They teach love and mutual sympathy to
their fellow-men, with measurable effects: 'the presence or
absence of poetry in its most perfect or universal form, has been
found to be connected with good and evil in conduct or habit.'
(By whom? we might ask.) The spirit of poetry, as is evident
here, can withdraw from a world unsympathetic to it, and Shelley's
history of culture is a narrative of the fluctuating presence of
the poetic spirit. He dismisses the usual historical and

religious explanations of the Dark Ages, for example, since it
was the 'extinction of the poetical principle' that really
counted.   After the eleventh century, things began to improve
as the 'poetry of the Christian and chivalric systems' began to
manifest itself.   Soon the abolition of personal and domestic
slavery and the partial emancipation of women were accomplished -
again, thanks to poetry - and the poetic tradition reached its
highest point in the Renaissance in Dante's Beatrice and Milton's
Satan.   But the historical role of poetry, though something of
which Shelley is proud, is not quite the essence of the art as he
sees it.   'Let us not be betrayed from a defence into a critical
history of poetry and its influence on society': 'betrayed',
because the primary reality of poetry is its permanence and
eternality;   only secondarily is it manifested in history.   Thus
Shelley can speak of 'that great poem, which all poets, like
the co-operating thoughts of one great mind, have built up since
the beginning of the world.'   His outlook is fundamentally
idealist and anti-historical, however useful as a corrective to
Peacock's vulgar brand of historicism.   And his veneration of
poetry as something at once above history and decisively engaged
in history is evidently of a religious kind;   it is no accident
that he describes poets as 'hierophants of an unapprehended
inspiration'.   The 'Defence' is, in T.E. Hulme's term, 'spilt
religion', but it is also a bold attempt to expropriate what is
worth keeping in actual religions, especially Christianity, in
the name of poetry.   Shelley both discredits Christian transcendentalism and borrows metaphors from it freely for his
eulogistic rhapsodies.   Thus he can be misread as saying that
poetry is spiritual and other-worldly, whereas these are never
more than the metaphors of his evangelical humanism.   For all
this, it has to be said that he gives himself far too much
imaginative licence, and the spirit of the 'Defence' is arrogant
and Napoleonic.   Only by reading it in a far more ethereal and
unpolitical way than he intended can we make his view of the
social power of poets seem remotely plausible.   His sweeping
cultural history leaves him time to show no literary sensitivity
at all - except toward Dante and Milton - so that the 'Defence'
must be read more as a hymn to the ideal unity of humanist values,
than as any kind of poetic analysis or programme.   It might have
served as a rallying-call to contemporary poets, but it remained
unpublished until 1840, eighteen years after his death.

Shelley's criticism rests on the conviction that poetry and
philosophy are essentially at one;   the poet, in his view, is
virtually omnipotent.   Keats was more cautious and hesitant in
assuming the prophetic stance.   He was a realist who knew that
choices had to be made, and were not always easy to make.   'An
eagle', he wrote, 'is not so fine a thing as a truth.'   Keats's
sense of the rival claims of poetical justice and social justice
is paralleled by the frank acknowledgment of such a conflict in
the criticism of William Hazlitt.   Hazlitt's work is distinctly
uneven, but he was an original critic, not merely an indefatigable literary politician and a popularizer of stock romantic

attitudes. The complexity of his response to poetry is evident
from his contrast of poetic and political values in his essay on
'Coriolanus' in 'The Characters of Shakespeare's Plays' (1817).
It was a passage which achieved some notoriety: Gifford derided
it in the 'Quarterly', Hazlitt hit back in his 'Letter to William
Gifford' (1819), and Keats was sufficiently moved by the reply
to copy out a long extract in his journal-letter to his brother
and sister-in-law (February-May 1819). Hazlitt had originally
argued that in portraying the conflict of leaders and led in
ancient Rome, Shakespeare 'seems to have had a leaning to the
arbitrary side of the question', and 'spared no occasion of baiting
the rabble':

> What he says of them is very true: what he says of their
> betters is also very true, though he dwells less upon it. The
> cause of the people is indeed but little calculated as a
> subject for poetry: it admits of rhetoric, which goes into
> argument and explanation, but it presents no immediate or
> distinct images to the mind, 'no jutting frieze, buttress, or
> coigne of vantage' for poetry 'to make its pendent bed and
> procreant cradle in'. The language of poetry naturally falls
> in with the language of power. The imagination is an
> exaggerating and exclusive faculty: it takes from one thing
> to add to another: it accumulates circumstances together to
> give the greatest possible effect to a favourite object. The
> understanding is a dividing and measuring faculty: it judges
> of things, not according to their immediate impression on the
> mind, but according to their relations to one another. The
> one is a monopolizing faculty, which seeks the greatest quan-
> tity of present excitement by inequality and disproportion;
> the other is a distributive faculty, which seeks the greatest
> quantity of ultimate good, by justice and proportion. The
> one is an aristocratical, the other a republican faculty. The
> principle of poetry is a very anti-levelling principle.

The antitheses, which restate a quarrel that was already old when
Plato wrote of it, are suspiciously neat but nonetheless effective.
Hazlitt was a republican, proud of his political consistency and
a merciless critic of the apostasy of Coleridge and Wordsworth.
He was also an advocate of the romantic imagination in poetry.
In writing of the interests of poetry as essentially opposed to
democracy he was giving hostages to the enemy, but he was able
to turn this weakness into a strength - partly by habitually
separating literary from political criticism, and partly by the
vigour of his polemics against the Lake school, who from his
point of view had the worst of both worlds by adopting the
'arbitrary side of the question' in politics, and the levelling
principle in poetry. Hazlitt's is a parliamentary mind, conscious
of his allegiances and capable of switching between cross-bench
negotiation and vitriolic abuse of the other side. He is
prepared to concede the Tory affiliations of 'Coriolanus' if
that will aid a romantic interpretation of the play. While
recognizing and revering the imperiousness of the poetic imagination, he later made it clear that the imagination was not a
party-political weapon, but belonged in a higher sphere: 'When
it lights upon the earth, it loses some of its dignity and its

use.' (56) This suggests the essential ambiguity of his position. Though he was habitually and often pungently aware of
the ideological tendencies of art, his criticism played an
influential part in the nineteenth-century retreat into an
aesthetic kingdom separate from everyday life.

Hazlitt attacked poets like Coleridge who meddled in politics;
they lived 'in an ideal world of their own', and could only
bring confusion into public affairs. (57) He attacked Shelley,
a fellow republican, for his intellectual unreliability and
extremism. (58) But he also attacked the utilitarians, Shelley's
'reasoners', for the inhumanity and self-interestedness of their
abstract rationalism. His dissection of the Lake school in the
lecture On the Living Poets is done with a brilliance and
perversity which puts it in a class by itself. The true motive
of 'these sweeping reformers and dictators in the republic of
letters', he asserts, is the madness of egotism:

> They took the same method in their new-fangled 'metre
> ballad-mongering' scheme, which Rousseau did in his prose
> paradoxes - of exciting attention by reversing the estab-
> lished standards of opinion and estimation in the world.
> They were for bringing poetry back to its primitive simplicity
> and state of nature, as he was for bringing society back to
> the savage state: so that the only thing remarkable left in
> the world by this change, would be the persons who had pro-
> duced it. A thorough adept in this school of poetry and
> philanthropy is jealous of all excellence but his own. He
> does not even like to share his reputation with his subject;
> for he would have it all proceed from his own power and
> originality of mind. Such a one is slow to admire any thing
> that is admirable; feels no interest in what is most
> interesting to others, no grandeur in anything grand, no
> beauty in anything beautiful. He tolerates only what he him-
> self creates; he sympathizes only with what can enter into
> no competition with him, with 'the bare trees and mountains
> bare, and grass in the green field.' He sees nothing but
> himself and the universe.

This surely is the sort of line that Burke, whom Hazlitt much
admired, might have taken. Analysis reveals an extraordinary
mixture of motives in it. Though personal animus is undoubtedly
present, the attack on Wordsworth's egotism is consistent with
his analysis of the 'intellectual egotism' of 'The Excursion' in
'The Examiner' four years earlier - an analysis which stands
behind Keats's phrase for Wordsworth's style, the 'egotistical
sublime'. But it may be argued that the imperiousness of
Wordsworth's poetic attitude is precisely what is to be expected
of that 'exaggerating and exclusive faculty', the imagination.
Though a political radical, Hazlitt seems to prefer the status
quo in literature to a new initiative such as Wordsworth's. There
is a brooding pessimism in his outlook, which sometimes becomes
the bitter pride of the last adherent of a lost cause. Wordsworth's facile anticipation of the eventual triumph of liberty in
'The Excursion' particularly grated on him:

> The dawn of that day was suddenly overcast; that season of
> hope is past; it has fled with the other dreams of our youth,

which we cannot recal, but has left behind it traces, which
are not to be effaced by birth-day odes, or the chaunting of
'Te Deums' in all the churches of Christendom. (59)

Hazlitt as a cultural critic too often seems to be writing from
a position of self-defence. He distinguished between the diffusion
of taste, the object of the periodical press of his own time, and
its improvement - there was no principle of universal suffrage in
matters of taste. As an art critic, he attacked public patronage
of artists and the institution of the academy - genius would make
its own way in the world, and there was no point in encouraging
the second-rate - but supported the setting up of a national
gallery. Public taste might be improved by 'a collection of
standing works of established reputation, and which are capable
by the sanctity of their name of overawing the petulance of public
opinion.' (60) Late in life he became still more outspoken
against the philistinism of public taste:

I would rather endure the most blind and bigotted respect for
great and illustrious names, than that pitiful, grovelling
humour which has no pride in intellectual excellence, and no
pleasure but in decrying those who have given proofs of it, and
reducing them to its own level. (On Reading New Books, 1827).

In the matter of culture, then, Hazlitt himself leant towards the
'arbitrary side of the question'. And he was essentially a man of
letters: the choice is like a confession. Political passions
infused his writing (his final work was the 'Life of Napoleon')
but they do not seem to have moved him to political action. There
is a certain realism about the literary democrat who turns against
the mob in these circumstances. It costs him more than other
people to do so, so that the result is a heartfelt and not a
supercilious response. Nonetheless, the alternatives painted by
Hazlitt are so rigid that the passage seems little more than a cry
of frustration. We must conclude that for all his intelligence
and mastery of the telling phrase and the cutting polemic,
Hazlitt lacked the pertinacity of a genuine social thinker.

As a strictly literary critic his claims are stronger, though
he is at his best in discussing two areas of writing which do not
involve the conflict of poetry and philosophy at its sharpest.
The first of these is realistic fiction, and the second the meditative or musical lyric. Hazlitt's 'Lectures on the English Comic
Writers' contain a superb discussion of the eighteenth-century
novel, which he warms to as a more human and democratic art-form
than poetry. Best of all is his appraisal of Hogarth (a curious
inclusion, in some ways) who he sees as the culmination of English
realism. Hogarth, however, is a representative of the 'familiar
style' in painting, falling short of the 'grand style' because he
lacks an imaginative and ideal dimension. Hazlitt finds the same
falling-short in a 'painterly' poet like Crabbe, and in the art
of painting in general. Though an excellent art critic and a fine
judge of the realistic mode, he looked upon realism as firmly
subordinated to the mode of imagination.

His fullest statement of the imaginative nature of poetry comes
in the essay On Poetry in General, the first of the 'Lectures on
the English Poets' (1818). Read superficially, this essay seems
no more than a vague romantic rhapsody; it is an oration rather

than a treatise, presenting an impassioned list of the attributes
of poetry in an appropriately florid and extravagant prose. But
though his method is metonymic rather than definitive, Hazlitt
intended his statements to be rationally defensible (he defended
them vigorously against the legalism of Gifford), and at times
they are effective and precise. The 'general notion' of poetry
with which he opens sounds Shelleyan in its expansiveness, though
it actually says a good deal less than at first appears:

> Many people suppose that poetry is something to be found
> only in books, contained in lines of ten syllables, with
> like endings: but wherever there is a sense of beauty, or
> power, or harmony, as in a motion of a wave of the sea, in the
> growth of a flower that 'spreads its sweet leaves to the air,
> and dedicates its beauty to the sun,' - there is poetry, in
> its birth.

It is not that poetry subsists in the wave of the sea or the growth
of the flower; rather, these can inspire us with a poetic 'sense
of beauty, or power, or harmony'. Hazlitt opposes poetic power to
the mere representation or description of an object. Poetry is
the result of internal processes of apprehension and contemplation:

> It is strictly the language of the imagination; and the
> imagination is that faculty which represents objects, not as
> they are in themselves, but as they are moulded by other thoughts
> and feelings, into an infinite variety of shapes and combina-
> tions of power.

The difference from Wordsworth's and Coleridge's accounts of
imagination is that they tended to stress its cognitive and
visionary nature, while Hazlitt presents it as a wholly aesthetic
process, appealing to a particular (and, of course, particularly
desirable) kind of sensibility. His distinction between imagination and description is strongly reminiscent of Schlegel's and
Schiller's contrasts of the ancient and modern spirit; Hazlitt,
in their terms, is claiming poetry as an essentially modern or
romantic art-form. (61) He goes on to discuss the differences in
aesthetic potential among the fine arts. Poetry is more imaginative than painting: 'Painting gives the object itself;
poetry what it implies.' Here again is the distinction between
the expression of the reflective mind and the mere pictorial representation of objects. Poetry is further enriched, however, by
its possession of the quality of harmony, which is associated
with the third of the fine arts, that of music. Hazlitt calls
poetry the 'music of language':

> Wherever any object takes such a hold of the mind as to make
> us dwell upon it, and brood over it, melting the heart in
> tenderness, or kindling it to a sentiment of enthusiasm; -
> wherever a movement of imagination or passion is impressed on
> the mind, by which it seeks to prolong and repeat the emotion,
> to bring all other objects into accord with it, and to give the
> same movement of harmony, sustained and continuous, or gradually
> varied according to the occasion, to the sounds that express
> it - this is poetry. The musical in sound is the sustained and
> continuous; the musical in thought is the sustained and con-
> tinuous also.

If this is peculiarly evocative, it is surely not because it is

generally applicable to poetry, but because it is an uncanny
prediction of the concentrated lyric poetry of the nineteenth
century. The passage virtually provides the formula of Keats's
Odes.

Modern scholars are agreed that most of Keats's theories were
developed from Hazlitt, and that his poetry was in some respects
a deeply theoretical endeavour; but I am not sure that all the
connections have yet been made. (62) In general, Hazlitt may have
prompted Keats to discover how natural objects could be treated
in a poetry of refined and synaesthetic, rather than directly
moral or sensual, appeal; the Odes avoid both the stolidness of
Wordsworth and the cloying richness of 'Endymion'.

There is a more precise point of connection between On Poetry
in General and Keats's Odes. It springs from a passage discussing
the Elgin Marbles, which were of such consuming interest to
Hazlitt, Keats and their circle:

> It is for want of some such resting place for the imagination
> that the Greek statues are little else than specious forms.
> They are marble to the touch and to the heart. They have not
> an informing principle within them. In their faultless excel-
> lence they appear sufficient to themselves. By their beauty
> they are raised above the frailties of passion or suffering.
> By their beauty they are deified. But they are not objects of
> religious faith to us, and their forms are a reproach to common
> humanity. They seem to have no sympathy with us, and not to
> want our admiration.

Ian Jack has written that 'It would be curious to have the comment
of Keats on this passage.' (63) I shall argue that in effect we
have that comment: it is the 'Ode on a Grecian Urn'. The difficulty that Keats appears to have missed the first of Hazlitt's
lectures, though he became a regular attender later on in the
course, may be overcome by supposing either that he read it in
manuscript or book form (the 'Lectures' were published several
months before the 'Ode' was written), or that he knew Hazlitt's
earlier and more diffuse discussion of the Marbles in his
'Encyclopaedia Britannica' article on the 'Fine Arts' (1817). As
for the difference between a vase and a sculptured frieze, this is
a complication, but no more. Ian Jack identifies the heifer led
to sacrifice in Stanza IV as that in the South Frieze of the Elgin
Marbles. Keats's 'Attic shape' surely stands for the whole of
Greek plastic art, as does Hazlitt's account of the 'Greek
statues', written in the tradition of German analyses of the
Hellenistic spirit.

The 'Ode on a Grecian Urn' is a poem about the relations between
the arts, which comes directly out of the aesthetic debate of its
time. Keats calls the Urn a 'Cold Pastoral'; that is his concession to Hazlitt's viewpoint, but it is belied by the very
choice of the Urn as subject for a poem. The poem reveals the
nature of the Urn's 'sympathy with us', and yet Keats is, so to
speak, cheating by weaving around the Urn the expressive harmonies
of another medium. Hence the poem opens with a riddle about
inter-aesthetic relations:

I

Thou still unravish'd bride of quietness,
  Thou foster-child of silence and slow time,
Sylvan historian, who canst thus express
  A flowery tale more sweetly than our rhyme:
What leaf-fring'd legend haunts about thy shape
  Of deities or mortals, or of both,
      In Tempe or the dales of Arcady?
  What men or gods are these? What maidens loth?
What mad pursuit? What struggle to escape?
  What pipes and timbrels? What wild ecstasy?

The first four lines present a backhanded compliment, since Keats
addresses the Urn as a literary narrator, a 'sylvan historian'.
He inevitably translates the object itself into what it implies,
and what it implies is a story, a 'leaf-fring'd legend'. And
then, at the premature climax of the story, he invokes the art of
music, with its 'pipes and timbrels' of ecstasy. The sudden still
ness of the second stanza is not produced by ordinary music,
however, for it consists of 'unheard melodies' and 'ditties of no
tone':

II

Heard melodies are sweet, but those unheard
  Are sweeter; therefore, ye soft pipes, play on;
Not to the sensual ear, but, more endear'd,
  Pipe to the spirit ditties of no tone:
Fair youth, beneath the trees, thou canst not leave
  Thy song, nor ever can those trees be bare;
    Bold lover, never, never canst thou kiss,
Though winning near the goal - yet, do not grieve;
  She cannot fade, though thou hast not thy bliss,
    For ever wilt thou love, and she be fair!

We are now in a state of synaesthesia, since it requires the
presence of all three arts, the pictorial, the musical and the
poetic, to realize the image of the fair youth's eternal song.
The unheard melodies are those of the imagination, and it would
still seem that poetry is the most imaginative of the arts, since
'unheard melodies' can only exist as a conceptual image, to be
represented in language.

III

Ah, happy, happy boughs! that cannot shed
  Your leaves, nor ever bid the Spring adieu;
And, happy melodist, unwearied,
  For ever piping songs for ever new;
More happy love! more happy, happy love!
  For ever warm and still to be enjoy'd,
    For ever panting, and for ever young;
All breathing human passion far above,
  That leaves a heart high-sorrowful and cloy'd,
    A burning forehead, and a parching tongue.

IV

Who are these coming to the sacrifice?
  To what green altar, O mysterious priest,
Lead'st thou that heifer lowing at the skies,

And all her silken flanks with garlands drest?
  What little town by river or sea shore,
    Or mountain-built with peaceful citadel,
      Is emptied of this folk, this pious morn?
    And, little town, thy streets for evermore
      Will silent be; and not a soul to tell
        Why thou art desolate, can e'er return.

The third stanza involves a return to 'poetic' elaboration, becoming increasingly hot and over-excited in contrast to the coolness of the Urn. The fourth explores a different part of the 'poetic' register, being a narrative description poised between realism and speculation. The little town of the poet's invention is either a port or a hill-town (a painter would have to choose between these alternatives): while the last lines remind us that the town's desolation is a fact deserving narrative explanation, although the town is a hypothesis existing only in the medium of the poem we are reading.

Through these minor riddles of the relation between different art-forms we reach the major riddle of the final stanza.

V

O Attic shape! Fair attitude! with brede
  of marble men and maidens overwrought,
With forest branches and the trodden weed;
  Thou, silent form, dost tease us out of thought
As doth eternity: Cold Pastoral!
  When old age shall this generation waste,
    Thou shalt remain, in midst of other woe
  Than ours, a friend to man, to whom thou say'st,
    'Beauty is truth, truth beauty,' - that is all
      Ye know on earth, and all ye need to know.

Though a 'Cold Pastoral', the Urn has a touch of eternity about it, and 'teases us out of thought'. And finally the 'silent form' speaks. Hazlitt had described the forms of the Elgin Marbles as a 'reproach to common humanity', but the Urn is a friend to man and does not reproach. Far from rejecting our admiration, it holds it spellbound. Nonetheless, the Urn's message reveals its own self-sufficiency and aloofness from human considerations, since no mundane 'philosophical' sense can be attached to the words '"Beauty is truth, truth beauty"'. After the unheard melodies, the poem now offers an unrecognized, perhaps unrecognizable truth. We should, of course, notice the wonderful contextual subtlety with which Keats has hedged around the Urn's flat statement, which could be seen as at once a rebuke to Hazlitt's brash impatience with the Greek statues, and as a tacit confirmation of his general principle that the values of the imagination are paramount only within the 'aesthetic' realm. What Keats conveys is not an objet d'art speaking to us directly, but a poetic statement put in the mouth of another art and then translated back into the art of language; the statement is not didactic but oracular, a direct 'expression of the imagination' reported to us by an admirer rather than authored by Keats himself.

Keats's poem expresses the full allure of aestheticism, without quite taking the leap into vulgar commitment. Similarly, Hazlitt's essay steeps itself in the literary emotions and in less sensitive

hands than Keats's could be made into a thoroughgoing aesthete's
charter. The essay can offer some general guidelines to the other
Odes, directing us to their more symbolistic features. The idea of
poetry as the 'music of language' is present in the third stanza
of 'To Autumn', where the first two lines invite us to number the
poem itself among the songs of autumn:

Where are the songs of Spring? Ay, where are they?
   Think not of them, thou hast thy music too, -

The list of autumnal sounds that follows is introduced by two lines
of landscape-painting describing the sunset; once again, the three
art-forms are fused. In the 'Ode to Psyche', the poet offers himself as choir, priest and builder of a temple for the goddess of
his choice. Psyche is forgotten and unworshipped, the 'latest
born and loveliest vision far/Of all Olympus' faded hierarchy'.
The poet, and he alone, can commemorate her and restore the 'faded
hierarchy'; but the music, painting and architecture of the temple
subsist in 'some untrodden region of my mind', so that this revival,
so typical of the solipsistic use of classical motifs by the
romantic poets, can be an imaginative achievement only. The 'Night-
ingale' Ode is, again, a poetic brooding and dwelling upon its
subject, weaving together visual beauty, musical harmony and the
'magic casements' of literary tradition in its striving for the
maximum intensity. These are all intensely literary poems, not in
the simple name-dropping sense (though literary names are dropped
throughout Keats's minor verse), but in their presentation of nearly
all experience in terms evocative of literature and the other arts.
This process of aesthetic mediation involves a new poetic diction
which deliberately transmutes life into art, sensation into dream
and message into oracle. 'The Fall of Hyperion' suggests that
Keats was acutely conscious of the divorce between poetry and ordinary discourse that this entailed. In some rather naked lines in
the Induction scene, the poet begs the priestess to explain why he
is alone in the temple, and she seems to confirm his anxieties:

'Those whom thou speak'st of are no vision'ries,'
  Rejoin'd that voice - 'They are no dreamers weak,
'They seek no wonder but the human face;
'No music but a happy-noted voice -
'They come not here, they have no thought to come -
'And thou art here, for thou art less than they -
'What benefit canst thou, or all thy tribe,
'To the great world?

The poet may become a humanist, but first he must incur the guilt of
turning his back on humanism. Hazlitt sought to persuade his
hearers to a proper respect for the imagination, but he still spoke
of poetry as a 'dream'. His view of the opposition between imagination and social concern helps to illuminate the secular other-
worldliness of Keats's poetry, his fascination with the Immortals
and with a supremely sensual initiation into mysteries that transcend the world of the ordinary senses. In a few great poems,
Keats was able to choose the ground on which to reconcile the warring
poles of critical dialectic. In life, however, he, like Hazlitt,
remained struggling irresolutely between poetry and philosophy.

Hazlitt's influence on Keats was the last and most fortuitous of
the interactions between criticism and original creation which so
profoundly mark the romantic period. The points of similarity
between them initiate the line of development from romanticism
to aestheticism, which emerged as a conscious movement in England
in the second half of the nineteenth century. Keats was
undoubtedly able to overlook the journalistic flaccidity and the
amount of borrowed finery that creep into Hazlitt's writing. For
Hazlitt's critical personality is evidently that of the bookman
rather than of the more refined and fastidious aesthete. He may
have been the first to describe critics as 'middlemen', and he
plays at least four roles with varying success in his criticism -
those of polemical reviewer, aesthetician, literary connoisseur
and public educator. His literary surveys are probably most read
today, although they were composed in a great hurry to meet a
public demand. 'The Characters of Shakespeare's Plays' and all
three lecture-courses came out between 1817 and 1820. These lectures contain some splendid passages, but they also tend to lapse
into the superficiality of literary history without tears. In his
comments on the task of criticism, Hazlitt invariably speaks for
the impressionistic method of the connoisseurs and bookmen whose
ethos was sketched at the beginning of this chapter. He believed
that the appreciation of poetry was a matter of 'instantaneous
sympathy', and that the literary imagination delighted in 'power,
in strong excitement' at the expense of humanity and principle. (64)
The critic's task was to express the joys of poetic excitement
and passion, when taken under licence and in moderate draughts.
Hazlitt deplored Johnson's incapacity for 'following the flights of
a truly poetic imagination', (65) and attacked the analytic methods
of Dryden and the French:

> A genuine criticism should, as I take it, reflect the colours,
> the light and shade, the soul and body of a work: here we have
> nothing but its superficial plan and elevation, as if a poem
> were a piece of formal architecture .... That is, we are left
> quite in the dark as to the feelings of pleasure or pain to
> be derived from the genius of the performance or the manner in
> which it appeals to the imagination. (66)

It is only one step further to the Pavlovian responses of Lamb,
when confronted by a passage from 'The Revenger's Tragedy': 'I
never read it but my ears tingle, and I feel a hot flush spread
my cheeks.' (67) This is a translation of the ecstatic response
of the romantic poet to literary experience (compare Coleridge's
'Schiller! that hour I would have wish'd to die') (68) into
the domestic language of bookish sensibility. Hazlitt usually
works on a more intellectual or comparative level than this; he
praises writers for their 'poeticality', their 'gusto'. He
describes his aim in his lectures as being to 'read over a set of
authors with the audience, as I would do with a friend, to point
out a favourite passage, to explain an objection; or if a remark
or a theory occurs, to state it in illustration of the subject,
but neither to tire him nor to puzzle myself with pedantic rules.'
(69) This combines Lamb's desire to make his private experience
public (his remark on 'The Revenger's Tragedy' is the kind of
intimate confidence that carries no risk) with a lightly pedagogic

concern. A great deal of nineteenth-century criticism exists
somewhere between these two alternatives, and Hazlitt's own work
is weaker and more patchy where - as in the 'Characters of
Shakespeare's Plays', which were not delivered as lectures - the
pedagogic motive is lacking.

A different blend of cognitive and affective elements is found
in his collection of Contemporary Portraits, 'The Spirit of the
Age' (1825). These essays combine vivid portraiture with an intellectual apparatus of concepts - such as mechanism and impulse,
method and imagination, authority and democracy - which serve to
relate the individual sitter to the 'Zeitgeist' or 'Spirit of the
Age'. At his best, on Bentham, Malthus, Jeffrey or Sir James
Mackintosh, Hazlitt clearly anticipates the cultural criticism of
Carlyle and Mill. But he never gets down to a precise exposition
of the 'Spirit of the Age', or straightforwardly declares his own
attitude to it. He is very much the reporter, hedging his bets.
Wordsworth's levelling genius is a 'pure emanation of the Spirit
of the Age', but then so is the 'Edinburgh Review'. Hazlitt may
be dissociating himself from both, but just where he stands is
uncertain - why, except as his patron, should Jeffrey be so much
more favourably treated than Wordsworth? The volume was published
anonymously, and it may be that Hazlitt took pleasure in
intriguing his readers while exploiting the idea of the 'Zeitgeist'
for all it was worth. Where his own preferences do emerge, they
suggest an impulse towards literary escapism. The carriers of
the Zeitgeist such as Wordsworth and Jeffrey are portents to be
wondered at, but they cannot exactly be liked; and old enemies such
as Coleridge and Gifford are treated as harshly as ever. The tart
edge to Hazlitt's commentary on his times is only forgotten in his
final essay on Charles Lamb and Washington Irving ('Elia, and
Geoffrey Crayon'). He affectionately portrays Lamb as an antiquarian who prefers 'byeways to highways', a poetic soul who is
untainted by the Spirit of the Age and stands aloof from its
animosities. Hazlitt, too, seems to be hinting that life is best
when one can take flight on the wings of imagination. His gallery
of 'contemporary portraits' ends with two sentences (they refer
to the dramatist Sheridan Knowles, another friend of Hazlitt's)
which conjure us out of the contemporary world altogether:

We have known him almost from a child, and we must say he
appears to us the same boy-poet that he ever was. He has been
cradled in song, and rocked in it as in a dream, forgetful of
himself and of the world!

Long disappointed in his political hopes, and embittered by a series
of desertions from the republican cause, Hazlitt in 'The Spirit of
the Age' seems emotionally incapable of feeling at home in the
contemporary world. Intellectually he responds to it; but finally
he can only gesture towards a resting-place in the cult of childhood and literary reverie. Once again he was putting his weight
behind that withdrawal of the poetic sensibility from social
concerns which constitutes romantic decadence.

As a contrast to Hazlitt's escapism, we may look finally at
Thomas de Quincey - famous for his opium reveries, and yet a very
practical and socially-committed literary critic. De Quincey's
most famous essay, On the Knocking at the Gate in 'Macbeth' (1823),

seems at first like an ordinary product of bookish impressionism.
'From my boyish days I had always felt a great perplexity on one
point in "Macbeth"'; this is how it opens. But what follows is
not an exercise in buttonholing intimacy, but a meditation of
Wordsworthian discipline and austerity. De Quincey goes on to
outline the solution of a critical problem that has puzzled him
for twenty years. He shows how the knocking at the gate inten-
sifies our sympathy with the complex feelings of the murderers,
and distracts us from simple horror at their crime. This is a
superb empirical demonstration of the 'manner in which it appeals
to the imagination' - the kind of criticism which Hazlitt recommends, but can never achieve with such force. Nearly two decades
later, when Coleridge, Hazlitt and Lamb were dead, de Quincey
re-emerged as a critic of far broader literary and cultural interests. His 'Reminiscences' of the Lake Poets, his remarks on the
poetic diction controversy and his distinction of knowledge and
power show him as the critical heir of Wordsworth and Coleridge,
reinterpreting in rational terms the prophetic insights of romantic poetry. In an essay on Goldsmith (1848), de Quincey reasserted
the international character of great literature and its embodiment
of a kind of power which is a challenge and an alternative to the
social power wielded by the state. Literature, he argued, was a
force tending towards international brotherhood and cultural
unity, and this was why poets were so often slighted in their own
homeland. This idea owes much to Wordsworth, and clearly anticipates Arnold; it represents a critical approach in complete
contrast to Hazlitt's disillusionment and solacing aestheticism.
Thus de Quincey, unlike Hazlitt, proved able to respond to the new
energy of social thought and the revival of liberal hopes in the
1820s and 1830s, so that his final incarnation was as a minor
Victorian sage and not as a romantic critic. The mixture of
public educator and private daydreamer in both Hazlitt and de
Quincey sums up the essence of the nineteenth-century literary
culture which their generation had done so much to create.

Chapter 4

VICTORIAN CRITICISM:
THE REPUBLIC OF LETTERS

1 THE DEFINITION OF LITERARY CULTURE

In Shelley's poem 'Julian and Maddalo', the poet's friendship with
Byron is recaptured at certain moments with supreme naturalness.
Arriving before Maddalo is up one morning, Julian observes the
Count's baby daughter, whose eyes gleam
>   With such deep meaning, as we never see
>   But in the human countenance:
He then starts to play with the child, and so
>   after her first shyness was worn out
>   We sate there, rolling billiard balls about,
>   When the Count entered...

In romantic criticism, as well as poetry, we are able to meet the
creative genius face-to-face. Romantic egotism, even while it
exalts the poet and puts him on a pedestal, can include this
interest in personality and in the everyday life of oneself and
one's friends. Hazlitt, Lamb and de Quincey were the intimates of
great poets; but they also felt themselves their equals, and
cherished their own experience as Shelley does in these lines. The
early Victorian critics inherited the romantic beliefs about
genius, but these beliefs had now solidified; they were becoming
a teaching, a body of doctrine.

'Julian and Maddalo' is set in Venice. Whether in Italy or
the Lakes, the community of poets was best able to flourish far
from the metropolitan centre of culture. Meanwhile, Londoners such
as Hazlitt and Lamb resorted to bookmanship, a deliberate, make-
believe isolation of the self from the sense of a present cultural
context. To be immured in the library was to be taken out of
time and into permanence. The early Victorian generation of intellectuals - Carlyle, Newman, Macaulay, Lewes, J.S. Mill - had no
time for such escapism. Instead, when they looked at poetry at
all they were concerned with locating it within a cultural framework. The notion of romantic genius had to find its place amid
the institutions of society and the general body of concepts
ordering intellectual life. One thing that happened was that the
intellectuals themselves became 'sages', taking it as their mission

to pronounce upon the totality of social life in the prophetic
manner exemplified by Wordsworth.

The sages were opposed to many features of nineteenth-century
society, yet they arose in response to a demand which that society
had created. The industrial revolution brought about the spread
of literacy and education, and the dissemination of more intellectual modes of consciousness, in many areas of life. George
Eliot records such a process, the 'bringing to consciousness' of
a small market town, in 'Felix Holt'. This is an elusive concept,
but is clearly related to the disturbance of settled religious
faith and political quiescence. 'Consciousness', then, means
receptivity to new ideas propagated from the metropolis; the
most certain evidence for it lies in the spread of reading-rooms
and libraries and in the existence, popularity and influence of
the sages themselves. The mode in which the sages write is that
of the lay sermon, an instructive and edifying discourse which,
however dogmatic in content, must exploit the questionable
authority of the book rather than the customary authority of the
pulpit. The nineteenth-century reader of the sages could not but
be aware of disagreement and the necessity of choice among them,
and he turned increasingly to this choice as a substitute for, or
at least a supplement to, religious orthodoxy.

The sages wrote for a mass audience, not for their peers; for
this reason they used a far more strident rhetoric than their
predecessors, even those with propagandist aims such as Burke.
They were writing to be heard at a time of social change, and
combined an appeal to traditional sanctities or absolute values
with an expression of the new historical awareness that came in
with the romantics. Change was visibly taking place, but it
was frequently attributed to unthinking forces - the machinery in
the factories, the iron laws of supply and demand, or the
unpredictable risings of the people. The sages unanimously
insisted that the decisions of men determined their own history.
Carlyle's idea of 'Hero-worship' and Mill's concept of the
'collective mind' are attempts to determine the agency through
which historical development is made. This agency could be seen
in terms of politics, but the sages tended to locate it outside
the directly political realm, in the field of what Arnold was to
call 'culture'. It was in defining culture that they took over
the prophetic mantle of the romantic poets.

When Mill discusses Bentham, and when Carlyle and Marx denounce
the 'cash-nexus', they are insisting that men and not the machine
must be the measure of social relationships. In their attacks on
rival ideologies, the sages upheld the ideal of a balanced culture in which man's general spiritual welfare was held to over-
rule all merely sectional interests. Carlyle's attacks on
utilitarianism, Ruskin's denunciation of political economy, and
Arnold's defences of culture against the nonconformists, the
working-class activists and the natural scientists, may all be
read as protests against the attempts of the champions of
particular sectors of culture to dictate to the whole. The idea
of a general culture in which all social and intellectual institutions have their appointed place became an increasingly conscious
one; and this idea formed the basis of a critique of the

materialism and spiritual anarchy of current society. In one
tradition of thought carried forward into the twentieth century,
literary criticism came to dominate the ideal of culture. The
early Victorian prophets were not primarily literary critics,
however, and they did not follow the romantics in looking upon
poetry as a source of the highest wisdom or an end in itself.
Nonetheless, literature in the broad sense was felt by most
writers to be central to the cultural ideal. The older associations of the word remained important in this context: 'literature'
could be used to indicate the humane education imparted at Oxford
and Cambridge, as well as the reviews and other media of contemporary debate.

   Looking back, it seems clear that the Victorian intellectual
world was far more 'literary' in its bias than the intellectual
world of today. One of the signs of this is the extent to which
literary interests and values were taken for granted. After the
deaths of Byron, Keats and Shelley, poetry virtually dropped out
of public controversy. Carlyle argued in Signs of the Times (1829)
that the way in which thought was now propagated was by 'machinery',
by the formation of societies and the holding of public dinners.
In fact, the range of Victorian learned societies and pressure-
groups provides an excellent indication of the broadening of
culture, and the discovery of controversial new matters of social
and intellectual concern. Very few of these societies were
literary. They were predominantly concerned with new scientific
and social-scientific fields, religion, ethics and politics, and
architecture and the visual arts. In the field of imaginative
literature the societies were concerned with writers' conditions
(the Society of Authors was founded in 1884), with Old English
(the Early English Text Society, 1864) and with the study of single
authors. The single-author societies suggest that in literature
it was a writer's 'oeuvre' which constituted a field of study
equivalent to one of the new disciplines such as sociology or
anthropology. As it happens, they were almost entirely the
creations of one man, F.J. Furnivall, who founded the Chaucer,
Wycliffe, New Shakspere, Browning and Shelley societies, all within
a period of twenty years. General literary societies were not
needed, except on an urban and regional basis. Literature -
outside the new industrial towns - was still held to be the
preserve of all educated men.

   There was one group of nineteenth-century intellectuals,
however, who did wish to see literature deprived of its privileged status. These were the utilitarians of the 'Westminster
Review'. Various writers in the early volumes of the 'Westminster'
(founded in 1824) set out to unmask literature as part of the
façade of social reaction. Literature, they argued, was the
preserve of the aristocracy, the occupation of a leisure class.
Its benefits for the individual were greatly exaggerated, and its
privileged place in education served to bolster conservatism and
repression. Literary ability was the gateway to posts in the
civil service and the Excise (even a poet could be made a
Distributor of Stamps). The study of the humanities was the one
indispensable qualification for political advancement. No wonder
that reform was so slow and industrial progress so hampered, for,

as one writer put it, 'woe be to the state whose statesmen
write verses, and whose lawyers read more in Tom Moore than in
Bracton.' (1)

The immediate target of these attacks was the classical curriculum. The reviewers were prepared to countenance the study of
English and modern languages for utilitarian purposes. (It is
notable that Mill, Arnold and Newman all went out of their way to
defend classical studies in the university. Training in classical
literature was essential to their conception of culture; the
status of modern literature was not so clear.) The early Benthamite reviewers seem also to have encountered the ideology of the
romantic movement, and show hostility and prejudice against
literature as such. 'Literature, we have said it before, is a
cant word of the age; and, to be literary, to be a "litterateur"
(we want a word), a "bel esprit", or a blue stocking, is the
disease of the age. The world is to be stormed by poetry, and to
be occupied by reviews and albums', proclaimed the 'Westminster
Review' in 1825. The reviewers' identification of literature with
aristocratic values was at best a half-truth (though one not lost
on Arnold); yet it was to be through the classical education
provided by the public schools, and the study of the humanities
in the universities, that the merger between the old aristocracy
and the new industrial plutocracy in nineteenth-century England
was cemented. The late Victorian statesman or administrator did
not merely know Greek, he had probably passed numerous examinations in it. But when the 'Westminster' reviewer spoke of
literature as the preserve of gentlemen of leisure, he seems to
have mistaken the image for the reality. I have argued that the
idle, unworldly bookman of the 1820s was the fiction of busy and
harassed literary journalists. Byron apart, the romantics are
not notable for their aristocratic connections. In the next generation, the image of the bookman virtually disappeared; the new
intellectuals were missionary and restless. A dilettante like
Leigh Hunt, whose 'Imagination and Fancy' was published in 1844,
was an anachronistic survival in the Victorian world - if not a
Skimpole who would turn a starving orphan away from the door. It
was only much later, in the wake of the Aesthetic Movement, that
the languid bookman came back. Pater spoke of Lamb's 'Specimens'
as the 'quintessence of criticism', and their author was
belatedly canonized as the choicest spirit of the early nineteenth
century.

The hostility of the utilitarians raises the question, what
were the class affiliations of Victorian literary culture? There
can of course be no simple answer to this. Not only were there
differences between writers, but the leading writers, above all
Dickens, were divided in themselves. Frequently Dickens reflects
the values of the commercial bourgeoisie. Acquiring culture and
becoming a writer are portrayed in his works as among the means
of self-help. Mr Brownlow with his book-lined study represents
the ideal of the good life in 'Oliver Twist', but when Oliver,
asked if he would like to be an author, replies that it would be
a much better thing to be a bookseller, he is felt to have said
something preternaturally smart. Authorship for Dickens was a
fundamentally entrepreneurial activity. In this he was at the

opposite pole from Matthew Arnold, whose advocacy of literary values is inseparable from his advocacy of a corporate ideology which would take the place of 'laissez-faire'. Despite the aristocratic associations of Arnold's 'grand style', he was really the prophet of the new ethic of service to the state, which was elicited by the growth of the middle-class professions and of the civil service both at home and in the colonies. Arnold envisages an international culture which, however, seeks to ratify rather than to deny the unique characteristics and individual spheres of interest of its constituent nation-states. And though they lacked Arnold's far-sightedness, many other Victorian critics saw themselves as middlemen in an essentially corporate process of production and consumption. Critics discussed such 'administrative' questions as those of anonymity, the relation between specialist and general reviewing, and the right choice of manner and tone. Men of letters such as Macaulay, Bagehot, Lewes and Stephen were superlatively competent reviewers, able to give a trenchant and searching account of almost any book that came to hand. The pace of Victorian reviewing at its most frenetic may be seen in one of George Eliot's surveys of Arts and Belles Lettres, which appeared in the 'Westminster Review' for April 1856. The article begins with a review of volume three of Ruskin's 'Modern Painters' - a crucial influence on Eliot's theory of literary realism. It continues with notices of fiction including Meredith, Wilkie Collins and Kingsley, foreign-language books by Stendhal, de Nerval and some German writers, Francis Newman's version of the 'Iliad', four volumes of Bohn's classics, and a batch of new poetry concluding with 'Leaves of Grass' - a total of twenty-nine volumes in all.

The reviews themselves in the mid-nineteenth century - the 'Fortnightly', the 'Cornhill', the 'Saturday', the 'Nineteenth Century' - were far more professional, open and objective than the old 'Edinburgh' and 'Quarterly'. The increasingly complex mechanism of publishing and reviewing itself affected the attitude of the critics. At least one anonymous mid-century reviewer felt that the machine had taken over:

> The manufacture of novels goes on with increasing activity. For the last two months novelists have been at work 'full blast.' We have, in consequence, some thirty volumes before us. Now, as each volume contains on the average about three hundred pages, and as we cannot possibly read more than one page a minute, especially when we have to cut the pages, it would take us, reading and cutting for five hours a day, a month to get through the pile. If, however, novelists write their tales by machinery, critics must review them by the same means. (2)

Mill's essay on Civilization (1836) is a classic study of the process of 'massification' in advanced societies; and in it he denounces the commercialization of literary values and suggests the formation of an authors' 'collective guild' to bypass the apparatus of booksellers and publishers. The apotheosis of the middleman is satirized in Gissing's 'New Grub Street' (1891), where the prosperous journalist and literary agent are contrasted with the starving novelist and scholar.

What has become of literature, in this mechanized, corporate
world of letters? The early Victorian critics were in two minds
about the industrialization of the press. On the one hand, it
gave the literary journalist a feeling of power, importance and
cultural centrality. On the other hand its characteristic
products seemed ephemeral, meretricious and crude. One way of
expressing this ambivalent feeling was to have two alternating
definitions of the term 'literature'. Carlyle is the main
exponent of the idea of literary culture before Arnold, and he
supplies his readers with such definitions. There is the expansive definition, by which Carlyle conjures up the whole empire
of the written word:

> Could ambition always choose its own path, and were will in
> human undertakings synonymous with faculty, all truly ambitious
> men would be men of letters ... all other arenas of ambition,
> compared with this rich and boundless one of Literature,
> meaning thereby whatever respects the promulgation of Thought,
> are poor, limited and ineffectual. (1829) (3)

The alternative is the evaluative definition, strongly resembling
de Quincey's 'literature of power':

> for that finer portion of our nature, that portion of it which
> belongs eseentially to Literature strictly so called, where our
> highest feelings, our best joys and keenest sorrows, our Doubt,
> our Love, our Religion reside, [Johnson] has no word to
> utter; (1828) (4)

Keeping a refined and intensified definition of literature in
reserve is a typical strategy of the literary apologist; what it
does is to insist that literature has its appointed place in the
realm of values, while not for a moment relinquishing its control
over culture as a whole. In the work of Newman and Mill, as well
as Carlyle, there are proposals for repairing the division between
fact and value, by bringing the conditions of intellectual and
spiritual debate closer to the desired ideal. Yet these two
critics, though deeply sensitive to the power of poetry, differ
from Carlyle in the equivocal value they assign to literature.

Mill's early Benthamism was modified by the spiritual crisis
in which he discovered Wordsworth and the place of the poetic
'culture of the feelings' in human life. A by-product of the
crisis was his attempt (which will be discussed below) to take
the romantic view of poetry to its logical extremes. Yet even in
those of Mill's essays which stress the importance of poetry for
men of intellectual culture, there is an undercurrent stressing
what intellectual culture can do for poets. An entry in the diary
he kept for 1854 rejects Carlyle's use of the term 'Artist' to
express 'the highest order of moral and intellectual greatness';
this honour, Mill says, belongs to the philosopher. (5) It is
unlikely that he had ever thought otherwise. His public views on
literary culture and education are expounded in the essay on
Civilization and in his Inaugural Address, delivered at St
Andrew's University in 1867. In Civilization he is concerned with
the threat to 'individual character' posed by the trend towards
a corporate society in which power is in the hands of masses. The
erosion of literary values by 'quackery' and 'puffing' makes a
graphic illustration of the pressures of the age. But Mill's

assertions about falling standards are backed up by very little
evidence. The causes of his anxiety seem to be the growth of the
periodical press and the adverse terms of the market for serious
publishing. Mill, in fact, was the first post-romantic critic
to write in defence of literary culture in the urgent, prophetic
tone we now associate with F.R. Leavis. He had two concrete proposals to make: the first was to change the economic basis of
publishing, while the second - far more significantly - was for
the reform of the universities. In universities, freed from
religious tests and thrown open to competitive entry, the pursuit
of truth could continue untouched by commercial pressures, and so
the moral and intellectual character of the middle classes would
be restored. Events were to show this as a highly practical
vision; Mill's fears were unfounded, and his 'higher classes'
emerged from the first century of mass advance with all their
privileges intact.

Mill sketched a curriculum that would include classics, history,
philosophy and the sciences. Although modern literature is
granted a place, it appears as part of history. He enlarged upon
the content of school and university education much later, in the
three-hour Inaugural Address that he delivered as Rector of St
Andrew's. Here he distinguishes between the two main branches of
education - those of intellectual and moral instruction - and adds
almost as an afterthought that there is a third branch, the
aesthetic, which deserves to be regarded far more seriously than
it is. The arts serve to 'keep up the tone of our minds'. (6)
Clearly this was only lip-service; Mill would seem to have thought
that the 'culture of the feelings' was too private an affair to be
assigned any more definite a place in academic studies. Classical
languages and literature continued to occupy the central place
in Mill's educational ideas, but then he himself had been taught
Greek from the age of three.

John Henry Newman also paid his tribute to the imagination in
the form of a youthful essay, 'Poetry with reference to Aristotle's
Poetics' (1829), which expresses romantic and aesthetic sympathies
while never quite contradicting the beliefs of the author's
maturity. There are important parallels between the two men's
discussions of university education, as well. Newman's starting-
point, once again, was that the universities had largely lost
their intellectual authority to the new institutions of periodical
literature. His defence of liberal education was an attempt to
restore the position. Both he and Mill see the branches of
knowledge as related to one another by considerations of intellectual utility, and ask for liberal education to be judged by
the effect it produces on the student. Thus, for Newman

A habit of mind is formed which lasts through life, of which
the attributes are freedom, equitableness, calmness, moderation,
and wisdom; or what in a former discourse I have ventured to
call a philosophical habit. (7)

Here he is defining culture in intellectual terms, and in a way
that is calculated to favour classical studies. 'Wisdom' is
almost inevitably that of the ancients, 'moderation' is in all
things Greek and 'calmness' is all too easily attained in the
study of dead civilizations. Newman uses the term 'literature' to

mean the humanities as a whole, as opposed to the faculties of
science and theology. Each branch of study in his idea of a
university has to justify itself as an intellectual discipline.
The central discipline in his view is theology. Poetry does not
constitute an authentic discipline, though a place is reserved
for philological study. A strict follower of Newman could, no
doubt, find a place for literature by seeing it as the heir of the
classics; Arnold, with more temerity, was to suggest it as the
heir of theology.

Both Mill and Newman foresaw something like the modern division
of intellectual life. Their direct influence has counted against
the university study of literature, rather than in its favour.
They are prophets of specialization, lamenting the decline of
learning in the face of the periodical press with its continuous
diet of instruction and commentary. Newman became a university
Rector in Dublin, and a Cardinal of the Church of Rome; but Mill,
notwithstanding his brief term at St Andrew's, remained an independent man of letters. At the time when Civilization appeared,
he was editing the 'London and Westminster Review'. His early
career, as much as any Victorian's, evinces the literary bias of
the reviews and periodicals which became the focus of Victorian
intellectual life. The seat of culture, as Arnold later saw, lay
not in the universities but in the metropolitan world of letters.
While Mill and Newman viewed this with distaste, their contemporary Thomas Carlyle wrote of it with unabashed enthusiasm. The
man of letters, he announced, was the modern Hero.

Like so much else, Carlyle's view of literary heroism can be
traced back to German romanticism. In a discussion of the 'State
of German Literature' (1827), he cited Fichte's view of the
artist as the interpreter of the Divine Idea to mankind:

Literary Men are the appointed interpreters of this Divine
Idea; a perpetual priesthood, we might say, standing forth,
generation after generation, as the dispensers and living
types of God's everlasting wisdom, to show it in their writings
and actions, in such particular form as their own particular
times require it in.

The elevation of the artist was also the elevation of the critic,
who stood 'like an interpreter between the inspired and the
uninspired'. Carlyle's essay might have been entitled 'State of
German Criticism'; he reports that criticism has taken a new
form in Germany, concerning itself not with externals such as
biography and craftsmanship, but with the 'essence and peculiar
life of the poetry itself'. Its method, moreover, is not
impressionistic, but scientific and systematic, appealing to
principles deduced from the 'highest and calmest regions of
philosophy'. And it is into those regions, and not into the
peculiar life of poetry, that Carlyle, like the later Coleridge,
is ultimately anxious to lead us. However, the heroes of his
early essays - Burns, Novalis, Jean Paul and above all Goethe -
belong to that romantic notion of literature in which poetry and
philosophy are as one.

Or is it that all forms of human greatness are ultimately as
one? This is the underlying proposition of the lectures 'On
Heroes, Hero-Worship and the Heroic in History' (1840). Though

perhaps his most influential performance, they are something of a
mixed bag. Carlyle tells the stories of his heroes superbly,
especially when they are slightly unfamiliar; he is much more
memorable on Thor and Odin, Mahomet, Dante, Knox and Cromwell
than on Shakespeare, Johnson and Burns. It is easy to enjoy his
narrative gifts without taking the underlying mystical belief in
the Hero as participator in the 'open secret' of the universe too
seriously. Moreover, Carlyle was expounding an evolutionary history of human society, as well as a redemptive saga of the
universe. Each form of society, he argued, generates its own
particular mode of heroism. Hence the historical series: God,
Prophet, Poet, Priest, Man of Letters and King or Dictator. Such
a series, which ends up with Johnson, Burns and Napoleon as
legitimate successors of Odin and Mahomet (Carlyle tactfully
doesn't mention Jesus), might well suggest a historical decline,
but Carlyle argues that the case is not so simple. Instead of our
reverence for the hero diminishing, it is that the standards we
exact of our gods and heroes are constantly rising. The result
is that the story of modern heroism is invariably a story of
failure. This lesson is seen in the histories of Cromwell and
Napoleon, who laid claim to the divine rights of kingship, and
also in the modern Men of Letters who are the successors of the
great poets such as Dante and Shakespeare.

The view of history in 'On Heroes' was not particularly new,
and in many ways the book is a culmination of the romantic age.
The idea of the modern author overshadowed by the burden of the
past had been familiar at least since Gray and Collins. Carlyle's
selection of heroes must have struck some as archaic and literary
in the 1840s, since he failed to celebrate such new types as the
scientist, the statesman and the captain of industry. His view of
literature as a power in the state echoes the truculence of the
romantic poets:

'Literature will take care of itself,' answered Mr Pitt, when
applied-to for some help for Burns. 'Yes,' adds Mr Southey,
'it will take care of itself; and of you too, if you do not
look to it!'

('The Hero as Man of Letters')

Yet the conclusion that Carlyle draws from this anecdote is a new
one:

The result to individual Men of Letters is not the momentous
one; they are but individuals, an infinitesimal fraction of the
great body; they can struggle on, and live or else die, as they
have been wont. But it deeply concerns the whole society,
whether it will set its light on high places, to walk thereby;
or trample it under foot, and scatter it in all ways of wild
waste (not without conflagration) as heretofore! Light is the
one thing wanted for the world. Put wisdom in the head of the
world, the world will fight its battle victoriously, and be the
best world man can make it. I call this anomaly of a disorganic
Literary Class the heart of all other anomalies, at once product and parent; some good arrangement for that would be as
the 'punctum saliens' of a new vitality and just arrangement for
all.

This is a crucial modification of romantic individualism. Carlyle is not concerned with the rights and privileges of 'mighty poets', but with a whole literary class and its place in the social organism. He is looking towards the organization of that class in the corporate state at the very moment of celebrating the role of individual genius in history. Carlyle believes that 'it is the spiritual always that determines the material', (8) and that it is men of genius who originate social developments, acting as interpreters of the 'sacred mystery of the Universe' for ordinary mortals. Modern society has generated in the Men of Letters a whole class of such seekers after the light. The Man of Letters, in effect, is a phenomenon for the cultural critic rather than for the epic storyteller, and it is as a cultural critic that Carlyle speaks in his lecture on Johnson, Rousseau and Burns.

Books, says Carlyle - 'that huge froth-ocean of Printed Speech we loosely call Literature' - are the university, church and parliament of the modern spirit. The literary world is the central cultural institution. But the man of letters is not recognized in the state, at least in the British state; he is an 'unrecognised unregulated Ishmaelite', living in a garret, ruling 'from his grave, after death' whole generations who would not have given him bread while living. This 'curious spectacle' is symptomatic of a wider cultural disability, reflected in the fate of the other modern hero, the political revolutionary adulated during his life-time only to have his reputation blackened for posterity. Such a disability is reflected, too, in the shortcomings that Carlyle discovers in Johnson, Rousseau and Burns, the products of an enlightened and sceptical age who never found the spiritual truths they sought. This essay, like all Carlyle's work, is a programme for the moral regeneration of society. But it is also a defence of his own class, expounding at once a vision of a time when the failing and unrecognized Man of Letters will exude 'palpably articulated, universally visible power', and a view of history which makes him the legitimate heir of the ages.

Carlyle, then, is the representative literary prophet before Arnold, and the romantic idealism and archaism of his view of society are representative too. Yet, it might be asked, has any writer talked more about literature, and given us less literary criticism? He is concerned with the state of soul revealed by his men of letters, but hardly at all with their prose and verse. In his essay on Burns in the 'Edinburgh Review', he says somewhat breezily that 'True and genial as his poetry must appear, it is not chiefly as a poet, but as a man, that he interests and affects us'; (9) and for criticism in the modern sense on Burns we turn straight to Matthew Arnold. This is evidence more of a difference of interest, however, than of any more fundamental incompatibility. Arnold and the other Victorian critics may have had more respect for the literary text, but they all regard the task of criticism as being to arrive at a series of responses to individual authors. Invariably the author was seen 'as a man' and the response was framed in moral terms. Carlyle as well as Johnson stood behind the monumental 'English Men of Letters' series of critical mono-graphs, founded by John Morley in 1877. While Johnson pioneered the brief critical Life, Carlyle's influence suggested that those so honoured should be a carefully chosen gallery of writers from

the past whose personalities stood out against their times.   The
contributors to the 'English Men of Letters' included R.H. Hutton,
Leslie Stephen, Henry James, Mark Pattison, T.H. Huxley, George
Saintsbury and Frederick Harrison.   Perhaps it is not too much
to claim that Carlyle's discovery of the identity of the modern
hero indicated the course of critical work for the next two
generations.   His conclusions about particular authors, too, have
often been echoed by more determinedly 'literary' critics.

Nevertheless, it is one thing to proclaim the poet as a great
man, and another to show an informed interest in his poetry.
The major irony of the Carlylean view of culture, half exultation
over the 'huge froth-ocean of Printed Speech' and half celebration
of the poetic heroes of the past, is that it may be the contemporary poet who feels most excluded from it.   The private, daydream
world of the romantics and the bookmen was a more natural habitat
for poets than for the energetic Victorian critics, and it was
the poets, after all, who were closer to the realities of
Carlyle's garret.   There is a fine expression of the poet's
helplessness in the new literary world in one of the lyrics of
'In Memoriam':

What hope is here for modern rhyme
   To him, who turns a musing eye
   On songs, and deeds, and lives, that lie
Foreshorten'd in the tract of time?

These mortal lullabies of pain
   May bind a book, may line a box,
   May serve to curl a maiden's locks;
Or when a thousand moons shall wane

A man upon a stall may find
   And, passing, turn the page that tells
   A grief, then changed to something else,
Sung by a long-forgotten mind.

But what of that? My darken'd ways
   Shall ring with music all the same;
   To breathe my loss is more than fame,
To utter love more sweet than praise

(LXXVI).

The 'mortal lullabies of pain' are materialized as an artefact
and set adrift in the public world where they become waste paper
or at best something idly glanced at on a secondhand bookstall.
We remember Johnson's contemplation of the futility of human effort
as enshrined in libraries.   It would not suit Tennyson's case to
admit that he can be in any way affected by neglect and oblivion,
however; as a modern lyric poet, it was his fate and duty to go
on ringing with music regardless of whether anyone heard him.   The
'darken'd ways' are at once ways unillumined by heavenly light
(the contrast is with the beatified Hallam of the preceding poem)
and the pages of an unopened book.   A sturdy private faith is
invoked to bolster the poet against neglect.   We may suspect a
certain posturing in this, when we remember the enormous success
of 'In Memoriam', and the public standing it gave its author.

Tennyson inherited the romantic duality of public exhortation and private daydream, but the emotions of his poetry are so generalized that any number of people besides poets could draw sustenance from its pious resolutions and inward sorrows.

Tennyson's poetry was felt to epitomize 'modern rhyme' by its earliest admirers. The lesson in 'pure poetry' which critics such as A.H. Hallam and Mill found in 'Mariana' and 'The Lady of Shalott' forms a convincing link between the aims of the romantics and those of the aesthetes and symbolists later in the century. Yeats, for example, acknowledged a debt to Hallam's review of Tennyson's 'Poems, Chiefly Lyrical' (1830), and this review, though necessarily immature, is one of the most important attempts to establish and clarify the definition of poetry inherited from the romantics. Hallam distinguishes between pure poetry, which is unpopular because it demands an active response, and fashionable verse which beguiles the reader with 'mere rhetoric'. Poetry is losing ground in the present age, since its 'subjective power' is overshadowed by the increase in social activity with its 'continual absorption of the higher feelings into the palpable interests of ordinary life'. (10) Modern poetry must expect to become, not a popular art-form, but an affair of votaries and sects. So far Hallam is giving a highly intelligent restatement of themes from Wordsworth's prefaces. But he accuses Wordsworth's poetry of too often resorting to mere rhetoric, and argues that the highest poetic mode is not that of reflectiveness but of sensation, as represented by Keats and Shelley. Tennyson, clearly, is in the Keatsian tradition.

Hallam did not live to elaborate a complete theory of 'pure poetry', but such a theory is to be found in Mill's two essays 'What is Poetry?' and 'The Two Kinds of Poetry' (1833). These essays had long been neglected when M.H. Abrams gave them a prominent place in his exposition of romantic theory in 'The Mirror and the Lamp'. They are, in effect, an attempt to give philosophical substance to the romantic use of the word 'poetry' to denote a quality common to all the arts. Thus Mill is committed to 'pure poetry', though he does not seem interested in 'poetry for poetry's sake'. He investigates it as a psychological phenomenon (it was, of course, as a psychological phenomenon or anti-depressant that he had first taken up poetry). The questions he asks are, what kind of mind produces poetry, what sort of communication does it constitute, and how do we respond to it? The discursive content of the communication is of little moment. In this respect, Mill's essays, for all their romantic attitudes, are less part of the mainstream of nineteenth-century thought than a prolegomenon to I.A. Richards.

Mill's view of poetry appears when he asks the question, how does a poet describe a lion? The answer is that he does so by imagery. He must try to suggest the likenesses and contrasts which belong to the emotional state which the spectacle of the lion would excite. What is described, then, is the state of excitement in the spectator, and the description must be judged not by its representation of the lion itself, but by its truth to the emotion aroused. Thus Mill distinguishes between poetry, a purely subjective utterance, and narrative fiction, which he

speaks of somewhat contemptuously. Poetry is a higher form than
narrative, a 'delineation of the deeper and more secret workings
of the human heart.' But it is also a more esoteric form,
appealing only to those whose imagination is more highly developed.
And just as poetry is more subjective than narrative, it is more
private than 'eloquence' or rhetoric, so that all poetry is of the
nature of soliloquy:

> eloquence is heard, poetry is overheard. Eloquence supposes
> an audience; the peculiarity of poetry appears to us to lie
> in the poet's utter unconsciousness of a listener. Poetry is
> feeling confessing itself to itself, in moments of solitude,
> and bodying itself forth in symbols which are the nearest pos-
> sible representations of the feeling in the exact shape in
> which it exists in the poet's mind. Eloquence is feeling
> pouring itself forth to other minds, courting their sympathy,
> or endeavouring to influence their belief, or move them to
> passion or to action. (11)

This translation of feeling into symbols and imagery is reversed
in the process of poetic response.

In 'What is Poetry?' Mill outlines the definition of poetry and
suggests how it may be applied to the arts of music, painting and
architecture. In 'The Two Kinds of Poetry' he distinguishes pure
from didactic poetry, and argues that pure poetry issues from a
specifically poetic cast of mind. The born poet is the 'poet of
nature'; his counterpart, who uses verse as a vehicle for thoughts
which could have been expressed in prose, is the 'poet of culture'.
Shelley is the example of the first, Wordsworth of the second.
Shelley's lyricism is a spontaneous product, an inspired and
exuberant stream of images controlled only by the poet's dominant
state of feeling and his natural 'fineness of organization'. The
result is poetry 'in a far higher sense than any other'. Wordsworth's attempts in the lyrical mode are 'cold and spiritless',
however, and he remains distressingly earth-bound:

> Wordsworth's poetry is never bounding, never ebullient; has
> little even of the appearance of spontaneousness: the well is
> never so full that it overflows. There is an air of calm
> deliberateness about all he writes, which is not characteristic
> of the poetic temperament; his poetry seems one thing, him-
> self another; he seems to be poetical because he wills to be
> so, not because he cannot help it: did he will to dismiss
> poetry, he need never again, it might almost seem, have a
> poetical thought. (12)

Written at the age of twenty-seven, 'The Two Kinds of Poetry' is
a brilliantly precocious theoretical exercise. If it falls short
of total clarity, this is probably because Mill remains tied to
the Wordsworthian psychological vocabulary of 'feelings', 'associations', 'states of excitement' etc. Yet the essay is also a
notable example of biting the hand that has fed one. Mill's
determination to expose the contradictions of Wordsworth's theory
and practice seems coldly wilful in the passage quoted above. In
view of the admiring tone in which he reported his first meeting
with Wordsworth in 1831, and the role later ascribed to
Wordsworth's influence in his 'Autobiography' it is impossible
not to suspect him of unconscious dishonesty in the 1833 essays.

(Did he really like Shelley? Though he may have assuaged some disappointment with Wordsworth's personality and later poetry by turning to the younger poet, it was surely only a passing phase.) In any case, though he denies Wordsworth a place among the born poets, he never suggests that Shelley attained creative maturity. A philosopher may not be able to become a poet, he writes, but 'a poet may always, by culture, make himself a philosopher'. Poets, providing that they are indeed poets, can only benefit by acquiring some intellectual culture. Here Mill betrays his under-lying concern with education and the constitution of the well-balanced mind. He mentions two poets who possessed a 'logical and scientific culture', Milton and Coleridge; and thence we may trace the line leading to his later work through the magnificent essays on Coleridge and Bentham. There are two other pieces closely linked to the essays of 1833, those on Tennyson (1835) and Alfred de Vigny (1838). In his review of Tennyson's first two collections, Mill shows how the theory of pure poetry as the expression of subjective emotions may be applied to poems such as 'Mariana'. But he also speaks of Tennyson's growing 'maturity of intellect', the advancing 'intellectual culture' that was enabling him to ripen into a true artist. A poem such as 'The Palace of Art' was not merely a rendering of sensations but a symbolic representation of spiritual truths. In welcoming this aspect of Tennyson's work, Mill does not seem at all far from Victorian orthodoxy.

   Mill's theoretical insight is great, but his critical judgments are not quite to be trusted. A wider question poses itself. What are we to make of a utilitarian philosopher whose poetic theory comes so close to that of the aesthetes? Mill is a psychologist adapting the theory of 'pure poetry' to his own uses, very much as I.A. Richards, ninety years later, was to construct a psychological theory of poetic communication under the influence of Clive Bell's notion of 'significant form'. Both 'Principles of Literary Criticism' and Mill's early essays reveal a hidden compatibility between apparently opposing doctrines. Aesthete and utilitarian are united by their opposition to the belief that poetry has a rational content and must therefore be treated on a level with other forms of discourse. The aesthete's religion of art serves to disguise a retreat from the romantic poet's claims for the moral and cognitive value of the poetic activity. Poetry for the aesthete is largely self-validating; too proud to compete in the intellectual market-place, he claims privileged access to a mode of reality which can only be embodied in poetical forms. The utilitarian is only too glad to assign to the poet a unique psycho-logical function, so long as this esoteric, purely emotive function disqualifies any claims he might have as a philosopher and social reformer. Both Mill and Richards write eloquently about the pure poet whom they confine, in effect, to uttering 'pseudo-statements'. (13) Poetry for the aesthete is a solipsistic, for the utilitarian simply a specialist, pursuit. Either emphasis is a denial of the romantic ideal of the poet as a man speaking to men - speaking to our whole being, with as much claim to our full and general attention as any other man can have. Nothing in Mill's work contradicts the idea that the highest offices of art are, first, to give moving expression to pre-existent truths, and second, to act as a therapy or cure for depression.

Although the doctrine of art for art's sake was familiar from the time of Gautier's preface to 'Mademoiselle de Maupin' (1835), it was not until the time of Pater and Swinburne that aestheticism emerged as a coherent force in England. The particular forms of English aestheticism will thus be dealt with in the final section of this chapter. The debate between romantic and utilitarian views of art is, however, one which has cropped up in varying forms since its inception in the 1820s. It is surprising, perhaps, that it was not taken further by the early Victorians, and that there is not more to refute George Saintsbury's observation of the 'general critical poverty' of the period 1830-60. (14) The advocates of 'pure poetry' were virtually unread in their own time. At the other extreme, Victorian positivism did not address itself to the development of a science of criticism; the nearest approach to this comes in the elaborate classifications of E.S. Dallas's 'Poetics' (1852). (15) The mid-Victorian reviewers such as Bagehot, G.H. Lewes and R.H. Hutton were all opposed to the idea of criticism as science; they failed, however, to put anything very much in its place. The reason why literature was felt to elude scientific codification was, broadly, that it was a medium of individual, idiosyncratic expression. This suggests that the true alternative to the aesthetic and the utilitarian positions would be found in the moralistic doctrine of art which received its most decisive critical formulation in the work of Arnold in the 1860s. Arnold's immediate predecessors here were first Carlyle, and then John Ruskin.

Mill and Carlyle provide us with critical texts which are clearly distinct from the rest of their intellectual enterprise. In Ruskin's case there is no such convenience, and anthologies of the 'Literary Criticism of John Ruskin', like other selections from his works, have a somewhat haphazard air. A prophetic conviction of the unity of culture is fundamental in his thought; yet the place of literature in this, though a central one, is never that assigned to it by Victorian cultural orthodoxy. He is nearest to orthodoxy in the concern with the morality of great art and with the ranking of geniuses that he shares with Arnold. Poetry for Ruskin is an evaluative term, applying to all the arts and defined as 'the suggestion, by the imagination, of noble grounds for the noble emotions'. (16) The best poetry, this seems to imply, is that which most closely expresses the divine plan of the universe. But any idea that he is returning to the eighteenth-century Sublime is undercut by his sharp disagreement with Reynolds over the nature of the grand style. Ruskin's text in his discussion 'Of the received Opinions touching the "Grand Style"' is a quatrain from Byron's 'Prisoner of Chillon'. Great poetry, he argues, inheres not in generalities but in the vivid presentation of minute particulars. Ruskin's conception of genius, however, is brought out in his discussions of Turner and Tintoretto rather than of his literary heroes, and it is the minute particulars of visual representation that he hunts out and dissects throughout the five volumes of 'Modern Painters'. Nonetheless, the literary sections of the book involve a kind of direct dealing with poetic

imagery and statement, exemplified in his analyses of Byron,
Wordsworth and Scott, which is exceedingly rare in Victorian criticism. Only Arnold, among the merely literary critics, even began
to take the object to pieces and to look at the parts as they
really were. Ruskin did this without effort. His inspiration,
as with his exhaustive analyses of natural forms, was, like
Coleridge's, a kind of natural theology. 'Modern Painters' ends
on an apocalyptic note, as Ruskin affirms his ever-growing
reverence for Turner's genius and portrays the act of criticism
as a frail human counterpart to God's task on the Day of Judgment.
In his later work his mode of analysis became an excessively
literal iconography, based on the interpretation of sacred texts.
The 'objective' interpretation of 'Lycidas' that he offers in
'Sesame and Lilies', for instance, has what Buck Mulligan would
call the true scholastic stink. Thus it is somewhat equivocal
praise, in my view, for Harold Bloom to call Ruskin the 'linking
and transitional figure between allegorical critics of the older,
Renaissance kind, and those of the newer variety, like Northrop
Frye.' (17) Professor Bloom is right to trace Ruskin's evolution
from a Wordsworthian concern with natural representation to a
mode of myth or archetypal criticism; but it may be that loss
rather than gain was involved.

   Ruskin could be a more forthright critic of contemporary
literature than almost any of his rivals, though his power of
harnessing contemporary criticism to cultural diagnosis was best
exercised in architecture and the visual arts. Throughout his
criticism he is concerned with art as the expression of man's
history, which he traces in its social, psychological, religious
and topographical aspects. His overall design is so grand that
it is only too easily misrepresented in isolated (and frequently
eccentric or dogmatic) extracts. What are we to make of the
astonishing discussion of Shakespeare, for example, in the Mountain
Glory chapter of 'Modern Painters' volume four? Bred on the
'plains of Stratford', Shakespeare, Ruskin tells us, was on a
level with his race; yet this is cited as proof, not as negation,
of his thesis of the 'mountain power over human intellect'.
May it not be that certain hills around Stratford, or even a
fleeting glimpse of the white cliffs of Dover, were essential to
the development of the Shakespearean genius? And in any case,
he lacks the 'ascending sight' of a great visionary such as
Dante, who could look up in the mornings towards Fiesole! Taken
in isolation, this mode of argument seems weirdly ramshackle,
but the conclusion does bring into focus an aspect of Shakespeare's
sensibility which had not often been seen so sharply. And set in
the whole context of 'Modern Painters', such a confrontation with
Shakespeare is an almost inevitable product of Ruskin's systematic
exploration of the nature and principles of creative imagination,
and of his fervent, Wordsworthian awareness of the influence on
mankind of the beautiful and permanent forms of nature.

   Ruskin, in fact, was the one Victorian who inherited the
ambitions of the major romantic critics. The conclusion of
'Modern Painters' is an elegy for the romantic genius of Scott,
Keats, Byron, Shelley and Turner, condemned by a godless society
to 'die without hope'. Homer, Dante and Milton, as well as the

romantics, were among his formative influences; but his deep understanding of poetry usually comes across in passing references, instead of being explored for its own sake. The literary text is just one of the subjects of his massive project of cultural analysis. This is why Ruskin seems distinct from the merely literary world of so much Victorian criticism, with its restricted discussions of individual works in relation to the author's personality, his literary milieu and the reader's responses. The effect of Ruskin's criticism was to set up alternatives to Victorian bookishness, rather than to broaden its scope. In later books like 'Sesame and Lilies', he expresses a view of culture which is essentially religious and constitutes a subordination of the imaginative spirit to doctrinal and iconological concerns. (He had, however, abandoned the sectarian Evangelicalism of his youth.) In the earlier work his vision is of a culture centred not upon literature but upon man's relation to nature as expressed in the visual arts, especially painting and architecture. At all times, however, he was moving away from the individuality of literary expression to more communal notions of culture. He was anticipated in his stress on the visual arts by Pugin, whose condemnation of modern building in 'Contrasts' (1836) was part of an explicit programme to restore the Catholic faith. Ruskin in turn decisively influenced William Morris, who became the propagandist of a radically socialist idea of culture in which literature as the nineteenth century knew it would cease to exist.

Ruskin describes his basic approach to art criticism in the Nature of Gothic chapter in 'The Stones of Venice'. He speaks of the necessity of 'reading a building as we would read Milton or Dante'. His own method of 'reading', however, was almost unprecedented; it involved relating architectural style, not merely to the spirit of a culture, but to its material base. Gothic architecture for Ruskin is the direct expression of the religious beliefs and the social and economic organization of the medieval community. It is also an expression of the eternal romantic spirit, engaged, as the German romantics had suggested, in a perpetual conflict with the principles of classicism. Ruskin ranges dialectically from level to level of sociological, technological, cultural and religious discussion, at the same time as he lays down rules for restoring freedom of expression to the contemporary arts and crafts. Architecture and the decorative arts, he implies, have a more genuinely communal basis in the skills and traditions of the people than literary culture has ever had. At the same time, architecture no less than poetry is illuminated by the 'Seven Lamps' of Sacrifice, Truth, Power, Beauty, Life, Memory and Obedience. It has - or should have - no deficiency in expressive power.

The implications of this were drawn by Morris, whose vision of a civilization based on the practice of the handicrafts was a deliberate rejection of literary culture. Morris believed that worthwhile art was the expression of a whole people, and not of the individual or of a coterie. As a poet, he stood for the revival of the primitive, oral forms of legend and saga, but in his lectures and essays he expounded a definition of culture as based on the arts of building and ornamentation, and not of literary expression. It was here that he combined the stress on architecture as the truly communal art, inherited from Ruskin and Pugin, with a socialist critique of the distortions of culture under capitalism. Marx and Engels had described the exclusive concentration of artistic talent in particular individuals as a 'consequence of division of labour'. (18) Morris in 'Hopes and Fears for Art' denounced the 'hierarchy of intellect in the arts'. (19) He was attacking the individualism of the artist, the cultural snobbery which placed the artist above the craftsman, and the coterie attitude of aestheticism. To speak of the 'hierarchy of intellect' was to link high art, with its academic standards and traditions of exclusion, to the whole existence of intellectuals as a class and the prevalence of 'ranking' and 'grading' attitudes in society. (George Eliot's novels, for example, are full of processes of assessment of the characters by the author and by one another, and show how the critical attitudes of high culture reflected the habits of ordinary life.) Morris's view of art was an openly revolutionary one; he was prepared to see art die, if it was not already dead, to compel the birth of a new tradition.

    Morris, as has often been pointed out, was a prophet of desirable rather than of possible worlds. His conception of a new art seems to have been dogged by triviality; we can find this in his own very diffuse creative work, in the 'epoch of rest' por-trayed in 'News from Nowhere' and in the sense that his lectures give of ignoring the highest potentialities of art (Beethoven, Rembrandt, Tolstoy), not to mention its capacity to revolutionize itself from within. (20) The Nowherians are penetrating critics of nineteenth-century fiction, although they have no impulse or need to construct artistic works which go beyond the texture of their everyday lives. (21) Morris's value for criticism, in fact, lies in the light he can shed on our inherited literary ideology. The idea of the man of letters as hero was an attempt to assert the cultural authority of the intellectual class. Morris links this to the privileged status of intellectuals and the need for an army of workers to process their ideas for transmission to the public. In his exposure of the luxury status of contemporary art he anticipates the doctrine of 'commodity fetishism' in a twentieth-century Marxist such as Christopher Caudwell. His anarchistic and collectivist view of the creative process remains a sympathetic and subversive ideal, even though a major movement of twentieth-century Marxism, notably in the work of Lukács, has been the repossession of bourgeois high culture. As for the actual cultural policies of socialist states, these have been far closer to the letter of Matthew Arnold than to the spirit of William Morris.

2   MATTHEW ARNOLD

It was Morris who denounced the 'hierarchy of intellect in the arts'; but Morris was a gentleman of leisure, with an unearned income that he was free to devote to aesthetic or to socialist ends as he chose. He, and not Matthew Arnold, was in that sense

the 'literary man'. A speech that Arnold made at a Royal Academy
banquet in 1875 serves to underline the point. Called upon to
reply to the toast of 'Literature', in a company which included
Gladstone, Disraeli, the Prince of Wales and a large section of
the British establishment, Arnold began as follows:

> Literature, no doubt, is a great and splendid art, allied to
> that great and splendid art of which we see around us the
> handiwork. But, Sir, you do me an undeserved honour, when, as
> President of the Royal Academy, you desire me to speak in the
> name of Literature. Whatever I may have once wished or inten-
> ded, my life is not that of a man of letters, but of an
> Inspector of Schools (a laugh), and it is with embarrassment
> that I now stand up in the dreaded presence of my own official
> chiefs (a laugh), who have lately been turning upon their
> Inspectors an eye of some suspicion. (A laugh.) ('The Times',
> 3 May 1875) (22)

The audience, of course, found this hilarious fun; they knew their
man, and knew he wouldn't embarrass them, and punctuated with their
laughs it all sounds dashing in 'The Times' report. We need not
stress the irony that Arnold, the champion of literary culture,
felt driven beyond that culture to make a living. He took up
school-inspecting, it seems, partly to provide himself with an
income and partly as a 'philosophic gesture' to establish his
social identity. (23) The problem of social identity is central
to a consideration of his literary criticism, as well as of his
failure as a poet. Arnold was the classic Victorian exponent of
culture because he saw with an unrivalled clarity the path that
literature must take to remain free from the encroachments of
positivism and political ideology on the one hand, and from a
trivializing aestheticism on the other. And Arnold taught that
integrity in the literary sphere was above all a question of style
and tone. The literary critic, therefore, could unmask the moral
and intellectual habits of his contemporaries in a way that other
commentators could not. But who was the literary critic, and what
was revealed in his tone? Arnold has a vivacious, an unmistakable
personality, but he has no settled voice, as Wordsworth and
Johnson have in their prose; he has a remarkable range of
rhetorical inflections, and even in a performance as integral in
conception as 'Culture and Anarchy', he proves astonishingly
difficult to pin down. The immediate cause of this, it would
seem, is histrionic; it arises from his attempt to command an
ever-increasing audience.

Arnold's early prefaces are examples of prose with a purely
intellectual appeal. They must have made a frigid impression
on some of the small band of admirers of his early poetry. His
Oxford lectures on Homer and his study of 'Popular Education in
France' (1861) show him addressing a wider, but still a
specialist readership. His sense of the general and acute
relevance of culture and literary criticism emerged in the 1860s.
By 1863 he was conscious of seizing his 'chance of getting at
the English public', writing to his mother that 'everything turns
upon one's exercising the power of persuasion, of charm'. (24)
So he developed into a licensed performer, dazzling the public
with inspiring rhetoric, withering irony and disarming self-display.

He is the most exhibitionist of the Victorian prophets. Mill
trusted in cold reason, and Carlyle in stump-oratory, to reach in
time their natural audiences. Arnold, however, feels compelled
to advertize himself, to put on an act in front of the footlights.
When the charm fails to work he seems less substantial and more
of a pretender than any of his rivals.

Arnold's poetry is intensely melancholy. The theme of loss
of self occurs in relation to the melancholia. Empedocles, who
is true to his own nature, throws himself into the crater of Etna;
Arnold, in suppressing morbid and suicidal impulses, perhaps also
suppressed himself. T.S. Eliot seems to have responded to this
when he wove references to Arnold's poem 'The Buried Life' into
'Portrait of a Lady'. (25) 'The Buried Life' (1852) expresses
the dichotomy of public and private selves. The buried self
exists at a 'subterranean depth', and can only come to the surface
in certain hours of private fulfilment 'When a beloved hand is
laid in ours'. (George Eliot often seems to echo Matthew Arnold,
and she portrays such a moment of 'surfacing' - though no
declaration of love is involved - when Lydgate is reassured by
Dorothea in Lowick library near the end of 'Middlemarch'.) (26)
For Arnold, the public adult is a 'baby man':

How he would pour himself in every strife,
And well-nigh change his own identity;
That it might keep from his capricious play
His genuine self ....

The extent of worldliness in this may be judged if we compare it
with the Tennyson poem quoted above; Arnold's darkened ways on the
whole do not 'ring with music all the same'. It may have been
precisely the indirectness involved in essays in criticism which
proved so attractive to him. There is no necessary incompatibility
between criticism and self-definition, as the examples of
Johnson and Wordsworth show. Yet Arnold is far more of an
interpreter and 'appreciator' than they are. Many of his essays,
especially in the first 'Essays in Criticism' (1865), are contributions to a gallery of minor culture-heroes, and many are
expressions of his admiration for the French critics Scherer and
Sainte-Beuve. Arnold is alone among major critics in the space he
gives to reporting the judgments of others. Is there a 'genuine
self' in such work? What is certain is that, even when his manner
seems earnest and passionate, he is frequently engaged in
'capricious play'. And it is the capriciousness that justifies
Geoffrey Tillotson's description of him as the 'clever salesman'
of criticism. (27)

Arnold's worldliness exploits a kind of play which had origi-
nated in his youth, as the wayward son of Arnold of Rugby - the
pose of the dandy, or aesthetic man-about-town. Arnold's
relation to the aesthetic movement is a puzzling one, since his
urbanity is a far more complex thing than the swashbuckling
brilliance of Whistler and Wilde. Aestheticism as a fashion
involves the cultivation of the arts as a species of social
imposture. The aesthete disdains to meet the supporters of
utility at the level of rational argument, relying, instead, on
associating culture with elegance, snobbery and hauteur. By
outraging the bourgeoisie, they sought to strengthen their claim

to recognition as an élite. (Theirs was thus a spiritual
imposture, very different from the economic expedients of the
Grub Street writers celebrated by Pope and Johnson.) Arnold,
however, avoided the transparent cliquishness of the aesthetes,
and spoke for 'Oxford', for 'criticism' and the 'republic of
letters'; at times, for the whole class of the cultivated. If
there was affectation in this, there was also a high sense of
duty and responsibility. But it was no longer enough to state
that literature was more solid and permanent than any alternative
value-system. Arnold intended to make it seem more attractive and
glittering, too. His appeal was to the sensibility as much as
to the intellect. The brittle and self-validating assertions
that he sometimes let pass as cultural propaganda go beyond mere
affectation; yet, in a non-pejorative sense, imposture is a
feature not merely of Arnold at his worst, but at his most characteristic. Poet and charmer, preacher, polemicist, sage and school-
inspector - they were all roles which he played with equal
facility. His 'high seriousness' is serious enough, but such
things as the 'theory of the three classes' in 'Culture and
Anarchy' are pasted together for the occasion. Arnold was well
aware that the values he was struggling to assert were precarious
and almost undemonstrable. He set out to charm the reader because
plain statement was not enough. Perhaps it was that his life's
work was to preach the importance of a culture which, in certain
senses, 'wasn't there' - he was not a 'man of letters', he turned
down university posts, and literature couldn't provide him with
a comfortable living. Thus Arnold devoted far more time than any
previous critic to identifying and attacking the enemies of
literature, and made himself into a master-rhetorician, inventing
many of the watchwords and strategies which have been used in a
continuing (and continuously over-dramatized) struggle. But on
the intrinsic nature of literature he sometimes seems rather blank.
Reasons are given for this: it cannot be put into words for the
Philistines, or a French critic has already said most of what
there is to be said. But what cannot be put into words for the
Philistines cannot always be put into words for oneself. The
essence of culture, like the genuine self, almost remains
unrealized; this is the Arnold problem.

One word which suggests many sides of Arnold's achievement is
'Hellenism'. His classicizing tastes were evident in his first
volume of poems (1849), and especially in 'Empedocles on Etna'
(1852), a poem which recalls Keats in its mixture of classical
setting and romantic self-expression. His career as a critic
began with the Preface to the 1853 volume, from which 'Empedocles'
was omitted. Citing the authority of Aristotle and Schiller,
Arnold maintained that passive suffering was unsuitable for
poetry, since morbidity must not be confused with genuine
tragedy. 'Empedocles', with its thinly-disguised expression of
a modern poet's anguish, was condemned on the score of self-
indulgence. Arnold's search for an austerer version of classicism
led him to Aristotle's doctrine that poetry imitates human actions,
and that the actions should have a permanent appeal. Hence the

poet should avoid both modern settings and peculiarly modern
emotions. In fact, Arnold continued to use modern settings; 'The
Scholar-Gipsy', 'Thyrsis' and 'Dover Beach' were all written
after 1853. His critical conscience, however, led him to sup-
plant 'Empedocles' with the neoclassical tragedy 'Merope' (1858),
a frigid performance which he hoped to endow with the 'character
of Fixity, that true sign of the Law.' (28) (Lionel Trilling
has commented that 'perhaps no poet ever hoped a more inauspicious
thing for his work.') Fortunately, it was not only the writing
of 'Merope' that came out of the 1853 Preface. After discussing
the Aristotelian doctrine of tragedy, he went on to attack the
romantic poets for their idolatry of Shakespeare at the expense
of the Greeks. Too much study of Shakespeare, he wrote, encourages
the modern vice of concentrating on the value of 'separate thoughts
and images', at the expense of overall construction. Keats was
typical of the modern poets who lack the power of producing a
'total-impression', at which the Greeks had excelled. Arnold's
attitude to Shakespeare was always a little uneasy; the 1849
volume contains his well-known sonnet ('Others abide our question;
thou art free ...'), but it was long before he included the dramatist among his exemplars of the 'grand style'. What is shown in
the Preface, however, is Arnold's concern with the literary
culture available to the poet and the models he is likely to turn
to for imitation. It is the waywardness of Shakespeare's genius
that makes him a doubtful influence for modern poets. The implications of this would be drawn in the 'Essays in Criticism' in
1865.

   Arnold's 'anti-romanticism' of 1853 was in fact founded upon an
idealization of the Greek at the expense of the modern spirit.
To this extent, he was the heir of the German Enlightenment. His
declared allegiance was to Goethe, and he was influential in the
movement that separates Carlyle's Teutonic mysticism in the 1820s
from Pater's celebration of the classicizing Germany in his essay
on Winckelmann fifty years later. Arnold's idealization of the
Greeks has both a poetic and a broadly cultural aspect. His
endorsement of Greek poetry is characteristically vague. The
qualities he finds in it are first the 'grand style', and second
'Architectonicè' or the power of construction in order to produce
a unified 'total-impression'. The 'grand style', at this stage,
seems little more than a tag Arnold has picked up from Reynolds,
while 'Architectonicè', so much more impressive-sounding than
'design' or 'construction', is from Goethe. These are terms that
we shall meet again, but the Preface is also notable for its
expression of a theme that Arnold would leave behind in his mature
years, the nostalgia of the modern intellectual. The present is
an 'age wanting in moral grandeur', and 'age of spiritual dis-
comfort', an age when poetic excellence is unattainable. The
phrases pile up, and suggest the same effect of melancholy that
is so pervasive in Arnold's poetry. In his 'Memorial Verses' on
Wordsworth, for example, he had suggested that modern anxiety could
be counteracted by the example of a prophet and teacher:
   He too upon a wintry clime
   Had fallen - on this iron time
   Of doubts, disputes, distractions, fears.

> He found us when the age had bound
> Our souls in its benumbing round;
> He spoke, and loos'd our heart in tears.

Despite this act of public homage, Arnold's lasting cure for the
times was not to be found in Victorian sentiment. The 1853 Preface
is a plea on behalf of the young poet. What he needs, it declares,
is 'a hand to guide him through the confusion, a voice to pre-
scribe to him the aim which he should keep in view, and to explain
to him that the value of the literary works which offer themselves
to his attention is relative to their power of helping him forward
on his road towards this aim.' (29) The need, in effect, is for
a source of cultural standards, and it is to be provided in the
form of literary criticism.

Here Arnold is giving to criticism a new importance. What he
wants is not a return to neoclassicism - the critic as provincial
magistrate applying the laws - because literary value is now (in
a sense) relative and not absolute. The critic has a historical
role: he is crucially concerned in a major enterprise of civilization, the production of new art. He is at the centre of
culture, and responsible for its progress. Arnold, consciously
or not, was reversing the balance of relationship between critic
and poet, and calling upon the critic to mediate the influence of
the past in the way most relevant to the contemporary scene. This
is an essentially nineteenth-century notion, based on the
idealization of the reviewer whose job was to apply a standard of
'permanent' value to the shifting directions of the contemporary
intellect. Hence, as John Holloway has pointed out, 'criticism'
and 'culture' became virtually interchangeable terms in Arnold's
system. (30) Arnoldian criticism constructs a tradition, or
global view of the literary hierarchy, and is characteristically
preoccupied with assigning authors to their rightful places within
that hierarchy. Arnold alternates between the pretence that such
judgments are 'sub specie aeternitatis' and the open admission
that they are made from the point of view of the present.

The impact of Arnold's poetry was responsible for his election
to the Chair of Poetry at Oxford in 1857. His inaugural lecture
was entitled 'On the Modern Element in Literature'. Any hopes
that he was about to pass judgment on his contemporaries must
have been quickly dashed, for he defines a 'modern' literature as
one which is the product of an advanced civilization and which
has adequately come to terms with its own age. Hence the literature of Periclean Athens is as modern - no, it is more modern -
than that of Victorian England. Though paradoxical, Arnold's
definition is important on account of its implicit relativism.
'Adequate' writers, he strongly suggests, are those best able to
help us comprehend our own times. Lionel Trilling has pointed to
the novelty of this criterion in literary criticism; (31) its
closest precedents seem to lie in the cultural criticism of the
1830s. One thinks of Mill's exposure of the inadequacies of
Bentham, and Carlyle's of 'laissez-faire'. Arnold uses the
language of the Victorian prophets when he speaks at the beginning
of his lecture of the need for a moral and intellectual 'deliverance'. Intellectual deliverance, however, is to be sought
exclusively in the study of literature. It is only through

literature that we can relate the nineteenth century to certain
earlier periods 'founded upon a rich past and upon an instructive
fulness of experience': the Periclean, Macedonian and Augustan
periods of classical civilization, and the Elizabethan period in
England. Of these, the age which manifested the fullest literary
maturity was the Periclean. Arnold plays off Greece against
Rome, and when he comes to discuss the period of Augustus his
criticism takes on an inquisitorial note. Lucretius was 'morbid',
Virgil was not 'dramatic' enough and Horace was insufficiently
serious; all three failed to measure up to the highest demands
of civilization. Perhaps for Augustan Rome we are intended to
read Victorian England, since in fact all three charges could be
levelled at Arnold and other contemporary poets. It is as if he
was able to rationalize and survive his own sense of poetic failure
by projecting his problems onto a whole age. His conclusions in
this lecture, however, are much less important than the kind of
critical exercise in which he had engaged. Arnold later used the
broad term 'criticism of life' to define the function of poetry;
this implies that great poetry is of permanent value for its
comments upon unchanging human nature. 'On the Modern Element
in Literature', however, shows him evaluating the poets' criti-
cisms of life in a much more particular sense. Ostensibly a broad
review of cultural history, its method is to judge everything by
its relevance to the present day.

Arnold continued his indirect diagnosis of Victorian culture in
his lectures 'On Translating Homer' (1861-2). These begin with
deceptive simplicity. His name has been put forward as a translator of Homer, but he has 'neither the time nor the courage'; in
any case, two versions have just appeared. All that he can do is
to offer some practical hints to future translators. The practical
hints take the form of a major essay on poetic style, while the
two hapless recent translators are the occasion of Arnold's first
polemic against what he would soon call Philistinism. The result
is the first work of his critical maturity, and in some ways his
most unqualified success.

Arnold's analysis of Homeric translation is concerned entirely
with style, not with 'Architectonicè'. He argues that existing
translations utterly fail to convey the Homeric manner, and that
this manner is compounded of four qualities: rapidity, plainness
of diction, plainness of thought and nobility. His main thesis,
as we might expect, is concerned with nobility. This is an
elusive quality, demonstrated by means of subtle and penetrating
poetic analysis; but it is also a metaphor, leading inescapably
into the realm of ideology. Arnold exploited this duality, first
positing that Homer was 'eminently noble', and then going on to
formulate a broad philosophy of culture.

For a start, Homer's status affected the whole literary
tradition. G.H. Lewes had argued in 1846 that, far from being
the foundation stone of the tradition, he was essentially a primitive author:

  it seems to us impossible for any dispassionate reader of
  Homer not to be struck with the excessive rudeness and art-
  lessness of his style - with the absence of any great
  o'ermastering individuality, which, were it there, would set

its stamp upon every line, as in Dante, Milton, or Shakespeare -
with the absence, in short, of everything that can, properly
speaking, be called art. (32)

Such a view had been taken to heart by Homer's latest translator,
Francis Newman, brother of Cardinal Newman and Professor of Latin
at University College London. Newman, an eccentric rationalist,
had reproduced the 'Iliad' in a ballad metre reminiscent of Scott.
Still worse, he had studded his text with deliberate archaisms,
in order to suggest the primitive sound of Homer's language for
the Greeks of the classical period. But Arnold saw the 'Iliad'
and 'Odyssey' as major monuments of culture, which it was impera-
tive to rescue from the whims of scholars and charlatans. 'Mr
Newman' became the butt of the lectures, and Arnold treated him
mercilessly. The translator managed a lengthy and sometimes
spirited reply; Arnold responded with the decisive 'Last Words'.
His increasingly lofty manner as a controversialist was exemplified
by his treatment of Wright, the other recent Homeric translator,
in the Preface to 'Essays in Criticism' three years later. Wright
had been upset by Arnold's pronouncement that there was not 'any
proper reason for his existence'. Arnold was unashamed of the
'vivacity' of his expression, retorting that 'One cannot be
always studying one's own works, and I was really under the
impression, till I saw Mr Wright's complaint, that I had spoken
of him with all respect.'

Whatever may be said of the unfortunate Wright, it would be
wrong to see Newman as merely a butt for Arnoldian slapstick.
For all its clumsiness, his use of archaisms had been an attempt
to recapture the strangeness of Homeric poetry and its remoteness
to modern ears. He thought Homer should be rendered in a language
analogous to Chaucerian English. But though Arnold rejected the
primitivist view of Homer, he believed as strongly as Newman that
translation ought to convey a conscious view of literary history.
The question was, which was the appropriate 'revival' style for
the 'Iliad' to be done in? Arnold opted for a translation in
hexameters (an idea as eccentric as any of Newman's), and the aura
of an established classic. The sensitivity of his argument should
not blind us to the nature of the Homeric specimens that he himself offers:

'Xanthus and Balius both, ye far-famed seed of Podarga!
See that ye bring your master home to the host of the Argives
In some other sort than your last, when the battle is ended;
And not leave him behind, a corpse on the plain, like
                                        Patroclus.'...
    So he spake, and drove with a cry his steeds into battle.

Arnold here has achieved the goal of 'rapidity', but he has done
it at the cost of some fussy and crowded diction and some flat-
footed syntax. Even to the Victorians, accustomed to oral reci-
tation, the bouncing hexameters would soon become wearily monoto-
nous. Newman complained that Arnold's translations would eliminate
any sense of singularity or surprise in the Homeric style; 'no
one could learn anything' from such a translation. (33) Perhaps
this was what Arnold intended. One does not get the impression
that translation was for him, as it would be for an Augustan or a
modern poet, in any sense a creative exercise. Despite the

shrillness with which Newman defends himself, he does manage to
suggest that Arnold viewed the 'Iliad' as a piece of official
literature.

The Homeric controversy was exemplary from another point of
view. Newman argues as a scientific scholar, pedantically
blinding the reader with his professorial command of facts.
Arnold's approach is a forensic one; where Newman repeatedly
demands proofs from his antagonist, Arnold uses every method
except scientific demonstration to produce a strong conviction
in the reader. The result is an object-lesson in at least one
branch of literary argument, the art of teaching the scholars a
lesson. Scholarship is exposed as a blunt, crude instrument,
where what is needed is the 'poise', 'tact' and fine discrimi-
nation of an exquisite sensibility. Criticism must display 'the
finest tact, the nicest moderation, the most free, flexible, and
elastic spirit imaginable', since the perceptions with which it
has to deal are 'the most volatile, elusive, and evanescent'.
In the Homer lectures we can see Arnold creating a reservoir of
critical vocabulary which almost every subsequent English critic
has dipped into. Here was a mode of discourse (indebted, as he
acknowledged, to his French master Sainte-Beuve) which seemed for
the first time to convey the distinctive - the 'adequate' -
expression of literary as opposed to scientific culture.

In sharp contrast to his earlier prose, the Homer lectures were
couched in a highly emphatic and informal style, well suited to
the Oxford lecture-hall and, by extension, to the public stage
which Arnold now aspired to occupy. While it is cultivated writing
in the traditional sense, the range of reference is there for
comparative purposes and not for elaboration merely. George
Saintsbury later paid tribute to the originality of the synoptic,
evaluative method of 'On Translating Homer'. (34) In addition,
Arnold combines an assertive and truculent laying-down of
principles with a sustained procedure of arguing by example. The
following is typical (he has just referred to Horace's 'bonus
dormitat Homerus'):

> Instead, however, of either discussing what Horace meant, or
> discussing Homer's garrulity as a general question, I prefer
> to bring to my mind some style which is garrulous, and to ask
> myself, to ask you, whether anything at all of the impression
> made by that style is ever made by the style of Homer. The
> mediaeval romancers, for instance, are garrulous; ...

Very brief examples usually suffice for him. 'Last Words', for
instance, contains a succinct page or two on Tennyson, which goes
far to remedy the absence from Arnold's work of any extended consideration of the Victorian poets. A few brief quotations serve
to relate Tennyson to the wayward fancifulness of the Elizabethans,
and to the themes of modern self-consciousness and the lack of
critical standards. Arnold's boldness, his essential literary
arrogance, lay in applying this glancing method to the statement
of critical principles and definitions. Most provocative of all
is his definition of the 'grand style'.

The grand style is Homer's style; it is the style of nobility.
Moreover, it is a style that in its very essence defies adequate
definition:

Nothing has raised more questioning among my critics than
these words, - 'noble', 'the grand style'. People complain
that I do not define these words sufficiently, that I do not
tell them enough about them. 'The grand style, - but what
is the grand style?' - they cry; some with an inclination to
believe in it, but puzzled; others mockingly and with
incredulity. Alas! the grand style is the last matter in
the world for verbal definition to deal with adequately. One
may say of it as is said of faith: 'One must feel it in order
to know what it is.' But, as of faith, so too one may say of
nobleness, of the grand style: 'Woe to those who know it
not!'

('Last Words')

'Arrogant'; 'evasive'; 'hypocritical'; there are any number of
ways of being provoked by this, and Arnold would like nothing better
than for us to rise to the bait, thereby suggesting that our real
place is among the crying, parrot-like masses. The terminology of
faith is very deliberate here; culture is a kind of faith, and
like faith, it has its pontiffs. But the peculiar weapon of the
man of culture, such a passage insists, is his charm. The possession of charm is a licence to the critic to throw the normal conventions of rational discourse out of the window.

Just what kind of licence Arnold is taking in these sentences
is not immediately clear. 'Nothing has raised more questioning
among my critics ...'; the implication of this is that the terms
'noble' and 'the grand style' are in some sense Arnold's own possession.
The quotation comes from 'Last Words', his reply to Newman, so
there was clearly some warrant for this. But the derivation of the
terms, both in Arnold's work and outside it, is complex. Arnold,
as has been said, uses 'nobility' to describe a social as well
as a literary manner. The term 'the grand style' plays a major
role in another essay he wrote in 1861 besides 'On Translating
Homer'. This is the preface to his study of 'The Popular Education
of France', later published separately in 'Mixed Essays' (1879).
Here he speaks of the 'grand style' as the chief cultural legacy
of the aristocracy which had been swept away by the French Revolution. A successful aristocratic class - such as those of Rome and
eighteenth-century England - was able to foster the 'grand style'
in the people over which it ruled. Arnold believed that some
other body must be found to perform this function in modern democratic society, if anarchy and 'Americanization' were to be
avoided; hence the rule of the aristocracy must be superseded by
the authority of the state. Arnold's evasiveness about the 'grand
style' in poetry, however congenial to the 'flexible and elastic'
literary sensibility, was directly linked to his somewhat mystical
use of the term in politics.

Arnold, then, does not use these words as an innocent critic of
poetry. The 'critics' to whom he is replying may be civil servants
or educationalists as well as students of Homer, and he nowhere
tells us for certain to what category of concepts, political,
ethical or poetical, the 'grand style' belongs. Had a reader of
the early 1860s been asked with whom he associated the two terms
under discussion, however, he would have been as likely to mention
Ruskin as Matthew Arnold. Arnold had read and admired Sir Joshua

Reynolds, but he had also read the third volume of 'Modern
Painters' (1856), which opens with a famous chapter on the
'Received Opinions touching the "Grand Style"'.   Ruskin takes
up Reynolds's description of Michelangelo as the 'Homer of
painting', and glosses this with the statement that 'Great Art
is like the writing of Homer'.   In the same chapter, he defines
poetry, with 'some embarrassment', as 'the suggestion, by the
imagination, of noble grounds for the noble emotions.'   Arnold
had originally dismissed Ruskin's remarks on Homer with some
asperity; (35)   how much greater must his embarrassment have been
when it became apparent that he could not do better in defining
the 'grand style' than to invent a woolly variation on the
Ruskinian formula.   Hence - after the diversion caused by his
assertion that definition is superfluous - we read that 'I think
it will be found that the grand style arises in poetry, when a
noble nature, poetically gifted, treats with simplicity or with
severity a serious subject.'   Perhaps the outrageous 'vivacity'
is simply an attempt to cover his tracks.

At least both Ruskin and Arnold were embarrassed by such definitions, which in themselves are as nugatory as Hazlitt's or
Shelley's definitions of poetry.   How, it might be asked, could
the idea of the 'grand style' be seriously intended as an analytical
tool?   The answer is that Arnold distinguishes between levels of
style by a systematic discussion of examples, and by a method of
elimination.   In particular he is at great pains to distinguish
the ballad manner, from Chapman to Newman and Scott, from the epic.
He is a master at exposing the jerkiness and bathos of the ballads,
as in Scott's

    Edmund is down, - my life is reft, -
    The Admiral alone is left.
But how to demonstrate its alternative?   Here he approaches the
core of the difficulty, and discovers an empirical solution to it:

    I may discuss what, in the abstract, constitutes the grand style;
    but that sort of general discussion never much helps our
    judgment of particular instances.   I may say that the presence
    or absence of the grand style can only be spiritually discerned;
    and this is true, but to plead this looks like evading the
    difficulty.   My best way is to take eminent specimens of the
    grand style, and to put them side by side with this of Scott.
The 'eminent specimens' are from Homer, Virgil, Dante and Milton
(not Shakespeare), and they are the direct forerunners of the
'touchstones' in The Study of Poetry (1880).   Arnold is like
Ruskin in insisting that artistic value inheres in particulars;
the two-to-four-line specimens of style are as simplified and
portable as Ruskin's sketches of Gothic windows or cornices, or
his 'true' and 'false' griffins. (36)   Where Arnold is original
is in his deliberate flouting of the conventions of rational
logic.   He is like a matador dazzling us with his graceful,
taunting passes before the bull of positivism.   His lethal weapon
is the precise particularity and not the blunt generalization.
Yet this is a spectator-sport with a dubious, emotive appeal.   The
qualities of the touchstones are declared to be self-evident,
and nothing is easier than to persuade the suggestible reader that
he sees what Arnold tells him, particularly when to do so is the

mark of sensibility and taste. Argument from touchstones is a
subtly didactic procedure, relying as much on the appeal to
cultural snobbery as to imaginative intuition. Arnold's intention is to subject literary value to a direct, empirical test,
and to highlight the inability of rationalistic method to cope
with poetry's delicate nuances. Yet neither the polemical
context of 'On Translating Homer', nor the idea of the 'grand
style' with its associations of vague sublimity, are well calculated to bring this out. The 'grand style' passages commemorate
fallen greatness, from Homer's warrior-heroes to the 'noble
simplicity' of Wordsworth's Michael. Are they talismanic symbols
of a vanished aristocracy, or simply specimens of a certain sort
of literary style? Arnold does not disavow the link between
poetry and social ideology, though he is anxious that it should
not be too overt. After 'On Translating Homer', however, his
campaigns as a social and as a strictly literary critic part
company enough to invite a degree of separate analysis.

> About the year 1629, seven or eight persons in Paris, fond of
> literature, formed themselves into a sort of little club to
> meet at one another's houses and discuss literary matters.
> Their meetings got talked of, and Cardinal Richelieu, then
> minister and all-powerful, heard of them. He himself had a
> noble passion for letters, and for all fine culture; he was
> interested by what he heard of the nascent society. Himself
> a man in the grand style, if ever man was, he had the insight
> to perceive what a potent instrument of the grand style was
> here to his hand.

So Arnold introduces his examination of The Literary Influence of
Academies in 'Essays in Criticism'. He saw the literary academy
as a 'potent instrument' to counterbalance the pluralistic (or,
as he put it, the anarchistic) effects of democracy. Arnold
utterly rejected a Johnsonian sturdy complacency towards the
individuality of the English. Where Richelieu had founded an actual
social institution, however, he was content to posit the mental
analogues of such institutions. The habit was a pervasive one,
but the major social institutions of the spirit in Arnold's
writings are 'criticism' and 'culture', as defined in 'Essays in
Criticism' and later in 'Culture and Anarchy' (1869).

The theme of the contrast between real and spiritual institutions is introduced in the Preface to 'Essays in Criticism'. On
the one hand are the 'Saturday Review' and the Woodford branch of
the Great Eastern Railway - bastions of the Philistine middle
class - and on the other hand Oxford, 'queen of romance', the
beautiful city 'so unravaged by the fierce intellectual life of
our century'. Arnold is playing to the gallery throughout the
Preface, but he is certainly in earnest when he disavows any
professorial authority in what he has written. He is not an
'office-bearer in a hierarchy' - an actual hierarchy, that is - but
a 'plain citizen of the republic of letters'. The two essays which
introduce the volume, The Function of Criticism at the Present
Time and The Literary Influence of Academies, are studies in the
constitution of the 'republic of letters'. Arnold's criticism of

the literary world has none of the abstractness of Wordsworth,
or the venom of Coleridge. He writes not as a romantic outsider
but as a periodical essayist, providing the expected combination
of hard-hitting topicality and the confident assertion of permanent standards. But (and it is one of the many paradoxes of the
two essays) his is at the same time a prophetic voice, unmasking
the shoddiness of the whole gamut of contemporary debate. Most
of what passes for criticism at the present time is false, he
asserts - but true critics are the unacknowledged legislators of
the national life. That these essays have remained classics is
a tribute to their clarity of purpose and to Arnold's eloquent
championship of the literary intelligence.

His starting-point in The Function of Criticism is where he
left off in the 1853 Preface - the education of the poet. This
is a cultural problem, rather than a psychological one as it was
for Mill. Arnold sees the poet as essentially a communicator of
ideas. The critic's job is to see that the best ideas are
available to him. This might seem a largely utilitarian task,
but Arnold's enthusiasm for it, together with his vagueness about
the creative power, implies that criticism is a good in itself.
'Literary criticism' for him is something close to Carlyle's
'Literature', the current of ideas in society as a whole. The
poet may either have a naturally flourishing culture to draw
upon, as Sophocles and Shakespeare had, or, like Goethe, he may
be an intellectual Titan able to reconstitute such a culture by
his individual efforts. Either way, the poet exists in a
distinct relation to the spirit of the age, but the critic forms
that spirit. When Arnold says, '1789 asked of a thing, Is it
rational? 1642 asked of a thing, Is it legal?', it is of the
critical activity that he is speaking. He does not bother to say
what relevance these questions had for poetry.

Arnold's reversal of the relations between poetry and intellectual life lies behind his comments on the romantic age.
Goethe, he insists, was alone in combining a creative with a
heroic critical effort; English romanticism, by contrast, was
a 'premature' outburst unsustained by the critical spirit. This
was his most influential formulation of a theme which can be
traced back to his early letters to Clough, which are full of
outbursts against the English romantics. Nevertheless, there
is a large element of romantic idealism in the quality Arnold names
as the quintessence of the critical spirit - disinterestedness.
It has often been pointed out that he himself was not disinterested. T.S. Eliot spoke of him as 'rather a propagandist for
criticism than a critic'. (37) Yet the full implications of this
have rarely been examined. If the critic is not disinterested,
what is the nature of the privileged, central status which Arnold
claims for him?

The aim of criticism is 'to see the object as in itself it
really is.' To do this, it must follow the rule of disinterestedness,

By keeping aloof from practice; by resolutely following the
law of its own nature, which is to be a free play of the mind
on all subjects which it touches; by steadily refusing to
lend itself to any of those ulterior, political, practical

considerations about ideas which plenty of people will be sure
to attach to them, which perhaps ought often to be attached to
them, which in this country at any rate are certain to be
attached to them quite sufficiently, but which criticism has
really nothing to do with. Its business is, as I have said,
simply to know the best that is known and thought in the
world, and by in its turn making this known, to create a
current of true and fresh ideas.

This, surely, is one of Arnold's pseudo-definitions; a mixture of
woolliness and polemic. The concept of disinterestedness represents him at his most suggestive and most elusive. As a
critical concept it has taken on an independent life, which goes
far beyond Arnold's specific usage. His own understanding of the
term emerges from the series of polemical passages which make up
The Function of Criticism. Pursuing a definition by opposites,
he cites the complacent chauvinism of Mr Roebuck and other
spokesmen of the middle class. His devastating response to these
is to quote the newspaper report about a child-murderer - 'Wragg
is in custody'. Arnold clearly feels some sympathy for Wragg (he
would hardly have been a school-inspector if he did not), but he
also invites Mr Roebuck to reflect on the grossness of her Anglo-
Saxon name. So nobody could accuse him of raising a case of
child-murder in order to get involved in the 'rush and roar of
practical life'. If disinterestedness partly means the ability
to take a whole and unblinkered view of society, it also refers to
an aloof, indirect and reflective mode of thought. The state of
being free from prejudice is more important to Arnold than any
humanitarian kindness toward Wragg herself.

    It is admirable that he raises the case of Wragg, but not that
he uses her to enforce an attitude of contempt for political
practice. He goes on to rebuke his predecessors in social
criticism, Cobbett, Carlyle and Ruskin, who failed to remain 'au-
dessus de la mêlée' in the Arnoldian manner. They are too
'blackened ... with the smoke of a lifelong conflict in the
field of political practice' to succeed in their aim of puncturing
British self-esteem. The praise of disinterestedness belongs not
to them but to Burke, who set intellectual truth above party and
was ready to follow the free play of the mind even when it under-
mined his own case. The quotation Arnold uses to show Burke in
this light is a highly untypical one, as he admits. But Burke's
concession that the French Revolution was a 'mighty current in
human affairs', to oppose which might come to appear 'perverse
and obstinate,' does indeed show a remarkable ability to see the
object as it really is. Arnold's perception of this is curiously
reminiscent of another great moment of nineteenth-century criticism: Engels's letter to Margaret Harkness (1888), in which he
speaks of the 'triumph of Realism' which compelled Balzac to
go beyond his own class sympathies and political prejudices in
his portrayal of France under the Restoration. (38) Burke
admittedly was a political writer, Balzac a novelist. But
perhaps a similar critical act is involved in pointing such
instances out. And what both Arnold and Engels possessed was
an 'interested' intelligence of a high order; something that
gave them the advantage, perhaps, over their disinterested

exhibits.   Balzac has long been enrolled in the cause of socialist realism - and Burke?   Part of Arnold's work is concerned with the acceptance of and adjustment to the new democratic age;   the other part with criticism of it.   Burke's denunciation of the French Revolution returns again and again to the evil of ideological politics - that is, of putting ideas into practice.   Arnold dissociates himself from the conservatism of Burke by calling him a product of an 'epoch of concentration', where the present time is an 'epoch of expansion'.   But he also was a counter-revolutionary. Culture, he believed, should refine the tone of the political establishment rather than attacking its substance as Cobbett, Carlyle and Ruskin had done.

Arnold often sounds supercilious toward the earlier Victorian sages.   It is as if he had to clear a space for himself, to wean the public from them in order to fulfil his own mission as a critic.   Though he could not surpass them in moral passion, he could do so in urbanity.   In The Function of Criticism he tries to subsume their message in his own - they are all enemies of the Philistines - and then claims that he alone has the tact needed to get this message across.   It is a bold, opportunist gesture, calculated to strike a chord with the more sophisticated part of the reading public.   But what he offers in place of the sages' bluntness can seem like a 'parliamentary language', a suave and decorous process of phrase-making:

> Where shall we find language innocent enough, how shall we make the spotless purity of our intentions evident enough, to enable us to say to the political Englishman that the British Constitution itself, which, seen from the practical side, looks such a magnificent organ of progress and virtue, seen from the speculative side, - with its compromises, its love of facts, its horror of theory, its studied avoidance of clear thoughts, - that, seen from this side, our august Constitution sometimes looks, - forgive me, shade of Lord Somers! - a colossal machine for the manufacture of Philistines?

Any explosion, evidently, is going to be as muffled as Arnold can make it.   The muffling is to be achieved by the critical virtues of 'flexibility' and 'tact', transposed into hesitations and modes of politeness.   The final phrase is not the thunderous bellow we should have had from Carlyle or Ruskin, but a little damp squib of 'vivacity'.

Later in the essay, Arnold returns to the attack on the liberal theologian, Bishop Colenso, which he had commenced in his essay The Bishop and the Philosopher (1863).   The earlier essay is notable for its statement of the centrality of criticism among the humanities.   The critic is not a specialist like the philosopher or theologian, but the 'appointed guardian' of general culture. It is he who is most fitted to assess the broad intellectual standing of specialist contributions.   Once again, this depends on the judgment of tone.   Colenso's demonstration of the literal falsity of certain Biblical passages might be true, Arnold wrote, but it was 'unedifying', lacking the 'unction' which might have conveyed reassurance to religious believers. (39)   This concern with cushioning religious faith against the impact of the dissolution of church dogmas was to become a major theme in Arnold's

work. In 'Literature and Dogma' (1873) and 'God and the Bible'
(1875), he set out to repair the damage wrought by scientific
theologians like Colenso by means of a 'literary-critical'
reading of the Bible, stressing imaginative rather than literal
truth. Whatever their value as theology, these books show Arnold
anxious at all costs to preserve the reconciling and cohesive
functions of faith.

They also remind us of the potency of criticism for him,
since one of its tasks was to redress the balance of Victorian
Christianity. The critic owes his authority, in Arnold's view, to
his command of tone. This is said to be the result of 'disinterestedness'. Now disinterestedness, as we have seen, may indeed be
demonstrated in the individual cases of a Balzac or a Burke. But
Arnold is suggesting that it should become the ethic of a social
group - the cultural élite. When disinterestedness becomes a
conscious, group ethic it must inevitably refer to some wider
'interest'. Arnold hardly makes this explicit; his strategy is
to evoke the notion of criticism as a pure activity informed by
romantic idealism. The underlying interest of the disinterested
critic is, however, quite clear from Arnold's other work. He
sees the critic as an intellectual civil servant, with a vested
interest in social cohesiveness. He works for cohesiveness by
confining fundamental antagonisms to the intellectual sphere and
by prescribing norms of polite discourse which presuppose a
mutually agreed social identity. Hence the justification that
Arnold offers for criticism is that, however tactfully and flexibly,
it represents the 'higher' interests of the state. Where those
interests conflict with the demands of rationality, Arnold
unhesitatingly chooses the interests of the state. This is the
message of the companion-piece to The Function of Criticism, The
Literary Influence of Academies, and also of the later 'Culture
and Anarchy'. Yet he remains conscious of being a lone voice,
the prophet of a minority, and his view of the state is far in
advance of the conventional Philistine one. At the end of The
Function of Criticism he contrasts the provinciality of English
thought and institutions with the 'great confederation' of which,
'for intellectual and spiritual purposes', Europe consists.
Through this vision of the critical mind we can attain to the
'promised land' of a new creative era. The final sentence, though
measured and urbane, shows Arnold deliberately taking his place
among the Victorian prophets:

   That promised land it will not be ours to enter, and we shall
   die in the wilderness: but to have desired to enter it, to
   have saluted it from afar, is already, perhaps, the best
   distinction among contemporaries; it will certainly be the
   best title to esteem with posterity.

In themselves, Arnold's attacks on English complacency, and
his slogans for the critical activity - 'a free play of the mind
on all subjects', 'a disinterested endeavour to learn and
propagate the best that is known and thought in the world' -
are unexceptionable. The problem arises from the social doctrines
which Arnold makes these phrases carry. Much of the underlying
rhetorical drama of 'Essays in Criticism' results from his
oscillation between the two poles of intellectual freedom and

constraint. One set of constraints that must be put on the free
play of the mind are what we call rationality. But in 'On
Translating Homer' we saw his rejection of conventional rationality
in favour of an alternative approach. In The Literary Influence
of Academies, he turns away from the exploratory deployment of
critical method towards a view of criticism as submission to
established authority.

Arnold is not proposing the formation of an English academy;
it is the model or idea of the function of an academy in the
republic of letters that counts. The Academy, he says after
Renan, 'represents a kind of "maître en fait de bon ton" - the
authority of a recognized master in matters of tone and taste.'
No doubt this is so, though many would deny that the presence of
an academy favours the critical spirit - that it fosters 'an open
and clear mind', or 'a quick and flexible intelligence'. But
Arnold's belief is that criticism flourishes most freely where
there are recognized social and intellectual standards - a 'bon
ton' that must not be offended against. In a libertarian,
anarchic culture like that of England, it languishes.

This, then, is an essay on the differences between the French
and the English. It shows Arnold at his finest and most vivacious
as the gadfly of the English intelligentsia. The crotchetiness
of vigorous English prose and the brutality of Victorian critical
invective are tellingly juxtaposed with examples of French clarity
and finesse. Shakespeare and the English poetic tradition are
made to seem liabilities rather than assets. An abundance of
individual genius, Arnold implies, is a poor complement to a
deficiency in intelligence; it is not enough to blunder hap-
hazardly into greatness. Within its own terms, Arnold's essay is
a triumphant demonstration of how an 'estranged' view of English
culture can shake the familiar picture, and shock us out of our
provinciality. Yet the issue of the Academy itself and its
supposed influence is clearly something of a red herring. The
sociological proposition contained in the title of the essay is
completely circular ('French culture is subjected to the discipline
of the Academy, therefore it is more disciplined'), and Arnold
gives no hint that there might be representatives of the French
spirit who consider the Academy a controversial, or an irrelevant
institution. Arnold's own view of contemporary French literature
has found few defenders, from his day to ours, though the
vivacity of this particular essay can still blind readers to the
essential stuffiness and - yes - provinciality of the picture he
gives. For example, his point about the virtues of literary
consolidation and the foundation of a tradition could have been
made perfectly by reference to the line of major novelists in
nineteenth-century France. But Arnold wrote essays on a series
of dismally minor contemporaries: Joubert, Amiel, the de Guérins
and (the nearest he came to celebrating a great contemporary
French writer) George Sand. Seven years after 'Madame Bovary',
he endorsed the ineffable Joubert's condemnation of realist
works, declaring that 'they have no place in literature, and
those who produce them are not really men of letters' (40) - a
pronouncement of academic anathema par excellence. His taste, as
far as France was concerned, was entirely dictated by a small

group of poets and critics around Sainte-Beuve and the 'Revue
des Deux Mondes', and his essays are inspired by the wish to
pass on the work of this group to the English. (41)   Thus Arnold
might be held not to have promoted but to have actually delayed
the reception of the best nineteenth-century French literature in
England. Although Swinburne had written on Baudelaire in 1862,
the major achievements of French realism and symbolism were not
a serious influence until the 1880s.

     If Arnold's view of France is untrustworthy, he does suggest
how a writer's very style and tone betrays deference to, or
independence of, a centralized cultural authority. There is only
the mildest admission in The Literary Influence of Academies that
such an authority might not be wholly desirable: 'There is also
another side to the whole question, - as to the limiting and
prejudicial operation which academies may have; but this side
of the question it rather behoves the French, not us, to study.'
One may, of course, find confirmation in this that the whole
essay is a tactical exercise, and even perhaps an example of
devil's advocacy. Certainly the dialectic of authority and the
free play of the mind is maintained throughout the 'Essays in
Criticism'. Arnold is at his most impressive as a champion of
freedom in his essay on Heinrich Heine. The battle-lines drawn
up here would have been recognized by any nineteenth-century
radical liberal. On the one side are the French Revolution,
Goethe, Shelley, Byron and the 'liberation' of the modern spirit;
on the other side are 'accredited dogmas', 'routine thinking' and
the 'Philistinism', Heine's 'ächtbrittische Beschränktheit', of
the British middle classes. Perhaps the real point for Arnold
lay in his depreciation of the English romantic achievement,
which is here at its most outspoken. Despite Shelley and Byron,
he writes, the English poets of the revolutionary era were
inward- or backward-looking; Scott became the 'historiographer
royal of feudalism', Wordsworth retired into a spiritual monastery
and Coleridge 'took to opium'. (He does not allow them the
excuse that he allowed Burke, of living in an 'epoch of concentration'.) English poetry is outside the 'master-current' of
the nineteenth century because, like the German mystics championed
by Carlyle, it has failed to keep abreast of modern ideas.
Arnold here was fulfilling the unfulfilled promise of On the
Modern Element in Literature, in language which at times echoes
the earlier essay. In depicting Heine, the Jewish successor of
Goethe, as a 'soldier in the war of liberation of humanity',
joining the forces of Hebraism and Hellenism in battle against
middle-class Philistinism, he had at last specified the nature of
the 'modern spirit', and traced its embodiment in the work of a
major, if flawed, contemporary poet.

     The Arnoldian pendulum, however, swung only briefly toward
'liberation'. After 'Essays in Criticism', he turned to still
more popular modes of communication. 'Friendship's Garland'
(1871), a series of newspaper columns, was a knockabout farce
in which his message to British Philistia was put in the mouth
of the German Baron Arminius von Thunder-Ten-Tronckh. Having
tried the roles of cultural critic and cultural ambassador,
Arnold then put himself forward in 'Culture and Anarchy' as its

lay preacher. The book has a playful resemblance to a sermon
in its repetition of key phrases, in its overt appeal to faith at
certain points and its expansion of a text from Bishop Wilson -
'To make reason and the will of God prevail!' Culture has
substantially taken the place of the will of God in this essay,
but Arnold is as coy about defining Culture as most Victorian
churchmen were about the deity. Like his ecclesiastical contemporaries, too, Arnold immediately found himself under attack from
a stubborn rationalist, Frederic Harrison, whose Culture: A
Dialogue (1867) set out to ridicule the blithely unphilosophical
approach of his opening chapter. Arnold was delighted at this
confirmation of the success of the role he was playing, and it
may even have led him on to the further extravagancies of, for
example, the class-analysis in Chapter Three. (Harrison, for
his part, consoled himself in later years with the idea that
Arnold's gospel of culture was only a restatement of the doctrines
of his own master, Comte. (42))
     The dazzling surface of parts of 'Culture and Anarchy' does
not disguise its seriousness of purpose. Like The Literary
Influence of Academies, it is an examination of the nature of
social authority. Arnold begins by summoning up the spirit of
the Academy, defining its purpose as to bring into the 'main
current' all the vital elements in the national life. He
develops a crucial analogy here between a cultural establishment -
whatever form it might take - and the Established Church. Both
institutions ought to serve the Hegelian concept of social
'totality', which is one of the key terms of the book. The
Established Church, however, is weakened by the political indifference revealed in the debate over Irish Church Disestablishment,
and, more fundamentally, by the strength of Nonconformity.
Arnold exposes the puffed-up provinciality of the Nonconformists
so relentlessly that the book might well have been named
'Culture and Bigotry'. (43) His underlying case is that
Puritanism, the religion of the middle classes, has never been
openly absorbed into the national life, so that British culture,
which should be unified, is distorted by sectarian conflict.
The existence of sects whose values and customs challenge the
dominant culture is thus a violation of the principle of totality.
But there is one crucial exception to this general rule that
Arnold makes - that of Culture with a capital C. No sooner has
he finished denouncing the Nonconformists for preserving their own
separate identity, than he extols the role of the intellectual as
a conscious alien standing outside the three classes of
Barbarians, Philistines and Populace. The difference is that
where the Puritan tradition stands for 'Doing As One Likes',
intellectuals, in Arnold's view, are the apostles of 'right
reason' and hence of a centralized spiritual authority. He then
suggests that this authority may be identified with the interests
of the state.
     In 'Culture and Anarchy' the political analogy underlying the
'Essays in Criticism' is brought out into the open. The result is
clearly explosive, since some of his statements now seem authoritarian and reactionary. On the other hand, it may be argued that
he is attacking 'laissez-faire' and that his support of the state

interest is simply prophetic of the commonplace assumptions of twentieth-century social democracy. The vast majority of intellectuals have, after all, followed Arnold in becoming 'public servants' within the education sector, and in accepting a corporate morality, even though many would prefer to trace this back to figures such as Huxley, Tawney or Beatrice Webb. It would, however, be whitewashing Arnold to accept him as a social democrat 'tout court', and even Lionel Trilling, his most sympathetic modern interpreter, who discusses this whole problem very fully, speaks of the 'reactionary possibilities of Arnold's vagueness'. (44) The important question, in my view, is whether and to what extent he abandons his own ideals of Hellenism - defined in 'Culture and Anarchy' as 'spontaneity of consciousness' - and the free play of the mind.

Arnold distinguishes between a realm of pure speculation and a realm of applied or cultural thought, and he invariably suggests that what is to be said in the latter realm should be governed by tactical considerations, by what he calls 'flexibility':

> For the days of Israel are innumerable; and in its blame of Hebraising too, and in its praise of Hellenising, culture must not fail to keep its flexibility, and to give to its judgments that passing and provisional character which we have seen it impose on its preferences and rejections of machinery. Now, and for us, it is a time to Hellenise, and to praise knowing; for we have Hebraised too much, and have overvalued doing. ('Preface')

Following the dictates of 'flexibility' is sharply distinguished from 'Doing As One Likes', since 'flexibility' acknowledges a principle of authority outside the self. This principle lies in the objective needs of Culture. But Arnold is never concerned to admit that there could be deep and fundamental disagreement as to what those needs are. He writes of Culture as if it were a tangible institution invested with actual, not with merely hypothetical power; thus Culture for him is a 'religious' tenet. And he himself, of course, is the prophet of Culture, speaking with its inspired voice. Here it might be said that Arnold, who had failed in his career as a romantic poet, had discovered his own source of romantic power.

What did Arnold mean by the injunction to 'Hellenise' in 1869? The concept is deliberately vague and can refer to anything from compulsory state education to the cultivation of art for art's sake. In part the book is a response to Disraeli's Reform Act, and it may imply that the teaching of the working classes is more important than whether they are given the vote. Arnold's own background and profession are important here. He constantly addresses himself to the middle classes, but does not feel himself to be one of them. The son of Arnold of Rugby - a school for the sons of the aristocracy - he saw himself as a public servant, obliged to work for his living but separated by origin and ethos from the commercial bourgeoisie. His idea of loyalty to the state was first advanced in educational writings such as Democracy and 'A French Eton' (1864). Between these essays and 'Culture and Anarchy' there intervened the extension of the suffrage and the renewed stirrings of the working class. The

Reformist demonstration of 1867, London's largest mass-meeting
since 1848, had a violent effect upon Arnold, as also upon some
Hyde Park railings. The first edition of 'Culture and Anarchy'
carried a quotation from Thomas Arnold which was applied to these
events:

> As for rioting, the old Roman way of dealing with that is
> always the right one; flog the rank and file, and fling the
> ringleaders from the Tarpeian rock. (45)

Social change, he argues in all editions, must never be allowed
to disturb 'that profound sense of settled order and security,
without which a society like ours cannot live and grow at all'.
The servility of this is quite different from his earlier 'statist'
arguments, and it makes the claim that the men of culture are the
'true apostles of equality' ring somewhat hollow. The tactical
reading of 'Culture and Anarchy' that Arnold invites might conclude
that for the sake of urging the principle of state control, he
had accepted the conventional, establishment notion of law and
order. His assertions about loyalty in the book are suspiciously
'Hebraistic'.

Culture teaches us to follow the authority of right reason,
but to whom can that authority be entrusted? Arnold poses this
question with an air of gleefully stepping into the lion's den:

> And here I think I see my enemies waiting for me with a
> hungry joy in their eyes. But I shall elude them.

The answer, given at the end of a long cat-and-mouse game with
his enemies, is that right reason is to be found in the idea of
the state. The argument seems a deliberate reply to Mill's
'On Liberty'. (45) Mill had located ultimate authority in the
self, subject to certain constraints; Arnold rejects individualism
and class politics as merely selfish ideals, and puts his faith
in the state without any constraint. He distinguishes between
the 'ordinary self', self-interested and class-bound, and the
altruistic and reasonable 'best self' which culture develops in
us. By our best self, we are 'united, impersonal, at harmony'.
But whereas Mill's 'self' had the sanction of a whole philosophical and cultural tradition, Arnold's 'best self' is no more
than a chimera. We may ask how we are to know if it is the
'best' or the 'worst' (because most timid and self-interested)
self which supports particular law-and-order policies? Arnold
replies that our best self 'enjoins us to encourage and uphold
the occupants of the executive power, whoever they may be, in
firmly prohibiting' political demonstrations. Moreover, the
'best self', being independent of class-interest, does so with
a 'free conscience'. Thus a free conscience would submit to the
authorities 'whoever they may be'! What evidence is there in
Arnold's own writing of a 'best self' restraining his vivacity,
and preventing him from 'writing as he likes'? The question takes
us back to the 1853 Preface and the dropping of 'Empedocles';
the 'best self', it would seem, is a deliberately constructed
public identity, an antidote to the 'genuine self' of the
poetry. Yet Arnold's social writings tend towards uncontrolled
rhetoric, not towards restraint. Though 'Culture and Anarchy'
has its roots in Arnold's whole social experience, it does not
offer a satisfactory or even a consistent cultural ethic.

'The end and aim of all literature,' Arnold wrote in his essay on Joubert, is 'a criticism of life.' 'Culture and Anarchy' shows the conservative leanings of Arnold's own criticism of life, and its indications are confirmed, up to a point, by his strictly literary essays. The 'criticism of life' formula does not stress the variousness and conflict of values in literature so much as its adherence to a standard of right reason. Arnold's belief in authoritative and normative standards extends to the content as well as the social role of culture. Ephemeral and 'anarchic' elements must be stamped out in literature, as in society. (47) When speaking 'ex officio' for literary culture, Arnold tends to present it as a staid, established institution, even as a mausoleum.

An example in which many of the paradoxes of his work are con- tained is his essay Literature and Science in 'Discourses in America' (1889). This was a reply to T.H. Huxley's Birmingham lecture on Science and Culture (1880). Huxley had named Arnold as 'our chief apostle of culture' and had accepted his doctrine as to the end and aim of literature, adding, however, that science was as essential as literature to a criticism of life. This has been regarded as the opening shot in the 'Two Cultures' debate. Certainly both Huxley and Arnold are distinguished by the compla- cency with which they speak of their respective disciplines. Arnold could not 'really think that humane letters are in much actual danger of being thrust out from their leading place in education'; in any case, only the humanities could relate the results of science to the broader aspects of life, which he defined as 'the sense in us for conduct' and 'the sense in us for beauty'. How would the humanities achieve this? Partly, Arnold implies, by a critical scrutiny of the weaknesses of the scientific approach; but beyond this, he could only evoke their effect with some weary protestations of faith:

we shall find, as a matter of experience, if we know the best
that has been thought and uttered in the world, we shall find
that the art and poetry and eloquence of men who lived,
perhaps, long ago, who had the most limited natural knowledge,
who had the most erroneous conceptions about many important
matters, we shall find that this art, and poetry, and eloquence,
have in fact not only the power of refreshing and delighting
us, they have also the power, - such is the strength and worth,
in essentials, of their authors' criticism of life, - they
have a fortifying, and elevating, and quickening, and suggestive power, capable of wonderfully helping us to relate the
results of modern science to our need for conduct, our need
for beauty.

The archaic shift from 'the humanities' to 'art and poetry and eloquence' helps to underline that Arnold is not claiming some- thing for the contemporary intelligence, but for men who lived long ago (he goes on to cite Homer). He specifically denies that modern poets and moralists should relate the results of modern scientific research to life. Their lot, presumably, is to go on repeating the wisdom of antiquity. This is desperately inadequate. A large number of Victorian thinkers were concerned with relating the results of modern science to life; one thinks

not only of Huxley but of Ruskin, Tennyson, Pater, Hardy and
Leslie Stephen. It may be, since he is so vague, that Arnold
intended only to deplore the work of rigid social scientists
such as Herbert Spencer. But his description of the 'fortifying,
and elevating, and quickening, and suggestive power' of literature is merely obscurantist. Naturally he appeals to the inert
authority of the tradition rather than to its living representatives. It is hard to distinguish between what he says about
literature in relation to science, and what a devout believer
might be expected to say about religion.

Literature and Science, then, is a feeble reply to Huxley. But
perhaps it is fair to see it less in these terms than as an
expression of the changing interests of Arnold's later criticism.
The idea that poetry is taking the place of religion is present
in the famous opening passage of The Study of POetry (1880):
'More and more mankind will discover that we have to turn to
poetry to interpret life for us, to console us, to sustain us.'
Arnold in his later years ceased to stress the intellectual function
of literary criticism, and dwelt instead upon the creative and
therapeutic power of poetry. He saw criticism more as a mode of
creative writing than as an indispensable prelude to it. The
second volume of 'Essays in Criticism' (1888), with its stress on
the individual genius of the English poets, is in some ways
directly opposed to its predecessor and to the intervening
cultural polemics. But we are not dealing with a simple 'volte-
face', since these late essays direct attention to some permanent
aspects of Arnold's sensibility.

In a sense, he was returning to his own career as a poet and
to its bases in the romantic movement. Heine was the only poet
treated at length in the first 'Essays in Criticism', but the
second volume discusses English poetry systematically. Arnold
even introduces some new items of critical apparatus, such as
the distinction between the 'real', the 'historic' and the
'personal' estimates of poetry. This should serve as a reminder
that critical objectivity did not come easily to him; the
'historic estimate' seems to prompt his hostility to the English
romantics, and the 'personal estimate' accounts for his over-
praising such minor French writers as the de Guérins and Amiel.
Indeed, the unevenness of some of his critical essays may be
accounted for by the tension between his instinctive responses
and his striving towards an ideal of objective judgment, appealing
to semi-official and authoritative values, which he only rarely
convincingly attains.

The essays on Falkland, Amiel, George Sand and the de Guérins
are portraits of writers for whom Arnold has a personal affection.
These essays are a mixture of biography, lavish quotation, and
brief and extravagant critical comparisons, striking a somewhat
elegiac note. The name of Maurice de Guérin, he writes, is
'beginning to be well known to all lovers of literature', and
his talent has 'more distinction and power' than that of Keats.
He and his sister belong 'to the circle of spirits marked by this
rare quality' of distinction, a quality which 'at last inexorably
corrects the world's blunders, and fixes the world's ideals'. No
earlier critic had translated romantic idealism into quite this

language of culture-snobbery. Yet the writings of the de Guérins
are slender in the extreme, and their story has a conventional
romantic pathos. Maurice de Guérin, like Empedocles and like
Sénancour's Obermann (who served as the subject of two of Arnold's
poems) was a spiritual exile haunted by depression and passive
suffering whose only solace is his intense feeling for nature.
This feeling, 'an extraordinary delicacy of organization and
susceptibility to impressions' from nature, is said to be one of
the perennial sources of poetry; de Guérin has it, though more
in his prose journals than his poems. Arnold calls such respon-
siveness to nature 'natural magic', in contrast to the other
source of poetry, 'moral profundity'. The distinction may owe
something to Mill's essay on The Two Kinds of Poetry, but where
Mill's example of the pure poet was Shelley, Arnold finds
'natural magic' more characteristic of Wordsworth and Keats. In
the form in which we shall discover it in the later series of
'Essays in Criticism', the dichotomy of natural magic and moral
profundity took the place of his earlier, more academic and
classicizing distinction of style and 'architectonicè'. There
is much fine perception of English romantic poetry in 'Maurice de
Guérin', as well as in the later essays. Natural magic, as
must always have been obvious to admirers of 'Empedocles', was
something close to Arnold's heart.

     Where in most respects 'Maurice de Guérin' shows Arnold duti-
fully following Sainte-Beuve, the essays on Milton, Goethe, and
Amiel are indebted to another of the 'Revue des Deux Mondes'
circle, Edmond Scherer. In the Milton essay, Arnold turns to
France for an objective view of a poet whom the English are unable
to see disinterestedly. He accuses Johnson of narrow-mindedness,
Macaulay of rhetoric and Addison of neoclassical conventionality.
This part of the essay is vintage Arnold (he detects in Macaulay
'the inconsistency of a born rhetorician'), but his own efforts
as a critic of Milton are less satisfactory. The passages from
Scherer that he quotes are outspoken about the deficiencies of
the plan of 'Paradise Lost' and of the poet's Puritan temper.
But if 'Paradise Lost' fails in 'architectonicè' it remains an
exemplar of the Arnoldian grand style. His concluding remarks on
Milton's style are bland generalizations which do not resolve the
ambiguities of his attitude. He plays one of the ranking-games
of which, in his later years, he became increasingly fond.
Wordsworth is pilloried for a single line:

     And at the 'Hoop' alighted, famous inn,

and Thomson, Cowper, Shakespeare himself, are denied the mastery
of 'perfect sureness of hand':

     Alone of English poets, alone in English art, Milton has it;
     he is our great artist in style, our one first-rate master in
     the grand style. He is as truly a master in this style as the
     great Greeks are, or Virgil, or Dante. The number of such
     masters is so limited that a man acquires a world-rank in
     poetry and art, instead of a mere local rank, by being counted
     among them.

Scherer had described 'Paradise Lost' as 'a false poem, a grotesque
poem, a tiresome poem'. Perhaps Arnold did not give himself
space to fully elaborate his own attitude; or maybe he was

concealing a Johnsonian boredom. But it is doubtful if his praise
of Milton as Grand Stylist would win back many readers who took
the 'French Critic' to heart.

A far less calculated comment on Milton comes in one of the
lectures 'On the Study of Celtic Literature' (1867). Here Satan
in 'Paradise Lost' is used to illustrate the passionate, Titanic
melancholy of the 'Celtic fibre' in the English genius. Arnold
was greatly attracted to Celtic melancholy and natural magic,
and his rehabilitation of 'Ossian' and its influence pointed the
way for the Celtic twilight of the late nineteenth century. In
discussing Celtic literature, however, Arnold once again felt
the need to bring his subject before the European tribunal. He
chose to discuss the contribution of the Celtic poets to European
literature in specifically racial terms, analysing literature as
the expression of a national spirit which is determined more by
heredity than by strictly literary influences. Thus English
literature stemmed from the mingling of the Teutonic, Norman and
Celtic strains. The Celts possessed sensibility and intuitive
tact, the Mediterranean races excelled in style and 'architectonicè', while Philistinism came from the Saxons. The racial
mythology here parallels that of the nineteenth-century nationalistic historians and is Arnold's most direct endorsement of
imperialist ideology. His tone is at times frankly chauvinistic,
in contrast to his usual internationalism. The reader is left
with the impression that the study of Celtic literature has an
ultimately political purpose. The scattered remnants of the
Celts belong within the 'English Empire' and should be given a
recognized status in British culture. Arnold's concern with
defining an intelligent imperial policy was manifested in a whole
series of commentaries on Irish affairs, including his 'Irish
Essays' (1882). Yet there is an odd mixture of scholarly
enthusiasm and political opportunism in a literary-critical essay
which ends by calling for the foundation of a Chair of Celtic
at Oxford, on the grounds that it would be a 'message of peace to
Ireland'.

Arnold's strictly literary criticism up to the mid-1870s gives
the sense of an impasse. He was committed to authoritative,
academic judgments of literature by European standards which
would make no concessions to the insularity and local prejudice
of the English. He was committed also to the ideal of classical
decorum at the expense of romantic expressiveness; 'Merope' was
preferable to 'Empedocles'. Yet it is his arguments for disinterestedness, the academy and the grand style which hold our
attention, and hardly ever his 'disinterested' and 'academic'
literary judgments themselves. He seems to have adopted the
views and methods of classicism, of cultural nationalism and of
the Sainte-Beuvian study of individual temperament without ever
finding his métier, except in his lectures on Homer. In fact,
without the essays collected in the second 'Essays in Criticism',
Arnold might now be remembered in literary criticism solely as
a polemicist for cultural standards. But his criticism took on
new life with the essays on Wordsworth (1879) and The Study of
Poetry (1880).

As with Johnson's 'Lives of the Poets', the immediate cause was

a commission, involving him in the preparation of an anthology of
English poetry. This was the Macmillan 'Golden Treasury' series
of 'The English Poets', edited by T.H. Ward. Arnold edited Byron
and Wordsworth, wrote introductions to selections from Gray and
Keats, and published The Study of Poetry as the general introduction to the series. For the first time he was writing for
posterity, or at least for the instruction of the young, and not
to satisfy the topical formula of the intellectual reviews.

The Study of Poetry begins with the statement that 'the future
of poetry is immense.' Arnold is at once setting poetry in the
centre of the intellectual world, and stressing its individual
and therapeutic power, as something that can 'console' and
'sustain' the reader for whom religious dogmas have failed. He
then invokes Wordsworth as the prophet of the centrality of
poetry, something that he had only previously done in verse.
Poetry, and not criticism, is now his panacea for the dilemmas of
modernism and the crisis of faith. The high destiny of poetry,
however, necessitates high standards. Poetry is at once a
'consolation and stay' and a 'criticism of life under the conditions fixed for such a criticism by the laws of poetic truth
and poetic beauty'. But these laws are not scientifically
ascertainable, and nor in this essay does Arnold suggest that
they can be laid down by an academy. They must be the personal
discovery of every reader. Arnold continues to see literary
criticism as a process of ranking the poets against one another,
but stresses that the comparative process must be applied inter-
nally, in the reader's mind. The procedure that he suggests is
that of the 'touchstones', foreshadowed, as we have seen, by
the specimens of the grand style in 'On Translating Homer'.
Arnold's specimens in The Study of Poetry ('Short passages, even
single lines, will serve our turn quite sufficiently', he says)
are from Homer, Dante, Shakespeare and Milton:

> If we are thoroughly penetrated by their power, we shall find
> that we have acquired a sense enabling us, whatever poetry
> may be laid before us, to feel the degree in which a high
> poetical quality is present or wanting there. Critics give
> themselves great labour to draw out what in the abstract
> constitutes the characters of a high quality of poetry. It
> is much better simply to have recourse to concrete examples; -
> to take specimens of poetry of the high, the very highest
> quality, and to say: The characters of a high quality of
> poetry are what is expressed there. They are far better recog-
> nized by being felt in the verse of the master, than by being
> perused in the prose of the critic.

This is a classic statement, with none of the truculence of his
earlier refusal to define the grand style. Arnold now emphasizes
the tact with which the touchstones must be used, and not the
crassness of those unable to apply them. There is a new note of
humility in the procedure he recommends, as well as a concrete
empiricism which has been echoed by a large proportion of
twentieth-century evaluative critics.

Nevertheless, this has been and remains a highly controversial
passage. Partly this is because of the nature of the proffered
touchstones themselves, taken as they are from the 'grand style'

poets plus Shakespeare. Arnold's name for what they have in
common is 'high seriousness'; this is a development of his earlier,
largely unexplored concept of moral profundity, and signifies his
abandonment of the classical categories of style and 'architectonicè'. Lionel Trilling points out that his examples express not
seriousness in the broad sense, but solemnity and even a specifically Arnoldian melancholy. (48) Also, as brief passages torn out
of context, they can only assume knowledge of the whole poem from
which they are derived if they are to be effective. All this
is to say that we need to use Arnold's own method with exceptional
tact, but given that tact, I think it can be defended. Though
the comparative method is the staple of criticism, this is one
of the rare attempts to define an empirical procedure for such
comparisons, in order that they should combine the necessary
breadth of vision with sharpness of focus. And it might be seen
as a positive gain that the touchstones are reflections of
Arnold's personal taste, and not of the official values of the
grand style or the European academy. He emphasizes that the
touchstones must be 'lodged ... well in our minds', and that he
'could wish every student of poetry to make the application of
them for himself'. All that one might wish to add would be
that the choice would be made for himself as well. Be that as
it may, Arnold's method acknowledges the combination of conscious
decision and intuitive response in criticism, and is a far truer
account of the process of evaluation than the eighteenth-century
ideal of the Man of Taste who must have read everything before he
can judge of anything. The danger, which he is certainly prone
to, is to make 'high poetical quality' a fetish independent of
authentic personal response. Here the criterion of 'high
seriousness' is undoubtedly limiting; many of the absurdities
produced by I.A. Richards's experiment in practical criticism,
for example, were caused by the students' unnatural susceptibility
to high-minded cliché. Yet Arnold gave notably flexible examples
of its use in his praise of the 'Shakespearean' quality of Keats,
the natural magic of Wordsworth and the poetic personality of
Byron.

In the second half of The Study of Poetry, he applies the touchstone method to a review of English poetry from Chaucer to Burns.
The classic status of Milton and Shakespeare is taken for granted,
so that the main discussion centres on Chaucer and the poets of
the eighteenth century. Arnold's dismissal of Dryden and Pope as
'classics of our prose' is notorious and somewhat casuistical,
but the true test-cases are Chaucer and Burns. Chaucer's
historical importance, he argues, is to have founded the tradition
of 'liquid diction' and 'fluid movement' in English poetry; a
tradition which Arnold had previously overlooked in his search
for the grand and elevated style. Chaucer, however, and later
Burns, are found wanting in the earnestness and depth of feeling
which inform Arnold's touchstones. Perhaps this is unsatisfying,
but most readers would agree that the two poets are below the
rank of the very greatest, whether or not we choose to label
their deficiency one of 'high seriousness'. Arnold's argument
is a genuinely critical one, provocative in its discriminations
and explicit in its use of evidence; and it is a demonstration

of method, not an 'ex cathedra' pronouncement, being intended
'to put any one who likes in a way of applying it for himself'
in the anthology which follows.

'Essays in Criticism: Second Series' consists of the introductions to the Golden Treasury volumes together with a
ceremonial address on Milton, a review of Dowden's 'Life of
Shelley' and essays on Tolstoy and Amiel. The Tolstoy essay is
an important, pioneering work in which 'Anna Karenina' is sharply
contrasted with 'Madame Bovary'. Apart from this, however, it
is the Golden Treasury essays which form a strong and distinctive
group. They show Arnold arriving at his mature assessment of the
romantic poets, and particularly of Wordsworth, who becomes the
yardstick for the others. Arnold's criticism here is essentially
judicial, being not a matter of close or brilliant insights but of
sober, general evaluation of the relative standing of the poets
with whom he deals. These essays come out of his long process of
personal reckoning, but they also stand forth as examples of a
genre looking back to the 'Lives of the Poets'. Arnold's
biographical comments ('Keats's love-letter is the love-letter of
a surgeon's apprentice') are perhaps consciously Johnsonian.
There is usually a gap between his evaluations of life and work,
as if he is refusing the romantic obligation to look into the
nature of creativeness itself. His comment in the Byron essay
that 'The ideal nature for the poet and artist is that of the
finely touched and finely gifted man, the ευφνης of the Greeks'
is singularly unilluminating.

The finest essay in the group, that on Wordsworth, is the
least biographical. It contains both a restatement of the theme of
the academy, and a further movement away from neoclassical principles. For while in The Study of Poetry he effectively adopted
the criterion of moral profundity, in 'Wordsworth' he at last
makes his peace with natural magic. The essay has been criticized by A.C. Bradley and, more recently, by Harold Bloom for its
stress on the nature-poet in Wordsworth at the expense of the
Miltonic visionary. (49) Arnold, indeed, says that Wordsworth
'has no assured poetic style of his own like Milton'; his
truest and most characteristic expression is to be found not in
his ponderous blank verse but in lines of unstudied simplicity,
such as the most elemental of all 'touchstone' lines:
And never lifted up a single stone.
As for his philosophical and visionary aspect, Arnold's Golden
Treasury selections reveal how little he felt that either
Wordsworth's or Byron's greatness depended on the long poem.
In the 'Wordsworth', the only passages from 'The Prelude' are
those which Wordsworth himself published independently. The
fragment of 'The Recluse' is one of the very few specimens of
the poet's Miltonic manner. And in his 'Byron', Arnold is still
more ruthless, restricting even his extract from the 'Vision of
Judgment' to a few stanzas. So much for 'architectonicè'.

The essay on Wordsworth begins with a history of the poet's
reputation, and a restatement of the Goethean ideal of the
spiritual confederation of Europe. Shakespeare and Milton have
been admitted to the European academy, but how will Wordsworth
find a place there? Arnold's argument is that Wordsworth is a

major classic, for reasons quite independent of the canons of
construction and style. His greatness is not a question of
philosophical eminence; here Arnold attacks the 'Wordsworthians',
and especially Leslie Stephen, who credit him with a 'scientific
system of thought' displayed to advantage in the 'Immortality
Ode' and 'The Excursion'. Wordsworth's greatness can only be
realized when a mass of verbiage is cut away, above all the work
done before and after the great decade of 1798-1808. This greatness, however, is a moral greatness, providing that a wide sense
is given to the term 'moral' (this is another of Arnold's contributions to critical terminology). For it lies simply in his
sense of natural magic, or the joy that sensibility to nature
brings into life. 'Joy', unprecedentedly for Arnold, is a key-
word of the essay, and the central statement is here:

> Wordsworth's poetry is great because of the extraordinary
> power with which Wordsworth feels the joy offered to us in the
> simple primary affections and duties; and because of the
> extraordinary power with which, in case after case, he shows
> us this joy, and renders it so as to make us share it.

After this we cannot be surprised when Arnold finally drops the
mask of disinterestedness, and avows that 'I am a Wordsworthian
myself'. The real and the personal estimate are at one.

Though it is a triumph, it should not be forgotten that
Arnold's exaltation of Wordsworth still depends on playing the
ranking-game, dismissing scores of rival poets ('Let us take
Klopstock, Lessing, Schiller, Uhland, Rückert, and Heine for
Germany; Filicaia, Alfieri, Manzoni, and Leopardi for Italy;
...'), many of them because they are quantitatively inferior;
it is 'in his ampler body of powerful work' that Wordsworth scores.
In reading Arnold we never for long lose the sense of literary
criticism as an endless round of European diplomacy, in which
the tactics of the Quai d'Orsai are singled out for particular
admiration and suspicion. Arnold takes up an internationalist
position - few critics are on balance less chauvinist than he -
yet he does so in order to preside over competing great powers
and to assess the export potential of their cultural products.
In its awareness of race and nationality as a primary fact about
literature, Arnold's is criticism for the age of imperialism.
It is also criticism which constantly looks to a supra-national,
judicial authority:

> The world is forwarded by having its attention fixed on the
> best things; and here is a tribunal, free from all suspicion
> of national and provincial partiality, putting a stamp on the
> best things, and recommending them for general honour and
> acceptance ('Wordsworth').

The 'tribunal', however, is an institution of the spirit only.
Arnold sees literature, for the most part, as an institution; he
often seems to deny the value of creativity for its own sake, and
he abhors anarchy in all its forms. His attempt to fuse the
notions of criticism as the free play of the mind and as an
impartial tribunal surveying the literary empire displays a Roman
as well as a Hellenistic spirit. Yet it would be quite wrong to
confuse him with the bland neoclassicism of a figure such as
Hume. The urgency and bite of his best writing are generated by

frustration and self-doubt, and among his many guises is that of Arminius, the German whose namesake led a revolt against the Roman Empire. The forces of Philistinism have displaced Arnold's empire of literary values from its rightful hegemony over the real, political empire. His object is to reinstate literary culture by assuring his readers that the essential balance of cultural power has not changed. Where such an assurance can be given, it is largely an achievement of tone; an achievement, in fact, of 'religious' assertion which uses the weapons of rationality to affirm a conviction which can neither be falsified nor proved.

Arnold, then, is a critical propagandist. In many ways he appears as one of Carlyle's Men of Letters, an embattled victim of his age who is forever groping towards prophetic detachment and a spiritual vision. He is a failed great writer, like Carlyle's heroes, but unlike them in that his failure brought him popularity, a captive audience and a series of roles to perform on a public stage. No doubt this is what nourished his tendency to pontificate and dictate. But he was alone among the Victorian prophets in the forcefulness of his advocacy of literature and the critical spirit. The choice made him a seminal figure, and provides the explanation of his 'modernity'; professional literary critics from Saintsbury to F.R. Leavis have striven to disentangle the element of 'true criticism' in his prolix and varied work. When we con- sider his prestige as a forerunner of modern English studies, it might be supposed that his main act of 'true criticism' was his discovery and propagation of the idea of the critical spirit as an institution of unrivalled virtue and power. Yet only the devotees of state control of the arts or of the mystique of the critical expert ought to accept the idea of a 'tribunal'. Criticism in its public aspect may be seen as a parliament perhaps - or a party conference - or even, without T.S. Eliot's distaste, as a 'Sunday park of contending orators'. (50) (Why not?) It is an ongoing process, and one in which real authority is frequently, but never finally, the property of individuals and small groups whose judgments and perceptions command the critical attention we give to an 'author'. In this sense Arnold's own 'tribunal', where it is persuasive, is only a mask for the self. Moreover, the desire to give his judgments institutional weight was only one side of the Arnoldian dialectic. The doctrine of the academy seems to leave little room for the creative sensibility in criticism; its sphere is reduced to that of providing 'flexibility' and 'tact'. The rhetorical brilliance of so much of his writing clearly goes beyond that, but it is only in the late essays, with their mellow empiricism, that the role of personal response in criticism is really acknowledged. (Even here, of course, Arnold warns against a merely personal estimate.) It might be said that the result, as in his selections of Wordsworth and Byron, was to bring him closer to conventional Victorian taste. Such a 'rapprochement' was necessary because Arnold's roots, like those of the taste of his period, lay among the English romantics. In the late criticism these buried roots receive a little water. The social apparatus of criticism is combined with a romantic naturalism which allows him to distinguish the 'characters of a high quality of poetry'

with unprecedented directness. The result is a personal vindication, even if it is not quite the canonical achievement which has
sometimes been claimed.

3   THE LATER NINETEENTH CENTURY

Matthew Arnold bore the brunt of propagandizing for literary
culture in the Victorian age. He saw literature as embodying the
spiritual life of modern society and taking over the edifying and
consoling functions of religion. Whether or not his contemporaries
agreed with this, he expressed for them the idea of literature
as an institution seeking to elevate their society and to legitimize
it at the spiritual level; through literature a people could
become vicarious participants in a power and perfection absent
from their everyday lives. Literature and criticism might be the
central source of spiritual authority, as Arnold himself maintained,
or merely one such source; but his writings did much to reclaim
for them the dignity and social respect whose loss had been lamented
by poets and critics since Wordsworth. How deeply was his influence
felt? The actual social effect of a writer like Arnold is almost
impossible to determine. Perhaps all that we can say is that he
wrote with a new urgency, that he found his audience and his impact
was widely acknowledged. His writings decisively named the enemy -
middle-class Philistinism - but were aimed to uncover latent dis-
affection with it as well as preaching to the already converted.
A fellow-critic like Leslie Stephen might wonder ruefully whether
he was not one of the 'Philistines', but the majority of
Arnold's readers must have found the label an apt one for their
neighbours rather than themselves. The gospel of culture made a
subtle appeal to the emotions of self-esteem, desire for self-
improvement, and snobbery.
   There were other, quite unconnected factors working to give
the 'republic of letters' a semblance of reality: the growth of
the Press, the rise of the novel (for so long cold-shouldered by
criticism) and its public, and the spread of literacy and elementary education. Before the development of television and radio
it must indeed have seemed that literature, and not just literacy,
was becoming the staple of mass communication. Of more lasting
relevance to criticism, however, was the growth of education.
Arnold became a school inspector, and in a later age he would
probably have become far more deeply engrossed in educational
reform. His emphasis on literary awareness as a 'pursuit of
perfection' adds the moral concern that is missing from Mill's,
Newman's and Huxley's more purely intellectualist views of the
curriculum. And Arnold's view of culture as part of the apparatus
of the state coincided with the first of the Education Acts which
asserted governmental control and responsibility over the schools.
Since the teaching of linguistic skills was the most essential
task of elementary education, this necessitated a supply of
English teachers who were trained by the colleges and, increasingly, by the universities. The emergence of university English
studies must be traced back to the 1820s and to the debate between
the utilitarians and their opponents; the first Chairs of English

were founded at University College, London in 1828, and at King's
College, its Anglican rival, in 1835. The majority of the civic
universities were founded in the last quarter of the nineteenth
century, and included English literature on the syllabus from the
beginning. By the end of the century, English was being taught
at the four Scottish universities and at Oxford, London, Birmingham, Leeds, Liverpool, Manchester, Newcastle, Nottingham and
Sheffield.

The late nineteenth century, unlike the early Victorian period,
has often been seen as an age of criticism. Partly this was due
to the growing educational demand for reprints, editions,
scholarly surveys, school text-books and school prizes. The
English Men of Letters and other series piled up, and the high
level of criticism continued in the intellectual reviews, the
finest practitioners being Leslie Stephen and Henry James. But
the most conspicuous new source of critical writing was the
aesthetic movement, from Swinburne and Pater through to Symons
and Yeats. The aesthetes, as much as the professors and the
reviewers, were the beneficiaries of Arnold's work and the
inhabitants of the area of culture that he had defined. At the
same time, all three groups look back past Arnold toward the
bookish and world-renouncing attitudes of the later romantics
such as Hazlitt and Lamb. The aesthetes in particular tended to
deny that culture had any edifying or instructive function for
the middle class. Culture was not for society's sake, but a mode
of enriching the self.

Walter Pater is the major intellectual representative of English
aestheticism, and the most closely connected to Arnold. T.S. Eliot,
in his essay on Arnold and Pater, spoke of the 'direction from
Arnold, through Pater, to the "nineties"'. The two had earlier
been less flatteringly linked by W.H. Mallock in his country-house
dialogue, 'The New Republic' (1877). Here Mr Luke (Arnold) and
Mr Rose (Pater) are somewhat reluctant allies as spokesmen for
culture against Huxley, Spencer, Jowett, Ruskin and other contemporary figures. The names indicate the difference between them;
Mr Luke is more Hebraic, and - in aesthetic matters - lukewarm.
Mallock credits Pater with all the languor and exoticism of the
aesthete, which Arnold conspicuously lacks. Public suspicions
about the morality of aestheticism had been aroused by the poet
Robert Buchanan's attack on the 'Fleshly School' of Rossetti and
Swinburne in the 'Contemporary Review' in 1871. Mr Rose, though
outwardly a gentleman, has a way of making the ladies feel as if
they had no clothes on, and he is last seen bargaining with his
host over a pornographic volume of the 'Cultes secrets des
Dames Romaines'. This caricature goes some way to explain why
Pater felt it necessary to delete the Conclusion from the second
edition of 'The Renaissance' in 1877, though it seems very far
from the real Pater, with his military moustache (one of his
pupils was General Haig) and his withdrawn and fastidious life
in Brasenose.

Pater, indeed, could more fairly be seen as the apotheosis of
the 'disinterested' critic; though his sort of disinterestedness
undeniably leads to narcissism. He is a much more subtle and
fastidious writer than Arnold, but his subtleties tend to seem

calculated and self-protective. His debt to his predecessor may
be judged from the Preface to 'The Renaissance' (1873). He
begins by stating the uselessness of abstract definitions,
endorsing Arnold's view of the aim of criticism as being 'to see
the object as in itself it really is'. But he adds that 'in
aesthetic criticism the first step towards seeing one's object
as it really is, is to know one's impression as it really is.'
It is not clear whether this is a refinement or a travesty of
Arnold's position; what it does, however, is to separate the
critical act itself from all the considerations of cultural
responsibility on which he had insisted. These considerations are
not necessarily denied; they are merely indefinitely postponed.
Pater's concern is with the subjective impression or effect
produced on the critic himself. His terminology, however, is
scientific; he speaks not of 'concern' but of 'primary data', and
adds that the critic must isolate the particular virtue of a work
of art and note it 'as a chemist notes some natural element'. At
moments we might be listening to I.A. Richards. But the critic
as Pater sees him is not only a chemist but a connoisseur, the
possessor of a 'certain kind of temperament' which enables him to
realize the virtues of 'the picture, the landscape, the
engaging personality in life or in a book' as he would of a herb,
a wine or a gem. Here we meet the idea, so fundamental in
aesthetic criticism, of the work of art as a luxury product,
demanding prolonged and leisurely tasting. In the mass of
Wordsworth's poetry, for instance, the critic has to discover 'the
action of his unique, incommunicable faculty, that strange,
mystical sense of a life in natural things'; in other words, his
natural magic. To do so, Pater writes, is to distinguish the
'virtue' in a body of poetry; the scientific imagery of the
Preface culminates in a metaphor taken (like Arnold's 'touchstone') from alchemy. 'The Renaissance', however, is a series of
historical studies, based on the Arnoldian themes of Hellenism
and modernity. The famous Conclusion states the dilemma of the
modern, 'relative' spirit, giving it a far more abstract and
philosophical formulation than Arnold had done. Pater's answer to
relativism is that you must 'give nothing but the highest quality
to your moments as they pass, and simply for those moments' sake'.
And the 'moments' he celebrates are moments in the art or thought
of Europe, from the middle ages to the time of Goethe, when the
Greek spirit was most amply recaptured and reinterpreted. His
purpose is not to draw didactic parallels with Victorian culture
in the Arnoldian manner. Instead, his interest centres on the
creative act of interpretation itself both in the artist and the
reader or spectator.
   Pater discussed the nature of artistic creation in his fine
early essay on Coleridge's Writings (1866; a much abridged
version was later included in 'Appreciations'). He sees Coleridge
as a metaphysical system-builder, struggling forlornly to give a
fixed account of the laws of art in the face of the sceptical and
relativistic attitude of modern scientific thought. Art, according
to Pater, emerges from a gradual, intellectual process, and not
from any single, all-embracing act of imagination. His account
of the artist at work is intended to challenge the 'blind' and

'mechanical' picture that Coleridge had given of the secondary
imagination:

> Here there is no blind ferment of lifeless elements to realize
> a type. By exquisite analysis the artist attains clearness of
> idea, then, by many stages of refining, clearness of expression.
> He moves slowly over his work, calculating the tenderest tone,
> and restraining the subtlest curve, never letting his hand or
> fancy move at large, gradually refining flaccid spaces to the
> higher degree of expressiveness. Culture, at least, values even
> in transcendent works of art the power of the understanding in
> them, their logical process of construction, the spectacle of
> supreme intellectual dexterity which they afford. (51)

We might say that Pater is no longer afraid to acknowledge the
'work' involved in artistic creation, because that work is so
specialized that none could confuse it with ordinary social processes of labour. It is the latter which are mechanical; the
artist's technique is clearly a craft, and as a result of
industrialism the handicrafts themselves have come to seem
distinguished and unusual, the repositories of a lost mode of
consciousness. There is a parallel between Pater's attitude and
that of his contemporaries who spoke of the 'Arts and Crafts'.
Moreover, Pater's language is calculated to suggest the particular
crafts of sculptor and painter, whose practice, he implies, is
at once intensely physical and intensely intellectual. As so
often, he is deepening the mystique of poetic creation by subtle
analogies with the visual arts and with science.

Pater goes on to distinguish between the artist's sensibility,
and his mode of expression - 'what may be called the talent of
projection, of throwing these happy moments into an external
concrete form - a statue, or play, or picture'. Projection, he
says, is 'of all shades of completeness', according to the
author's individual circumstances and those of his age; and
'when it is perfectly transparent, the work is classical'. The
critic's job is not to produce systematic theories of art but to
make an empirical classification of actual works in terms of the
sensibility expressed and the degree of projection. It is quite
startling how many of Eliot's main ideas are anticipated here:
the 'objective correlative', the relation between sensibility and
expression and the 'intellect at the tip of the senses'. Passages
like these in Pater's work invite us to consider him not as the
languid Mr Rose but as the first of the moderns.

Further analogies between writing and the visual arts are found
in his essays on The School of Giorgione, where he compares the
effect of lyrical poetry to that of music, and on Style where he
compares the creation of prose to architecture. Whether it is
a harmony or a logical structure that the writer produces, such
analogies inevitably suggest that his task is one of working in a
material rather than of working on a meaning. Pater's prose as
a whole notoriously possesses the air of being rather than meaning.
The explicit material is language; and not least among his
contributions to literary criticism is his contribution to its
vocabulary. (Much of this vocabulary was declared extinct by
the earlier twentieth century, but it is notable how recent
critics have again succumbed to the charms of 'comely', 'exquisite',

'contingent'.) Beneath the material of language, however, is the
material of personality. Most critics of Pater have noticed
that the critical essay in his hands becomes a mode of self-
portrayal. He himself provided an indirect commentary on this
when he discussed the dialectical method ('this continuous
discourse with one's self') in 'Plato and Platonism' (1893).
When the air of solipsistic intensity is lacking, his writing
becomes slack and belle-lettristic. Several of the essays in
'Appreciations' (1889) do nothing to redeem their conventionally
bookish choice of subject; Shakespeare, Wordsworth, Lamb and
Sir Thomas Browne all induce much the same level of pious
reverence.

   It is true that Pater distinguishes between mere style, that
in which writing resembles music or painting or architecture,
and 'great art'. Great art, he says in the final paragraph of
the essay on 'Style', depends upon subject-matter; he might
almost have defined it as a criticism of life. But perhaps his
most influential criticism was that which insists on the ideal
harmony of content and form. This harmony could be achieved in
prose and in drama, but it was most characteristically found in
lyrical poetry where there was 'a certain suppression or vagueness of mere subject, so that the meaning reached us through ways
not distinctly traceable by the understanding.' This prescription,
from the essay on Giorgione in 'The Renaissance', is backed up
by the account that Pater gives of the historical sequence of the
arts in his essay on Winckelmann. The progress of art, he argues,
is toward increasing complexity and individuality of expression;
hence architecture, the first of the arts, was succeeded by
sculpture, and later by painting, poetry and music. The idea that
painting, poetry and music are more adequate vehicles of modern
expression is close to Hazlitt:

   painting, music, and poetry, with their endless power of
   complexity, are the special arts of the romantic and modern
   ages. Into these, with the utmost attenuation of detail, may
   be translated every delicacy of thought and feeling, inci-
   dental to a consciousness brooding with delight over itself.
   Through their gradations of shade, their exquisite intervals,
   they project in an external form that which is most inward in
   humour, passion, sentiment.

Does the difference lie in an increased narcissism? In a tone
that is self-congratulatory rather than merely wistful? Certainly
there is a touch of Mr Rose in this, as there is when Pater
speaks of du Bellay as the poet of a 'refined and comely
decadence'. (52) Like every major critic after Hazlitt, Pater
had to struggle with the problem of classical and romantic.
Perhaps he did not intend the formula for 'musical' poetry in
The School of Giorgione to be construed, together with other
features of 'The Renaissance', as an aesthete's charter for a
poetry of private associations or 'pure' and meaningless sounds.
There are various signs that he came to regret the anti-
intellectualism of this essay. 'Marius the Epicurean' (1885)
is the story of its hero's growing realization that the luxuriant
religion of art must be absorbed in a wider and more mature
philosophy. In 'Plato and Platonism', the poetic language of

Wordsworth and Tennyson is praised for its philosophical power,
and Pater names the essay, the vehicle of sceptical rationalism,
as the characteristic modern literary form. The solipsism of
this last point is particularly striking, given his own unique
combination of prose-poetry and rational dialectic. But there is
a single theme underlying Pater's enthusiasms for lyrical poetry
in 'The Renaissance', for a vaguely Christian humanism in
'Marius' and for the dialectical method in 'Plato and Platonism'.
Each is a plausible mode of response to the modern, 'relative'
predicament. (53)

Pater's first definition of modernity comes in his review of
Poems by William Morris (1868). He is defending the escapist
impulses of Morris's poetry. Modern empirical philosophy, Pater
argues, leads us to an all-embracing sense of relativism and flux
(this argument later became the Conclusion to 'The Renaissance').
The necessary response to a world in transition is to cultivate
the passing moment, burning with a hard, gem-like flame. This
is the justification of the poetry of the earthly paradise, which
turns away from contemporary experience toward a beauty which
embodies the real fulfilment of our needs. Pater takes Morris
as the acme of the 'aesthetic' poet, describing his achievement
both as a decadence and a thirst for the exotic:

> Greek poetry, mediaeval or modern poetry, projects above the
> realities of its time a world in which the forms of things
> are transfigured. Of that world this new poetry takes
> possession, and sublimates beyond it another still fainter and
> more spectral, which is literally an artificial or 'earthly
> paradise'. It is a finer ideal, extracted from what in relation
> to any actual world is already an ideal. Like some strange
> second flowering after date, it renews on a more delicate
> type the poetry of a past age, but must not be confounded with
> it. The secret of the enjoyment of it is that inversion of
> home-sickness known to some, that incurable thirst for the
> sense of escape, which no actual form of life satisfies, no
> poetry even, if it be merely simple and spontaneous. (54)

This is a statement about historicism in poetry: Morris, as the
author of 'Guenevere' and 'Jason', has captured the essence of
Greek and medieval poetry, producing a sublimation of a sublimation. It is also, it seems to me, a statement about nostalgia,
despite the disavowal in the phrase 'inversion of home-sickness'.
The earthly paradise glimpsed beyond and through an earlier
period of history is another Eden - though an artificial, poetic
one. The process that Pater discovers in Morris does much to
illuminate his own intentions in 'The Renaissance'.

'Renaissance' itself means for Pater not so much a rebirth as
a successive recapturing of the Greek spirit. Thus the nostalgia
for Greece is his subject, and this gives to his view of the
historical Renaissance a plangent and unfulfilled cast. The
grandeur, sensual satisfaction and cruelty of Renaissance life
and art are wholly absent from his book. The process of turning
away from contemporary life to the Greek ideal, which is Pater's
theme, in fact confesses the modernity of the Renaissance. Pater
himself is, like Morris, producing a sublimation of a sublimation; he is nostalgically grasping the nostalgia of the

Renaissance at a higher degree of consciousness. He was in close
contact with the Oxford Hegelians, and his book embodies a deeply
Hegelian view of the relation of history and the intellect. (55)
It is the boldness of this embodiment which is Pater's originality as critic and cultural historian. The tradition that he
surveys is both internal and external, subjective and objective.
It is internal in the sense of being a sequence of spiritual
epiphanies, of engaging personalities and exquisite works of art
chosen idiosyncratically by a critic who was so little committed
to the necessity of their historical existence that he could
follow up 'The Renaissance' with the 'Imaginary Portraits', which
are fictional vignettes on precisely the same themes. (56) But
Pater's tradition has an external existence, both symbolic and
real. The symbolic existence is present, above all, in the
passage on La Gioconda. Pater's impression of Mona Lisa is
certainly fanciful, but given the enigmatic quality of the work
itself, it does not seem an ill-judged or inappropriate fancy.
His description has simply added itself to the complex of meanings
which Leonardo's picture today possesses. But this passage also
testifies more directly to the reality of the cultural tradition
which Pater is surveying. His theme is the modernity of Mona
Lisa, a modernity which in her is unconscious and 'but as the
sound of lyres and flutes':

> The fancy of a perpetual life, sweeping together ten thousand
> experiences, is an old one; and modern philosophy has con-
> ceived the idea of humanity as wrought upon by, and summing
> up in itself, all modes of thought and life. Certainly Lady
> Lisa might stand as the embodiment of the old fancy, the symbol
> of the modern idea.

Whether or not we can credit Mona Lisa's knowledge of the whole
of history, such knowledge is presupposed by the relativism and
universalism of modern culture. We can and do respond to 'art'
from all times and places, ranging it in a 'Musée Imaginaire'.
Pater is one of the earliest writers to celebrate this phenomenon,
(57) which is fundamental in twentieth-century aesthetics and may
even be seen as the essence of 'modernity' as it relates specifically to the arts. In twentieth-century criticism there is a
crucial division (say that between I.A. Richards and F.R. Leavis)
between those who accept a total relativism among modes and
styles of art, and those who erect a standard of values derived
from a specific, and limited, tradition. It is in keeping with
his dialectical evasiveness that Pater's sanction can be found
for either point of view. If in the Gioconda passage he is the
spokesman of relativism, in the essay on Winckelmann he defines
the European tradition in terms which, because they are more
specific than Arnold's, again look forward to Eliot. What he
says here of the standard of taste and its derivation in classical
Greece is not precisely new. But 'The Renaissance' gives to the
tradition of 'conscious Hellenism' a peculiar stress on the
element of consciousness, and this is taken up by the image of
a series of beacons passing on the light:

> There is thus an element of change in art; criticism must
> never for a moment forget that 'the artist is the child of
> his time.' But besides these conditions of time and place,

and independent of them, there is also an element of permanence,
a standard of taste, which genius confesses. This standard is
maintained in a purely intellectual tradition. It acts upon
the artist, not as one of the influences of his own age, but
through those artistic products of the previous generation
which first excited, while they directed into a particular
channel, his sense of beauty. The supreme artistic products
of succeeding generations thus form a series of elevated
points, taking each from each the reflexion of a strange light,
the source of which is not in the atmosphere around and above
them, but in a stage of society remote from ours. The standard
of taste, then, was fixed in Greece, at a definite historical
period.

Pater's purpose is to suggest how a society can support a
tradition of art which is autonomous; above it, beyond it and
irradiating it. He does so in tones combining romantic idealism
with classical serenity. But the tradition defined here, it ought
to be remembered, is not so much a fixed 'standard of taste' as
the idiosyncratic sequence of artists commemorated in Pater's
book. It is the individual critic rather than a remote 'stage of
society' who is the source of the 'strange light'.

   The Preface to 'The Renaissance' puts forward the ideal of a
'unity of spirit' occurring only in certain fortunate periods of
culture. Such unity is composed of individual thinkers and artists
coming together. Whatever the ambiguities of his notion of
culture, Pater never came near to the outlook of Pugin, Ruskin
and William Morris. History for him was the setting from which
individuals emerged, and the tradition, seen as a 'series of
elevated points', had a metaphorical rather than a real existence.
For Morris, tradition was the literal process of handing-down,
mediated through the systems of apprenticeship in the various arts
and crafts; modern high art was necessarily sundered from this.
But Pater's approach to cultural history is one that barely distinguishes between the results of the Renaissance studio-system, and
the spiritual elective affinities that brought Winckelmann to Rome
or Goethe to Winckelmann. The sense of deepening nostalgia obscures
any perception of real discontinuity. Pater was never more himself than in his serene acceptance - which was thereby also a
deflection - of the burden of 'modernity'. 'The Renaissance' is
among the most buoyant, as well as the most scintillating, works
of nineteenth-century criticism.

   Swinburne, beside Pater, is aestheticism vulgarized. His
output as a critic was enormous. Some of it was undoubtedly
influential in its time, and his work on the Jacobean dramatists
also made its mark on Eliot. Swinburne's early essays complement
his poetry; the 'fleshly school of poetry', as Buchanan called it,
goes with the romantic school of criticism. Later on, he produced
a series of critical books as part of his rather frantic bid for
social and academic respectability; the best known is his 'Study
of Shakespeare' (1879). But none of these do anything to justify
his recent editor's contention that 'Swinburne belongs among the
great critics'. (58) The most notable aspect of the early criticism up to 'Essays and Studies' (1875) is the style, yet this is
not charismatic, like Pater's, but merely ostentatious. Swinburne

makes deliberate use of ornate metaphor to insist on the unity
of the literary work with the other arts and with the natural
world. 'Appreciation' thus consists in building up the thickest
set of analogies for the work that the critic can muster. Such
a critical language quickly runs to cliché. Among Swinburne's
specialities are 'painterly' terms ('brilliance of point and
sharpness of stroke', 'delicacy and affluence of colour') and
musical terms ('weighty and sonorous harmony'). Another constant
resource in his work is sea-imagery. Shakespeare, predictably
enough, is oceanic in his inexhaustibility and profundity, but
Swinburne is also reminded of the sea by the rhythms of 'Don
Juan' and of Blake's 'Songs of Experience', while to enter the
Prophetic Books is to 'take a blind header into the midst of the
whirling foam and rolling weed of this sea of words.' (59) In
the midst of such whirling metalanguage it is not surprising that
Swinburne cannot define anything properly. Beside his attempts
to explain Arnold's 'clearness' as a poet, for example, Arnold's
own definition of the grand style appears a model of precision:

> I have used this word already more than once or twice; it
> comes nearest of all I can find to the thing I desire to
> express; that natural light of mind, that power of reception
> and reflection of things and thoughts, which I most admire in
> so much of Mr Arnold's work. I mean by it much more than mere
> facility or transparency; more than brilliance, more than
> ease or excellence of style. It is a quality begotten by
> instinct upon culture; one which all artists of equal rank
> possess in equal measure. (60)

In the last sentence he is relying on the reader's snobbishness or
sheepishness to give him a hearing; it is meaningless but is
meant to sound impressive. The tendency of his impressionism is
to suggest that art is at once the product of ineffable skills,
and a cherishable, luxury possession. Rossetti's 'Blessed Damozel'
is a 'mystic rose', 'a pure first sunrise', 'a thing too dear and
fair for promise or price'. (61) This is no longer something which
compensates us for worldly poverty and drudgery, as it would have
been for Hazlitt and Keats; it is the refined luxury of the
aesthete who shares the wealth of the bourgeoisie, has probably
been to Oxford and lives on a private income. With Swinburne,
commodity-fetishism, as Christopher Caudwell and others would
later define it, makes its most tangible entry into criticism.

It would be unfair to judge his review of Matthew Arnold's
New Poems solely by its more dandified aspects, however. Swinburne
uses the device of a fictitious 'French critic' to say the sharp
and abrasive things about Arnold which he doesn't wish to say in
his own person. Nonetheless, he does permit himself a telling
assault on Arnold's view of France. The idea that you can take
the Academy and the 'Revue des Deux Mondes' at their own valuation,
Swinburne asserts, is 'nothing short of pathetic'. He was the
only one of Arnold's contemporaries who had earned the right to
say this. Unhappily, Swinburne's invective became increasingly
violent as he grew older, and it was rarely employed as accurately
as it was here. He seems to have taken his poetic achievement as
a licence to set up as a one-man academy, handing down judgments
far more bluntly and pompously than Arnold himself had done. The

literary league-table became Swinburne's obsession. Of the
Jacobeans, for example, we learn that Marston is to Webster as
Webster is to Shakespeare, while Tourneur stands halfway between
Marston and Webster, but is no closer to Webster than Webster is
to Shakespeare. (62) It is all very prep-schoolish.

The essay from which this is taken, 'John Webster' (1886),
contains a typically paranoid attack on critics who accuse Webster
of horror-mongering. Swinburne delights in the cruelties of
Iago, Flamineo, Bosola and their like, and anyone who objects to
the sadism of these characters comes in for a good critical
caning. He accomplished some important revaluations, such as
his championship of Blake, Dickens and Emily Brontë; he also
persistently overrates second-rank writers such as Herrick and
Lamb. But the way in which he goes about it is almost uniformly
offensive. Once he had discarded the raptures of aestheticism,
Swinburne settled for a neurotic literary pomposity. 'The very
greatest poets' ... 'Webster's crowning masterpiece' ... 'his
other and wellnigh co-equally consummate poem' .... 'Here again,
and finally and supremely here, the purifying and exalting power
of Webster's noble and magnanimous imagination is gloriously
unmistakable by all and any who have eyes to read and hearts to
recognise.' (63) So the phrases roll off - in this case, all
within the same brief paragraph. The 'Study of Shakespeare' has
pages of turgid and muscle-bound rhetoric like this. Swinburne's
pretence to authority as a critic, in fact, is usually the worst
kind of imposture. As for his relation to earlier nineteenth-
century criticism, his own sense of this is summed up in his
final 'consecration' ('The time is wellnigh come ...') of his
book on Shakespeare to the memory of the 'three who have written
of Shakespeare as never man wrote, nor ever man may write again':
Coleridge, Landor and Lamb. The three, after all the flummery,
are named in the same breath, but for Swinburne himself, as is
seen in his dedication of 'The Age of Shakespeare' (1908), the
greatest of the three was Lamb.

Swinburne, then, began as an idolater of romantic genius and
ended as the Ancient Pistol of Victorian bookmanship. If there
was a school of aesthetic criticism, it took on new life at the
end of the 1890s in the work of Symons and Yeats, which will be
discussed below. In the meantime, the dialectics of aesthetic
criticism were converted into neatly turned paradoxes by Oscar
Wilde in his dialogue The Critic as Artist (1891). This is a
manifesto for a catholic, hedonistic attitude of seeking for
beauty 'in every age and in each school', 'ever curious of new
sensations and fresh points of view'. (64) Such a critic will
avoid the narrow-mindedness which Wilde attributes to creative
genius, but is likely to become a trend-hound defenceless against
the unending changes of fashion. Wilde's blithe assertions that
it is the manner not the matter which counts in aesthetic criticism are quite close to the mark, however:

Who cares whether Mr Ruskin's views on Turner are sound or
   not? .... Who, again, cares whether Mr Pater has put into the
   portrait of Monna Lisa something that Leonardo never dreamed of?
The logical outcome of this was realized by Yeats, when he chopped
up Pater's passage on the Mona Lisa and put it at the beginning of

the 'Oxford Book of Modern Verse' (1936). But perhaps the result
was no more than a companion-piece to Rossetti's 'Sonnets for
Pictures', which date from the foundation of the Pre-Raphaelite
Brotherhood in 1848, and look back in turn to Keats.   Throughout
the romantic tradition, in fact, we can find examples of criticism
taking possession of works of art and exploiting them as objective symbolizations of the mysterious something in the critic's
own soul. When Wilde pointed out the limited scope of creation
in his own day, declaring that 'it is to criticism that the future
belongs', (65) he was indicating the process of literature feeding
on itself that is fundamental to aestheticism. Despite their
stress on the esoteric and non-intellectual nature of poetry,
the aesthetes' religion of art in fact committed them to criticism
as never before. Critical impressionism was their basic mode of
experience. It is often surprising how literary this was; how
Pater, for instance, shows his visual artists as individual personalities seeking self-expression rather than craftsmen working in a
common discipline, and to what extent he puts them in the verbal
context provided by thought like that of Pico and poetry like that
of Michelangelo and du Bellay. It is this literary cherishing of
experience that links 'The Renaissance' to the conventional
belle-lettrism of 'Appreciations', and even to the frenetic
academicism of late Swinburne. The aesthetes continued to pursue
the duality initiated by the early romantics, of criticism as
public discourse and private daydream.

In 'The Renaissance', Pater presents the neoclassical tradition of
rediscovery of the 'ancients', and especially of Greek civilization, in an explicitly romantic light. In 'Appreciations', he
even gives qualified approval to Stendhal's opinion that all good
art was romantic in its day. (66) Thus he continued the process
of assimilation of the achievements and doctrines of the romantic
movement into the literary tradition, which had preoccupied
Arnold, Carlyle and Mill. This labour of incorporation went on
into the late nineteenth century, but alongside it there was a
consolidation of work on Augustan literature, culminating in the
criticism of Leslie Stephen and the scholarship of Saintsbury
and Birkbeck Hill. With the rise of English studies, criticism
and scholarship were becoming a professional routine, and no
century could expect to remain uncovered; but there were other
reasons for the rehabilitation of the eighteenth century. It was
the period which the conservative bookman found most congenial.
Nearly half of the volumes in the original English Men of Letters
series were devoted to Augustan authors. This movement, typified
by the apotheosis of Boswell and Boswell's Johnson (which had
begun with Carlyle and Macaulay), was one outlet for hostility to
the fashionable aesthetic attitudes of the 1870s. Another outlet
lay in the criticism of the novel, which at last began on a more
than occasional basis.
   Among the more extreme of the anti-aesthetes was Arnold's
antagonist Frederic Harrison. The leader of the English
Positivists, his artistic heroes were Ruskin and George Eliot.
His essay The Choice of Books (1879) is an attack on the frivolity

and dandyism of the literary world. Choosing a book was a heavy
and weighty responsibility; better that it should be Hume,
Gibbon or Adam Smith than a 'kind-hearted play-book' of the kind
rescued from the dung-heap by Lamb. (67) For a writer such as
George Eliot, he wrote in 1885, science, philosophy and social
ideals were the 'substance' of culture, while the 'graceful form
and the critical judgment' were merely the 'instrument by which
it speaks'. (68) Harrison, however, remained within literary
culture (as George Eliot and Lewes had done), mingling historical
and philosophical studies with collections of critical essays
with titles like 'Among my Books'. A less austere kind of bookmanship is exemplified by George Saintsbury, the most prolific of
the new professors of English. Saintsbury's only diversions from
literary scholarship were in the direction of wine and food.
Though remembered for his breadth of learning and his synoptic
literary histories, he was also a spokesman for scholarly minuteness, defending the study of the 'variations of the position of
a pronoun' against both the Arnoldian 'criticism of life' and the
impressionism of the aesthetes. (69) His study of 'Dryden' (1881)
attempts to restore the idea of literature as a craft, hard work
for the writer and still harder work for the critic, who is
obliged to toil through everything, regardless of its established
reputation, in order to develop a sufficiently catholic view of
poetry. Once he had that, however, he could rest on his intellectual laurels, and feel obliged to go no further. It is all
summed up in the title of his last, elegiac critical book, 'The
Peace of the Augustans: A Study of Eighteenth-Century Literature
as a Place of Rest and Retirement' (1916). Saintsbury's notion
of catholic taste is so clearly aimed at the academic with time
on his hands that he became the symbol of the relaxed, tradi-
tionalist attitude of early twentieth-century English studies;
English as a soft option, a place of sporting refreshment in which
the student, though he might be threatened by a surfeit of books,
would at least never have to think. Though it is not true that
Saintsbury never thought, he was a bookman of the old school in
that he made the thinking look fatally easy. His critical attitude
bears some resemblance to that of Leslie Stephen, though
Stephen's much more incisive and rigorous work demands more
detailed discussion. But first we must consider a critic who
makes a notable exception to the mildly Philistine air of late
Victorian critics of prose. This is Henry James.
    James as a critic began conventionally enough. Two years older
than Saintsbury, he wrote in 1867 of his desire 'to do for our
dear old English letters' something of what Sainte-Beuve had done
for the French. (70) He started as a regular contributor to the
'Nation', the 'North American Review' and the 'Atlantic Monthly',
and the style of the intellectual reviews is reflected in the
spacious, biographical studies collected in 'French Poets and
Novelists' (1878) and 'Partial Portraits' (1888). James's
development as a novelist, however, increasingly moulded his
criticism, culminating in the New York prefaces to his own works
(1907-9) which transmitted the 'lesson of the master' to
posterity. Our concern here is not with the specialist attractions
of the New York prefaces, but with the body of general criticism

in which James speaks both as reader and practitioner. His
achievement lies almost entirely in the discussion of fiction,
especially of French fiction. Consideration of James as a
practitioner-critic might well start from his polemical manifesto
on The Art of Fiction (1884), a reply to a lecture on the same
topic by the popular novelist Walter Besant. James's essay is
written quite explicitly from the 'producer's point of view',
and argues for an imaginative and organic, rather than a merely
commercial attitude to fiction. Criticism must confine itself
to the artist's execution, not his choice of subject-matter (a
rule that James himself seldom followed); nor must it stand in
the way of greater realism. Realism for James, unlike George
Eliot, is a subjective entity. A novel is a personal impression
of life, so that the novelist aims at the 'air of reality (solidity
of specification)', not at the concreteness of the thing itself.
James's famous reply to Besant's golden rule for beginners - 'a
young lady brought up in a quiet country village should avoid
descriptions of garrison life' - is that 'Greater miracles have
been seen than that, imagination assisting, she should speak the
truth about some of these gentlemen.' She must, however, be a
'damsel upon whom nothing is lost'. James's plea for realism
coincided with an increased emphasis on the distinction between
life and art, which Besant's common-sense rules had taken little
account of. Arguing against convention and for open-mindedness,
James declares that the novelist's task is to catch 'the very
note and trick, the strange irregular rhythm of life'. Even this
phrase is not quite what it seems; the 'life' suggested by its
fluttering rhythm is that of consciousness, or of external
events as they might be felt by a contemplative and introspective
observer. From the internal perception or 'impression' to the
transmuting artistic vision is not, it turns out, such a great
step. The rhetoric of 'life itself' in this essay may well have
been useful to later psychological novelists such as Virginia
Woolf. But it all leads back to the 'fine intelligence' of the
writer himself:

> There is one point at which the moral sense and the artistic
> sense lie very near together; that is in the light of the very
> obvious truth that the deepest quality of a work of art will
> always be the quality of the mind of the producer. In propor-
> tion as that intelligence is fine will the novel, the picture,
> the statue partake of the substance of beauty and truth.

'Fine intelligence' is a complex and qualified Jamesian idea.
The writer's intelligence must be nurtured in a rich soil; hence
the importance of the trip to Europe for the American writer.
James's distrust of a purely American literature was expressed in
his study of 'Hawthorne' (1879), where he wrote of the immense
accumulation of tradition and culture that was needed to 'produce
a little literature'. (71) In addition, the novelist's need to
translate his moral sense into artistic terms (James wrote to
H.G. Wells that 'It is art that makes life, makes interest, makes
importance ...', (72) may be met by the representation within the
novel of the viewpoint of the 'fine intelligence' observing and
commenting on life. James's 'fine consciences' are, of course,
partially naive figures, shown up by the surrounding characters and

the narrator's irony. Their presence in his fiction, however,
testifies to his convictions that objective realism is not enough,
and that adequate feeling or realization is the prerogative of
the subtle intelligence. James met his greatest challenge as a
critic where, as in the case of Balzac, he was forced to acknowledge an artistic power that was independent of subtlety or moral
delicacy.

James's criticism of other writers is largely concerned with
the 'quality of mind of the producer'. When we have digested
the expansive, fulsome urbanity of a James critical essay, it
often comes down to a study of the defects of the subject's sensibility. These are revealed as exemplary, or (in Jamesian jargon)
as constituting a 'case'; his criticism becomes a series of case-
histories enquiring into the peculiarities of his rivals and
peers. Thus Maupassant, for example, is unmasked as a wholly
sensual writer, barely getting beyond the visual, sensual and
olfactory aspects of life. The Preface to 'Pierre et Jean', with
its rejection of psychological analysis in favour of a purely
objective record of events, is diagnosed by James as a rationalization of the demands of the author's limited sensibility. There
was little evidence of 'fine intelligence' to be found in
Maupassant; or, for that matter, in Dickens. In his early
review of 'Our Mutual Friend' (1865), James laid down that a
story based upon the elemental passions 'must be told in a spirit
of intellectual superiority to those passions'. (73) He is at
his most involved and rewarding as a critic of writers who, if
not intellectuals, were at least systematizers like Zola and
Balzac. Though he speaks with admiration of Zola's massive
architecture in 'Les Rougon-Macquart', we soon realize that he
regards this as a merely mechanical achievement, a wonder of
the nineteenth century on a par with the Eiffel Tower, the steam-
ship and the railway. Zola, like Maupassant, excelled at the
coarser side of life, and he had also made the mistake of
confiding to James his ambition of writing 'Rome' on the basis
of 'a month or two with "introductions" and a Baedeker'. Zola,
in fact, wallowed in his material 'quite, if I may allow myself
the image, as we zoologically see some mighty animal, a beast of
a corrugated hide and a portentous snout, soaking with joy in
the warm ooze of an African riverside.' (74) (How much abuse
poor Wells has had to bear, for describing James in 'Boon' as
a hippopotamus picking up a pea! But that was not in another
country, and James (unlike Zola) was still alive.) Despite the
human qualities revealed by the Dreyfus affair, James finds
something disreputable in Zola as an artist, which is brought
out in the contrast with Balzac. Where Zola deliberately sought
out 'life', Balzac was overtaken by it. He stands in James's
work as the Shakespearian artist, the primal creator whose fervid
imagination projects a whole world which can stand as a historical
representation of the totality of France in his time. Yet this
is still not enough for James, who believes in a degree of 'art'
or conscious control which Balzac, for all his fascination, lacks.
He wrote a total of six essays on Balzac, and the finest of them
concludes with a note that is almost wistful:

Art is for the mass of us who have only the process of art,

comparatively so stiff. The thing amounts with him to a
kind of shameless, personal, physical, not merely intellectual, duality - the very spirit and secret of trans-
migration. (75)

Against the intellectual process of art is put a naked and
shameless kind of witchcraft.

Art, for James, is life covered up and held at arm's length.
The very expansiveness and rhetorical skill of his critical
essays suggest that he is really portraying himself, sustaining
the bubble of his own creative persona, which is never, it goes
without saying, shameless and physical. Much of his later
criticism suffers from a lack of any precise and explicit method
of analysis; at worst, it seems to express an intelligence
bombinating in a near-vacuum. Yet this criticism is only partially applicable, and least of all to his remarkable essays on
Flaubert. Flaubert presents the 'intellectual case' - a case
which James's essays on him crystallize both in biographical and
structural terms. Though Flaubert is the conscious artist 'par
excellence', the antithesis of the instinctive, unbuttoned English
novelists, James in his 1902 essay accuses 'Madame Bovary' and
'L'Education Sentimentale' of possessing a crucial formal defect,
in the poverty of consciousness of their central characters.
Neither Emma nor Frédéric is sufficiently dignified to bear the
leading part in a major novel. Flaubert's intellectual superiority
over them is not in doubt, but James strongly implies that the
'smallness' of the characters proceeds from a meanness of spirit
in their creator - a meanness which he had found abundantly confirmed in reviewing Flaubert's correspondence nine years earlier.
So, like all the writers James discusses, Flaubert becomes an
object-lesson to be rejected by the moral conscience. James
delivers the verdict in his most ingratiating way, paying his
respects to Flaubert as the 'novelist's novelist' and flattering
his audience with 'Are we not moreover ... pretty well all novelists
now?' The essay exhibits a fascinating combination of the seductive
literary aura that James creates, and the fastidious intelligence
operating within it.

All James's best criticism is concerned with his own artistic
mentors, who are either his contemporaries or the recently dead.
This is why he needs to present them as a series of 'cases'. His
essays on French novelists remain valuable for the completeness
of their survey of what has become a classical tradition. As
the major Victorian sages, poets and novelists died, it became
possible to see Victorianism as a tradition too; but there is
no equivalent to James's achievement here, let alone a 'Lives of
the Poets' or a 'Spirit of the Age'. Perhaps the sheer exhaustive-
ness of public discussion to which writers were subjected precluded
the magisterial overview. Besides, the nineteenth-century critic
had other, and newer obligations: to express his century's
historical consciousness, and to display his qualifications as
scholar and antiquarian. The literary public were not all
novelists, but all bookmen now. The greatest of late Victorian
historical critics was Leslie Stephen, philosopher, agnostic,
editor of the 'Dictionary of National Biography' and author of the
monumental series of critical essays collected in 'Hours in a

Library'. The title speaks of bookishness as surely as does
Harrison's 'Among my Books', and Stephen in fact was torn between
cosy antiquarianism and a bracingly judicial mode of criticism.
He prefaces 'Hours in a Library' with a selection of 'Opinions
of Authors', voicing the consoling solitariness of library
pleasures. He confesses that he loves a book 'pretty much in
proportion as it makes me love the author', (76) and writes
evocatively of hours spent savouring 'a page of Sir Thomas'.
Yet Stephen never indulges the emotions of bookmanship without
quietly deflating them as well:

> One should often stop to appreciate the full flavour of some
> quaint allusion, or lay down the book to follow out some
> diverging line of thought. So read in a retired study, or
> beneath the dusty shelves of an ancient library, a page of
> Sir Thomas seems to revive the echoes as of ancient chants in
> college chapels, strangely blended with the sonorous perorations
> of professors in the neighbouring schools, so that the inter-
> ferences sometimes produce a note of gentle mockery and
> sometimes heighten solemnity by quaintness.
>
>   That, however, is not the spirit in which books are often
> read in these days. (77)

One is reminded that Stephen gave up his Cambridge fellowship for
London, agnosticism and the republic of letters. A passage like
this is remarkable not for self-indulgence but for its 'gentle
mockery' and unobtrusive wit. There are limits to his geniality,
often quite narrow ones, so that it was possible for Q.D. Leavis
to portray him as a stern Cambridge moralist and ancestor of
'Scrutiny'. (78) Stephen himself seems to have been divided in
his aims. He was able to contradict himself over Lamb, for
example, speaking in 1876 of his 'singular excellence' as a
critic who 'only spoke of what he really loved', but then
accusing him five years later of having 'helped to start the
nuisance of "appreciative criticism"'. (79) A man of letters in
the Johnsonian sense, Stephen had no wish to be confused with the
aesthetes who had taken Lamb to themselves in the 1870s. The
rise of aestheticism may have intensified his own considerable
doubts about the value of literary criticism, to which he gave
up so much of his time and talents. His biographer, Noel Annan,
goes so far as to say that he 'despised the whole business' as
trifling beside the concerns of ethics and religion. (80)

'Hours in a Library', nevertheless, manifests the 'scientific
spirit' that he practised in all three of these fields. The
four volumes (with, to a lesser extent, the volumes of 'Studies
of a Biographer') are the nearest thing to a canonical series of
evaluations across the range of English literature that the
Victorian age produced. Their form is that of the periodical
essay devoted to a single author. Though Stephen is less ingratiating and pyrotechnic than most of his contemporaries, his
essays are finely judged for their audience, relaxed, slightly
sardonic and modulating from gossipy biography to scrupulous moral
analysis. There is nothing prophetic or eccentric about his
writing; nothing calculated to give the reader a jolt. The evenness of tone in essay after essay is the result of a deliberate
balancing act. Quite often, we feel, the final verdict could be

reversed, but the method and ethical intelligence glimpsed behind
it would be precisely the same. Stephen's formal sense of the
critic's role is set out in his essay Thoughts on Criticism, by
a Critic (1876), which is mainly concerned with the ethics of
reviewing. Criticism cannot be a science, though it should aim
at a scientific spirit; hence the writing of criticism is a
moral act. Stephen's view differs from Johnson's mainly in being
couched in more ideological terms. The problem for him is to
define 'the sense in which a critic should be liberal'. Liberal-
ism requires a deliberate effort to look from strange points of
view, and also 'a certain modesty in expression and diffidence in
forming opinions'; a non-authoritarian tone. Getting the tone
right, and elaborating a sensibility which is catholic enough to
respond to varying forms of literature, while maintaining a consistent moral standpoint, is his overriding concern.

The sense in which Stephen himself is liberal lies in devising
a mode of moral criticism which is applied to the individual alone.
His hours in the library are spent in scrupulous neutrality
towards doctrinal and social questions. Virtually the only nexus
between art and belief that he allows is that constituted by
individual morality - by judgments of the writer's personal integrity, his 'manliness' and his sensitivity to the world outside him.
Stephen writes on Pope as a Moralist, and on Wordsworth's Ethics.
His method, coupled with his relative insensibility to poetry and
to literary form, seems to reduce literary criticism to the level
of common-sense morality. Thus his virtues of reasonableness and
moderation are themselves the manifestations of an ideology,
which is closely connected with his religious agnosticism. The
analogy between criticism and religious belief is drawn at the
start of his essay on Charlotte Brontë in 'Hours in a Library':

> though criticism cannot boast of being a science, it ought
> to aim at something like a scientific basis, or at least to
> proceed in a scientific spirit. The critic, therefore, before
> abandoning himself to the oratorical impulse, should endeavour
> to classify the phenomena with which he is dealing as calmly
> as if he were ticketing a fossil in a museum. The most glowing
> eulogy, the most bitter denunciation, have their proper place;
> but they belong to the art of persuasion, and form no part of
> scientific method. Our literary, like our religious, creed
> should rest upon a purely rational ground, and be exposed to
> logical tests. Our faith in an author must, in the first
> instance, be the product of instinctive sympathy, instead of
> deliberate reason. It may be propagated by the contagion of
> enthusiasm, and preached with all the fervour of proselytism.
> But when we are seeking to justify our emotions, we must
> endeavour to get for the time into the position of an inde-
> pendent spectator, applying with rigid impartiality such
> methods as are best calculated to free us from the influence
> of personal bias.

In many ways this is an admirable statement. However ardent our
feelings for a writer, their justification should be a matter of
rational argument. Stephen here is directly confronting aesthetic
criticism, since his target is Swinburne's extravagant enthusiasm
for Charlotte Brontë. He goes on to demonstrate in memorable

fashion the provinciality of her art, and the failure of her male
characters in particular; the Brontë gospel has fallen on deaf
ears.   However, if such phrases as 'rigid impartiality' are more
than polemical devices, they sound somewhat chilling, and invite
the retort that 'Jane Eyre' is not - or should not be - a fossil
in a museum. 'Rigid impartiality' is a less humane and less
plausible quality to aim for than 'disinterestedness'; it is
the kind of thing Arnold would have associated with Bishop Colenso.
Stephen should have remembered Johnson. Literary faith is not
just a private affair, and even in the most justified arguments,
impartiality may be a somewhat ludicrous boast.

Stephen's criticism is not merely judicial, however. His
'scientific' liberal outlook led him in his later work to consider
literature as the expression of particular social groups, and not
simply of the moral individual. 'English Literature and Society
in the Eighteenth Century' (1904) is, as Noel Annan says, a 'new
kind of literary study', (81) and one which inaugurates the
'literature and society' approach in twentieth-century criticism.
In this he perhaps looks back to Macaulay, whose famous essay on
Johnson (1831) contained a brilliant general sketch of Augustan
culture. Macaulay both portrays Johnson the man with a Dickensian
vividness, and shows his character as the necessary product of
his environment and early struggles. Stephen lacks both Macaulay's
literary powers and his forensic obsession, but his best historical
essays (that on Pope, for example) are concerned with how the individual of genius is shaped by a particular milieu. The heroism of
the individual man of letters is surrounded with qualifications
in his essays, much as the heroes and heroines are given qualified,
muted roles in major Victorian novels. Stephen's gallery of
individuals in 'Hours in a Library' sums up the tendency of most
of the more pedagogic Victorian criticism. On the one hand,
Carlyle's analysis and prophecy had been vindicated; the men of
letters had indeed become cultural heroes. But though Stephen
holds up his subjects for our admiration, he also shows them as
typical products of their society, manifesting its spiritual
failings and possible mode of redemption. Their historical
environment forms their identity, rather than subjecting it to the
general constraints of human nature, as was the case in
Johnson's 'Lives of the Poets'. In this respect the portrayal
of 'character' in Victorian criticism parallels the achievements
of the Victorian novel, though the one is concerned with the past
and the other with contemporary life. The biographies of the men
of letters might be set against the stories of Pickwick and
Little Dorrit, Lydgate and Adam Bede; none of these strikes us
as an isolated moral agent. The task of the critic, as Stephen
interprets it, is to show how the gallery of classic authors
emerges from social history.

Stephen reflects the ideology of literary culture, but he does
not invariably endorse it. In 'English Literature and Society'
he speaks of literature as 'a kind of by-product', which is not
alone an adequate representation of the moral temper of the
society in which it occurs. His criticism seems to me to fall
short of classical status because of such hesitancies, which also
help to produce his remarkable evenness and consistency of tone.

His indifference to poetry, coupled with his contempt for anything smacking of literary 'effeminacy', is another severe
limitation. Stephen perhaps did not take literature seriously
enough. But he is an entertaining, shrewd and reflective writer
who stands out in his age for his sociological interests, his
Cambridge dryness and precision and the explicitness with which he
moulds his criticism to a liberal and rational ethic.

If Stephen's criticism is the product of Cambridge and London,
Oxford and the provinces at the turn of the century are represented by A.C. Bradley. Bradley left Balliol in 1882, but
returned to Oxford in 1901 as Professor of Poetry after holding
chairs at Liverpool and Glasgow. His 'Shakespearean Tragedy'
(1904) is dedicated 'To My Students' and is the one work of its
period to survive as an irreplaceable student textbook. Largely
this is a tribute to the centrality and meticulous sensitivity
of his readings of Shakespeare's major plays. Bradley's procedure is one of highly detailed, eclectic analysis, bringing
textual scholarship and aesthetic, moral, and psychological
approaches to bear on the text before him. Overarching it all,
however, is the Hegelian outlook he imbibed from his elder brother
F.H. Bradley and from Oxford. His synthesis of aestheticism and
moral analysis is put forward in the lecture Poetry for Poetry's
Sake (1901) and in the postscript to 'Oxford Lectures on Poetry'
(1909). The opposites are reconciled in a sort of kindly hazi-
ness. Though attracted to grand theories of poetry, Bradley
treats these as imaginative metaphors rather than as intellectual
statements demanding systematic confrontation and refutation. He
grants poetry an autonomy of means, but claims that its ends
are the same as those of philosophy and religion. Hence we can
each stay in our separate departments: 'the pursuit of poetry for
its own sake is the pursuit both of truth and goodness.' (82) It
seems a recipe for academic quietism.

That this is an unfair (though hardly an unprecedented) interpretation of Bradley is suggested by certain aspects of 'Shakespearean Tragedy' and by the essay on Wordsworth in 'Oxford
Lectures', which stresses the parallels between the visionary
imagination of 'The Prelude' and German idealist philosophy - an
insight which remained unpursued until the 1960s. L.C. Knights's
attack on Bradley's Shakespearean criticism in How Many Children
Had Lady Macbeth? (1933) is partly aimed at a man of straw.
Bradley, after all, had explicitly described the question of the
Macbeths' fertility as 'quite immaterial'. (83) The unifying
theme of his book is not one of character-biography but of concern
with the nature of the 'tragic' experience and Shakespeare's
response to it. In tragedy, men are brought up against the
universe as a blind and wasteful process; effectively this is
the chaos of meaningless flux as revealed by Huxley, Hardy and
Pater. An attitude of resignation would be the simplest response
to the tragic facts, but after long and earnest consideration of
the problem Bradley suggests that it is to be rejected. The
Shakespearean hero is as much part of the universal process as are
the forces that he confronts. Hence the nobility of the hero and
the survival of goodness must reconcile us to the tragic suffering.
This conclusion is a faintly consoling one, reflecting the

Victorian ethos of masculine duty. Nevertheless, Bradley
suggests that in tragedy we contemplate an ultimate mystery in
life, meriting much deeper consideration than the 'moral profundity' and 'natural magic' of Arnold or the health and manliness
of Stephen. His essay on 'Lear' in particular testifies to the
visionary nature of art and its power to overwhelm conventional
social and intellectual categories. It is as if Bradley is
hesitantly offering in tragedy an alternative to the orthodox
religious view of life. 'Shakespearean Tragedy', in its contemplative way, contains evidence of the survival of the high romantic
attitudes to art which the Victorian republic of letters had
progressively excluded.

'I cannot get it out of my mind that this age of criticism is
about to pass, and an age of imagination, of emotion, of moods,
of revelation, about to come in its place.' The dissenting voice
belongs to W.B. Yeats, writing in 1895. (84) Yeats is the one
critic of the late nineteenth century who stands out in opposition
to Arnold, inheriting a different aspect of the romantic revolution. For where Arnold claimed to speak for the authority of
culture, of literature in its relation to the social establishment,
we can now see that Yeats spoke, as nobody since Wordsworth had
done, with the singular and more absolute authority of the major
poet. His prophetic stance is reflected in every aspect of his
remarkable series of critical essays. With his habit of reminiscence and informal, circumstantial detail, Yeats often seems to
be half talking to himself, setting it down for the record no matter
who hears. But now and then comes a 'Diktat', and this is also
for the record. He does not waste energy in blandishments and
persuasions, as Arnold does; his poetry will carry conviction, or
nothing will. Yeats's prose is solipsistic, but (unlike Pater's)
it is the extrovert solipsism of a man secure in his identity
and proud of gifts that he knows must be reckoned with. At his
best, the result is prophecy, and at worst merely eccentricity -
the eccentricity that later twentieth-century poets such as Auden
have found it necessary to adopt as a social retreat. But Yeats's
Cassandra role is something with which he seems thoroughly content.
    In criticism, as in his poetry, he emerged out of Pre-
Raphaelitism, the aesthetic movement and the 1890s. One point
of emergence is perhaps indicated by a famous passage from the
critical book that he did much to inspire, Arthur Symons's 'The
Symbolist Movement in Literature' (1899):
    Here, then, in this revolt against exteriority, against rhetoric,
    against a materialistic tradition; in this endeavour to dis-
    engage the ultimate essence, the soul, of whatever exists and
    can be realised by the consciousness; in this dutiful waiting
    upon every symbol by which the soul of things can be made
    visible; literature, bowed down by so many burdens, may at
    last attain liberty, and its authentic speech. In attaining
    this liberty, it accepts a heavier burden; for in speaking to
    us so intimately, so solemnly, as only religion had hitherto
    spoken to us, it becomes itself a kind of religion, with all
    the duties and responsibilities of the sacred ritual. (85)

The theme of revolt, the magic word 'symbol' and the suggestion
that literature is as yet unliberated are new, as is the sequence
of poets, de Nerval, de L'Isle-Adam, Rimbaud, Verlaine, Laforgue
and Mallarmé, whom Symons introduced to English readers. When
all this is preparatory to the notion of art as 'sacred ritual',
however, we may feel that we have been here before. Arnold,
after all, had called on literature to take over the responsibi-
lities of religion. But one thing that both Symons and (more
pertinaciously) Yeats try to do is to redeem poetry from the conventions of the established tradition. Their incense, at least,
will be burnt on different altars. Yeats as a critic is far
less tied by the established reputations than, say, Swinburne.
Nor is he bounded by the slightly unctuous tones of Symons.

Yeats had been influenced not only by the decadents but by
William Morris; in addition, he was an Irish poet at a time of
national reawakening. Morris had championed and translated the
'folk-bibles' such as the sagas, and it was Yeats's originality
as a critic to draw connections between these and the 'sacred
books' of the modern symbolists. In his lecture Art under Plutocracy (1883), Morris defined tradition as 'that wonderful, almost
miraculous accumulation of the skill of ages, which men find themselves partakers in without effort on their part.' (86) The
idea of popular art suggested by this is derived from the Gothic
Revivalists, and especially Ruskin. For Yeats, too, tradition
was an 'effortless' acquisition, but its essence lay in folk-
tales and occult beliefs, rather than in the techniques of crafts
such as stonemasonry. The modern poet who studied mythology and
magic could bring himself back into contact with his forebears.
In What is 'Popular Poetry'? (1901), Yeats argued that true
poetry originates in the unwritten tradition of the peasantry,
and is carried on in a developed culture by a few coterie poets
who resist the temptation to make a rhetorical appeal to the
educated public. Such poetry is not direct and simple, as
Wordsworth thought, but 'strange and obscure', though immediately
comprehensible to those who have retained the folk 'mother-wit'.
It is at the furthest possible extreme from the 'Kitsch' served
out to the disinherited middle classes. Though a palpable
rationalization, like most such theories, this goes beyond
Wordsworth and Morris to stress that poetic origins lie in the
once universal faculty of visionary, magical understanding. Yeats
believed that criticism should be instinctive and 'hieratic',
and that the modern artist must be aware that 'it is what is old
and far off that stirs us the most deeply.' (87) His aim was to
write a 'sacred book' tapping these ancient sources, as previous
poets of educated culture had done. Thus he found the essence
of literature in a mythopoeic, rather than a lyrical or a moral
tradition. Belief in a mythopoeic tradition implies that poetry
is more deeply rooted than modern society, standing over it with
a prophetic, demonic power. Yet Yeats's examination of the
tradition in his essays on Shelley, Spenser and Blake is undeniably
rather bland. He follows Rossetti and Swinburne in recognizing
the importance of Blake, the one English romantic poet who
remained unassimilated by Arnoldian 'culture'. But it is the
fact of Blake's being a visionary, rather than the particular

details of the vision, which seem to move him. If he had paid
more attention to the details, Yeats could not have presented
Blake as an ancestral mage, lifted above place and time. As it
is, he can speak calmly of 'Blake's anger against causes and
purposes he but half-understood' as the necessary madness of one
who 'half lives in eternity'. (88) It seems more important to
use him as the occasion of a mystic thrill than to understand,
or even to sympathize with, Blake's anger. There is little that
is alarming or subversive about Blake in Yeats's account;
progression, in fact, without contraries. Yet in his early
essays he was seeking to enlist Blake and the other visionary
poets in a crusade to reassert the place of imagination in life,
and to arrest the 'slow dying of men's hearts'. (89)

'We are but critics, or but half create', he wrote in 'Ego
Dominus Tuus'. It might have been expected that, when the social
mission to which he dedicated himself in Ireland was overtaken by
events, criticism would lose its importance for him. Once he had
developed his own mythological system, what need could he have
for it? In fact, Yeats's continuing output of prose suggests that
his system was more of an intellectual construct than he liked to
admit; but only a small proportion of the later prose is criticism
in any normal sense. An important exception should be made for
his speculations on tragedy. Tragedy, he wrote, is a 'drowner of
dykes', a 'confounder of understanding' and in watching it 'we
feel our minds expand convulsively or spread out slowly like some
moon-brightened image-crowded sea.' (90) But tragedy for Yeats
was a lesser thing than for Bradley because it had its appointed
place in the cycles of history. He could fit his own colleagues
of the 1890s into that scheme as the 'Tragic Generation' - the
title of a brilliant autobiographical essay (1922), exploiting a
framework which is altogether too neat and deterministic.
Ireland's bitter road to independence was also fitted into the
tragic scheme, but the sense of tradition to which the later Yeats
appealed was not one in which the Irish peasantry figured very
prominently. It may be that the last stanza of 'Coole Parke and
Ballylee, 1931' constitutes his farewell to the ideal of the 'book
of the people' -

    We were the last romantics - chose for theme
    Traditional sanctity and loveliness;
    Whatever's written in what poets name
    The book of the people; ...

- even though 'mounted in that saddle Homer rode'. From his
eclectic later references to the art of Japan, of Byzantium, of
'ancestral houses' and the Quattrocento one could perhaps draw a
new theory of art as the by-product of aristocratic energy and
violence; but these are the subject-matter of his major poetry,
and not of a body of criticism.

Yeats loved to represent himself and his friends as a doomed
generation, the last romantics, which they were not. One of his
successors was Joyce; the romantic myth of the artist as priest
of the eternal imagination is recaptured in all its fervour by
Stephen Dedalus. Joyce deserves mention here for another reason;
there are times when his fiction turns into a final wake over the
corpse of Victorian criticism. His early work is a culmination of

aestheticism. The presentation of Stephen's aesthetic theory
fulfils Wilde's notion of the critic as artist, while every one
of Joyce's works meets Yeats's prescription for a 'sacred book',
becoming at once more strange and obscure, and more destructive
of the other-worldly aesthetic ideal as we move through 'Ulysses'
to 'Finnegans Wake'. In the Library chapter of 'Ulysses',
however, Stephen abandons aesthetic abstractions for the world
of the bookmen, steeping himself in the Shakespeare-biography
that was one of the main literary industries of the late nineteenth
century. Based on details cribbed from Dowden, Brandes, Sidney
Lee and others, Stephen's interpretation of Hamlet seems to repeat
all the worst excesses of the biographical approach. Yet what it
does, in the relentless process of Joycean parody, is to repeat
them to the point of philosophical absurdity. The simple pattern
that Stephen traces (the pattern of cuckoldry) turns up in so
many features of Shakespeare's works that it must lead to a view
of artistic creation, not so much as 'myriad-minded' but as anonymous and automatic. It cannot have been Shakespeare, but some
psychic urge or cosmic trickster working through him, which
produced an 'oeuvre' that was so transparently obsessive. As a
theory of Shakespeare this is absurd, and is meant to be, but as
a theory of Joyce's own writing it both hits the target and
destroys that target, since the author is both on exhibition
throughout his works, and laughing mockingly at his own manifestations. Thus the comfortable Victorian assumptions about the
author's personality hidden behind the work are frustrated, and
perhaps untenable. Individual human responsibility was concealed
or evaded, and the literary values which had rested upon it now
had to be reinterpreted. In modern criticism, the poem and not
its author becomes the guarantor of culture and source of its
power of prophecy.

Yeats spent a good deal of his life in public libraries, while
the literature on Joyce's literary borrowings itself fills a
good number of library shelves. Both authors lived the life of
the bookman, and both inherited the romantic tradition of the
artist. They are great writers partly because they took that
tradition out of the Victorian world, and remade it for the
twentieth century. The remaking was also a destruction. Yeats's
poem 'The Circus Animals' Desertion' might be read as, among other
things, an allegory of the end of Victorian art. The 'old songs',
the images and 'painted stage' to which he has given his life
represent the world of literature, enchanted, 'disinterested' and
cut off from life; but it is all an artifice, a lie which the
poet can no longer sustain:

> Now that my ladder's gone,
> I must lie down where all the ladders start,
> In the foul rag-and-bone shop of the heart.

The idea that that might make supreme poetry is one for which we
might look in vain in the Victorian age. Joyce's dismissal of
Victorian culture, in the Library chapter of 'Ulysses', could not
be on a more different plane. But here, quite explicitly, it is
a whole literary ethos which is rejected when Stephen, after the
fiasco of his Shakespeare lecture, redeems himself in the company
of a man whose visit to the Library was spent in checking an

advertisement and peering up the backsides of Greek statues.
Stephen's audience of 'AE', John Eglinton, Buck Mulligan and the
Quaker librarian might indeed have been intended as the last
gathering of nineteenth-century literary intellectuals: 1904 seen
through the eyes of 1919.

POSTSCRIPT

'Honest criticism and sensitive appreciation is directed not upon
the poet but upon the poetry.' (1) T.S. Eliot's theory of the
impersonality of great poetry may be taken as the starting-point
for the critical revolution which took place in the 1920s.
Eliot's essays form a bridge between the modern movement in
literature and the arts, with its stresses on abstraction, discontinuity and the disruption of humanist assumptions, and the
new methods of professionalized poetic analysis pioneered by
critics whom he deeply influenced. In England there was no conscious alliance between modernism and academic criticism, although
in America the founders of New Criticism were John Crowe Ransom
and Allen Tate, two poets. But these two forces together did
their best to kill off what was left of Victorian literary culture.

This culture was a strangely sheltered one. Although we think
of irony, nihilism and the use of art as an anti-bourgeois
weapon as typically modern, such attitudes had been current in
Europe since the mid-nineteenth century. Flaubert and Baudelaire
were read in England, but their ironies were little understood and
their sense of social alienation met with little sympathy. The
crisis of identity revealed in Matthew Arnold's poetry was also
'modern', but his way of resolving it was, by and large, a ratifi-
cation of Victorian society. Forty years later, Joyce's denizens
of the National Library are aware of Mallarmé, Wilde, Gustave
Moreau and the 'new Viennese school' - but this does little to
disturb the atmosphere of provincial bookmanship and gentility.

The Great War came, and with it the rejection of what Pound
called a 'botched civilization'. Millions had to die, among other
things,
    For two gross of broken statues,
    For a few thousand battered books
                    ('Hugh Selwyn Mauberley').
There is an echo here of the shell-torn cities, as in Eliot's
'These fragments I have shored against my ruins'. Out of this
crisis, however, Eliot, and later Leavis, emerged as critics with
a mission to reaffirm the authority of culture. Their prophetic
voices, Delphic in Eliot's case, evangelical in Leavis's, identify
them as the heirs of the nineteenth century. Eliot appealed to

the 'mind of Europe', an impersonal, classical tradition mysteri-
ously extended to incorporate the 'rock drawing of the Magdalenian
draughtsmen', which had just been discovered. (2)   Leavis appealed
to the richness of 'life' and the creative force inherent in the
English language.   Each sought to exercise a kind of cultural
dominance, through fiat and exhortation, through the editorship
of literary reviews, and through criticism impressed throughout
with the stamp of a masterful personality.

It is in the literary autocracy asserted by Eliot and Leavis
that we may find, to use Pater's term, a 'strange second flowering'
of the romantic and Victorian tradition.   Their influence reached
its peak during the 1950s, at a time of conservatism and political
retrenchment in Britain.   Eliot's death in 1965 marks the date
at which it became clear that their dominance had passed.   It
now seems unlikely that, as cultural critics, they will survive
for posterity with the force that Wordsworth and Arnold have long
possessed.   Leavis's criticism especially suffered from the strain
of asserting the absolute hegemony of a literary culture whose
social existence he felt to be incurably impotent and weak.   He
has always known where the enemy lay, to the point where he saw
whole reaches of intellectual life as harbouring a monstrous
'trahison des clercs'.   But as Leavis's despair has deepened, so
has his following diminished.   Like Ruskin in his old age, he can
still find any number of inquisitive listeners, but can no longer
command a chosen people.

Literary criticism today is commonly described as 'pluralistic'.
The term was coined by the Chicago critics, the first of the
purely academic modern critical schools.   The significance of
'pluralism', to my mind, is that the critic no longer cares or
perhaps knows how to assume an intrinsic cultural authority - a
general authority, that is, beyond his particular area of expertise.   This is the strength and weakness of most present-day
criticism.   On the credit side, the consciously pluralist critic
is committed to the obligations of rationality, and especially to
the idea of demonstration and not of mere assertion.   But against
this, great numbers of academic critics and scholars have become
what Kuhn calls 'normal scientists' working within frames of
reference which are taken utterly for granted.   There is no lack
of writers to point this out;   but are they 'pluralists'?   The
pluralist's greatest enemy might well be the reformer.

Pluralism, however, is not just a stance of the modern academic.
It has its roots in attitudes to art and culture going back to
Paterian aestheticism.   The modernists proclaimed that the whole
of culture was simultaneously present;   all was available, none
was inherited or prescribed.   In a sense, 'The Cantos' and
'Finnegans Wake' are pluralist books.   They say to the reader
'Take me or leave me'.   In criticism the most subtle and resource-
ful advocate of pluralist attitudes has been William Empson.   In
'Seven Types of Ambiguity' (1930), after his dazzling, simultaneous
presentation of texts from Shakespeare to Max Beerbohm, Empson
confides that 'The object of life, after all, is not to understand
things, but to maintain one's defences and equilibrium and live
as well as one can.' (3)   This is the ultimate, clinical
justification of his radically pragmatist methods.   But the later

Empson has become (without philosophical self-contradiction) a
bluff professor who says of 'Eng. Lit.' that 'with periodic
sanitary efforts it can probably be got to continue in a sturdy,
placid way, as is needed.' (4) Perhaps what all forms of
pluralism have in common is an air of professional self-
satisfaction - though at best this is only a mask - which again
has its antecedents in Pater.

   Today there are many signs that literary criticism is becoming
a more technical discipline, more remote from ordinary language
and at the same time less able to generate its own concepts. The
new culture in which we live is dominated by the rise of the
social sciences. There is, however, a fundamental difference
between the 'politicization' of criticism - a process which is
implicit in literary culture, at least from the romantics onwards -
and its absorption into social science. The intellectual tradition
studied in this book may be seen as a search for a unifying source
of cultural authority in great literature. Whatever the distortions to which this leads, they are not necessarily corrected
by searching instead for a unifying theory of cultural structure.
In studying the development of English criticism we become aware
of the bankruptcy of many customary, inherited assumptions about
literature. Today's widespread borrowing from other disciplines
must seem a necessary development. The historical strength of
English criticism lay, however, in a quite different affiliation:
that to the primary creative process. Today the split between
creator and critic has never seemed wider. It is hard to be
objective about this. Complaints about it are frequent; they
invariably come from novelists and poets and tend to sound shrill
or priggish or merely wistful. What can be said is that in the
absence of a new 'Aristotelian' synthesis in the social sciences -
or even in its presence - the next revolution in criticism will
probably also be a revolution in literary creation, and the new
voices of authority may once again be those of the authors themselves.

NOTES

(Many of the critical essays discussed in this book are well known and relatively brief. Often they are available in various modern editions and anthologies. Where this is the case, page references or references to a particular edition have been omitted.)

INTRODUCTION

1 See J.W.H. Atkins, 'Literary Criticism in Antiquity', Cambridge, 1934, vol. 1, pp. 11ff.
2 T.S. Eliot, Imperfect Critics in 'The Sacred Wood' (1920).
3 Paul Feyerabend, Consolations for the Specialist in 'Criticism and the Growth of Knowledge', ed Imre Lakatos and Alan Musgrave, Cambridge, 1970, pp. 197ff. See also the contributions of Kuhn and Lakatos to the same volume.

CHAPTER 1 SAMUEL JOHNSON: THE ACADEMY AND THE MARKET-PLACE

1 R.S. Crane, English Neoclassical Criticism: An Outline Sketch, in 'Critics and Criticism Ancient and Modern', ed R.S. Crane, Chicago, 1952, pp. 372ff.; and On Writing the History of Criticism in England 1650-1800, in 'The Idea of the Humanities', Chicago, 1967, pp. 157ff.
2 W.J. Bate, 'The Burden of the Past and the English Poet', London, 1971, pp. 16ff.
3 René Wellek, 'The Rise of English Literary History', New York, 1966, pp. 35-6.
4 Johnson, Life of Dryden.
5 There are more serious grounds for the equivocating Augustan attitude to Shakespeare. A great work of art in the heyday of neoclassicism existed less as an uplifting cultural monument than as a model to be copied. Shakespeare seemed a highly misleading model for the very reason that the possibility of imitating him was still there. Poetic drama still held the stage; it did not yet need to be revived in the poet's study out of piety towards a vanished heroic age.

6   George Watson, 'The Literary Critics', Harmondsworth, 1962,
    pp. 43-4.
7   Addison, 'Spectator' no. 409 (19 June 1712).
8   Reported by Spence in the last year of Pope's life. This is
    mentioned by Ian Jack, 'Augustan Satire', Oxford, 1966, p. 5.
9   See the notes to the text in the 'Yale Edition of the Works
    of Samuel Johnson', New Haven, 1963, vol. 2, pp. 185ff.
10 Johnson, 'Idler' no. 76 (29 September 1759).
11 There are many anecdotes of this, particularly in Mrs Thrale's
    memoir reprinted in 'Johnsonian Miscellanies', ed G. Birkbeck
    Hill, Oxford, 1897, vol. 1, pp. 141ff.
12 Boswell, 'Life of Johnson', Oxford, 1953, p. 939. See also
    p. 798.
13 See Paul Fussell, 'Samuel Johnson and the Life of Writing',
    London, 1972, pp. 183ff.
14 Johnson, Preface to 'A Dictionary of the English Language',
    London, 1755.
15 Johnson, 'Idler' no. 66 (21 July 1759).
16 See Johnson, 'Rambler' nos 156 and 158 for classic statements
    of this.
17 Burke, 'A Philosophical Enquiry into ... the Sublime and
    Beautiful', 5th edn, London, 1767, p. 91.
18 Raymond Williams, 'Culture and Society 1780-1950', London,
    1958, Introduction.
19 The phrase is from Fussell, op. cit.
20 Johnson, 'Rambler' no. 93 (5 February 1751).
21 Hume, Of the Standard of Taste in 'Philosophical Works',
    Edinburgh, 1826, vol. 3, p. 263.
22 Johnson, 'Rambler', nos 2 (24 March 1750) and 106 (23 March
    1751).
23 Johnson, journal entry for 2 April 1779, in 'Yale Edition',
    vol. 1 p. 294.
24 Boswell, 'Life', p. 442.
25 Johnson, 'Rambler' no. 208 (14 March 1752) and 'Preface to
    Shakespeare' respectively.

CHAPTER 2 WILLIAM WORDSWORTH: THE POET AS PROPHET

1   Johann Peter Eckermann, 'Conversations with Goethe', trans.
    John Oxenford, London, 1930, p. 32. The passage is quoted in
    Bate, 'The Burden of the Past and the English Poet', p. 6.
2   Flaubert, 'Selected Letters', ed Francis Steegmuller, London,
    1954, p. 94.
3   Cf. M.H. Abrams, 'The Mirror and the Lamp', New York, 1958,
    pp. 240ff.
4   Johnson demonstrated how much he stood apart from this cult
    when he defined the sublime (in the Life of Cowley) as a mode
    of rational statement ('Great thoughts are always general ...').
    Yet there is also his startling choice of a passage from
    Congreve's 'The Mourning Bride' as 'the most poetical para-
    graph' in English poetry (Life of Congreve). The passage -
    a surpassingly Gothic description in which the observer is
    struck successively by 'fear', 'dread', 'awe', 'terror',

'chilness' and 'fright' - is intended to give precisely that
thrill of sublimity which popular taste designated as the
quintessentially poetical. For a full discussion of Johnson's
attitude to the sublime, see Geoffrey Tillotson, Imlac and
the Business of a Poet, in 'Studies in Criticism and Aesthetics
1660-1800', ed Howard Anderson and John S. Shea, Minneapolis,
1967, pp. 296ff.

5 Joan Pittock, 'The Ascendancy of Taste', London, 1973, p. 65.
6 René Wellek, 'The Rise of English Literary History', New
York, 1966, pp. 70ff.
7 Cf. Lawrence Lipking, 'The Ordering of the Arts in Eighteenth-
Century England', Princeton, 1970, p. 11.
8 Quoted in Pittock, op. cit., p. 175.
9 Hume, Of the Rise and Progress of the Arts and Sciences in
'Philosophical Works', Edinburgh, 1826, vol. 3, p. 154.
10 E.g. Stephen A. Larrabee, 'English Bards and Grecian Marbles',
New York, 1943, p. 119. Larrabee argues that 'Blake accepted
the Platonic elements of Neo-classical theory.'
11 See Stephen Gill, The Original 'Salisbury Plain', in
'Bicentenary Wordsworth Studies', ed Jonathan Wordsworth,
Ithaca, New York, 1970, pp. 142ff., for a text of this poem.
12 See E.P. Thompson, Disenchantment or Default? A Lay Sermon,
in 'Power and Consciousness', ed Conor Cruise O'Brien and
William Dean Vanech, London, 1969, pp. 149ff. I am grateful
to Mr Kelvin Everest for drawing my attention to this article.
13 Hazlitt, On the Living Poets in 'Lectures on the English
Poets'.
14 See W.J.B. Owen, 'Wordsworth as Critic', Toronto and London,
1969, pp. 112-13.
15 Owen, op. cit., p. 12.
16 Coleridge, 'Biographia Literaria', chapter 18.
17 'An original may be said to be of a vegetable nature; it
rises spontaneously from the vital root of genius; it grows,
it is not made: Imitations are often a sort of manufacture
wrought up by those mechanics, art, and labour, out of pre-
existent materials not their own' (Conjectures on Original
Composition).
18 See Raymond Williams, 'Culture and Society 1780-1950',
Harmondsworth, 1961, especially pp. 48ff.
19 Wordsworth, Preface to 'The Excursion'.
20 Owen, op. cit., p. 151.
21 Lamb, review of 'The Excursion' in 'Quarterly Review' (1814),
reprinted in 'Lamb's Criticism', ed E.M.W. Tillyard,
Cambridge, 1923, p. 106.
22 Shelley, 'Defence of Poetry', and de Quincey, 'Reminiscences
of the English Lake Poets', ed John E. Jordan, London, 1961,
p. 99.
23 De Quincey, Letters to a Young Man ..., in 'Works', Edinburgh,
1863, vol. 13, p. 55. De Quincey's distinction was first put
forward in 1823 and elaborated in several other places. See
especially the essays on Wordsworth (1839), Goldsmith (1848)
and Pope (1848).
24 It was the utilitarians, however, who played a major part in
the establishment of the study of literature in the

universities. The irony of this has been noted by D.J. Palmer, 'The Rise of English Studies', London, 1965, p. 15. See also chapter 4 below.

CHAPTER 3   THE ROMANTIC CRITICS

1   Table-talk, recorded by T. Allsop, in 'Coleridge: Select Poetry and Prose', ed Stephen Potter, London, 1962, p. 476.
2   'The Poetical Works of Lord Byron', London, 1945, p. 910.
3   Hazlitt, Mr Jeffrey in 'The Spirit of the Age'.
4   J.O. Hayden, 'Romantic Bards and British Reviewers', London, 1971, p. ix.
5   Coleridge, 'Biographia Literaria', ed George Watson, London, 1956, p. 34. (Hereafter as 'Biog. Lit.')
6   For discussion of this episode, see 'Coleridge's Shakespearean Criticism', ed Thomas Middleton Raysor, London, 1930, vol. I, p. xxxi. (Hereafter as 'Shak. Crit.'); and Norman Fruman, 'Coleridge: The Damaged Archangel', London, 1972, pp. 141ff.
7   'Shak. Crit.', vol. 2, p. 260n.
8   A.W. Schlegel, 'A Course of Lectures of Dramatic Art and Literature', trans. John Black, London, 1846, p. 343.
9   Hazlitt, 'Complete Works', ed. P.P. Howe, London, 1931-3, vol. 6, p. 176.
10   'Shak. Crit.', vol. 1, p. 140.
11   John Gross, 'The Rise and Fall of the Man of Letters', Harmondsworth, 1973, p. 23.
12   'Shak. Crit.', vol. 1, p. 200; 'Biog. Lit.', p. 169.
13   'Shak. Crit.', vol. 1, p. 129.
14   Schlegel, op. cit., pp. 38ff.
15   Introduction to 'Jeffrey's Literary Criticism', ed D. Nichol Smith, London, 1910, p. xxi.
16   De Quincey, 'Reminiscences of the English Lake Poets', ed John E. Jordan, London, 1961, pp. 172 and 173.
17   See the testimony of Kathleen Coburn, in her I.A.R. and S.T.C., in 'I.A. Richards: Essays in His Honor', ed Reuben Brower, Helen Vendler and John Hollander, New York, 1973, pp. 237ff.
18   I.A. Richards, 'Coleridge on Imagination', London, 1934, p. 72.
19   See John Colmer, 'Coleridge: Critic of Society', Oxford, 1959, pp. 52ff, for an account of Coleridge at this period.
20   Quoted by George Whalley, The Integrity of 'Biographia Literaria', 'Essays and Studies' 6 n.s., 1953, pp. 87ff.
21   Letter to Robert Southey, in Coleridge, 'Select Poetry and Prose', p. 728.
22   'Biog. Lit.', pp. xiiff.
23   See M.H. Abrams, 'Natural Supernaturalism', London, 1971, pp. 236ff.
24   'Biog. Lit.', p. 88.
25   For discussions of Schelling, Coleridge and pantheism, see J. Shawcross's Introduction to his edition of 'Biographia Literaria', London, 1907; J.A. Appleyard, 'Coleridge's Philosophy of Literature', Cambridge, Mass., 1965, p. 205; and Thomas McFarland, 'Coleridge and the Pantheist Tradition', Oxford, 1969, which provides an exhaustive treatment of the

whole question. For the religious tensions in Coleridge's
life and work as a whole, see William Empson's Introduction
to 'Coleridge's Verse: A Selection', ed William Empson and
David Pirie, London, 1972.

26 McFarland, op. cit., p. 127.
27 J.R. de J. Jackson, 'Method and Imagination in Coleridge's
Criticism', London, 1969, p. 115. For the orthodox view, see
Shawcross, op. cit., p. lxvii.
28 McFarland, op. cit., p. 308.
29 'Biog. Lit.', p. 179. The reader may compare the discussions
by Shawcross, Appleyard and Jackson cited above.
30 Letter to Southey, in Coleridge, 'Select Poetry and Prose',
p. 729.
31 See his lecture On the Relation of the Plastic Arts to Nature,
reprinted as an appendix to Herbert Read, 'The True Voice of
Feeling', London, 1968.
32 An even more explicit statement may be found in the (slightly
garbled) report of the third lecture of the 1811-12 course,
in which Coleridge is quoted as follows:

> He would even venture to give the definition of poetry as
> being That which, from the always present, though always
> conscious idea that it is poetry in the mind of the
> reader, allows a greater attention to each particular part
> of a composition the greater power of giving pleasure and
> attracting attention from each part than would be permitted
> in ordinary language or ordinary writing, though writing a
> fiction. And the great rule by which poetry is to be
> judged is the balance between them: Is there more pleasure
> in the particular lines than is consistent with the whole?
> Is the sense of totality injured, or not injured, by the
> splendour of particular passages? For the great object of
> the poet must be to produce the great total effect ('Shak.
> Crit.', vol. 2, p. 79).

The origins of Coleridge's association of metre with the
pleasures of attention may be seen by comparing his various
statements with the 1800 Preface, and especially with
Wordsworth's discussion of the effects of pathos in Shakespeare
and Richardson.
33 Coleridge uses 'genial' as a synonym for 'creative'. Hence
the 'genial criticism' at which he aims ('Biog. Lit.', p. 149)
is perhaps that which 'furnishes a torch of guidance ... to
the poet himself' (ibid., p. 51).
34 'Biog. Lit.', p. 182.
35 'Biog. Lit.', p. 213.
36 Cf. Fruman, op. cit., pp. 199ff.
37 Quoted in Hayden, op. cit., p. 171.
38 'Biog. Lit.', p. 197.
39 'Biog. Lit.', p. 257. On The Thorn, see pp. 194 and 202.
40 Ibid., p. 251.
41 Wordsworth (in the Essay Supplementary), Hazlitt and Keats
were hard on his heels.
42 'Biog. Lit.', p. 180.
43 'Shak. Crit.', vol. 1, pp. 32-3.
44 'Shak. Crit.', vol. 2, p. 171.

45 'Shak. Crit.', vol. 1, p. 91.
46 'Shak. Crit.', vol. 1, p. 136.
47 Shawcross, op. cit., p. lxxiii.
48 Quoted by Jackson, op. cit., p. 149.
49 Coleridge, 'The Friend', ed Barbara E. Rooke, London, 1969, vol. 1, p. 507.
50 Coleridge, 'Miscellanies, Aesthetic and Literary', ed T. Ashe, London, 1892, p. 6.
51 'The Letters of John Keats', ed Maurice Buxton Forman, Oxford, 1935, p. 52.
52 Ibid., p. 31.
53 Ibid., p. 384.
54 Quoted in 'Peacock's Four Ages of Poetry, Shelley's Defence of Poetry, Browning's Essay on Shelley', ed H.F.B. Brett-Smith, Oxford, 1921, p. xiii.
55 See J. Bronowski, 'The Poet's Defence', Cambridge, 1939, p. 82, for an interesting examination of this point.
56 Hazlitt, 'A Letter to William Gifford, Esq.' in 'Complete Works', vol. 9, p. 50.
57 Hazlitt, 'Complete Works', vol. 16, p. 137.
58 Ibid, vol. 16, p. 268.
59 Ibid, vol. 19, p. 18.
60 Ibid, vol. 18, p. 101.
61 For Hazlitt's derivation of this idea, see his essay Schlegel on the Drama, 'Complete Works', vol. 16, pp. 62-4.
62 On Keats and Hazlitt, see Ian Jack, 'Keats and the Mirror of Art', Oxford, 1967; Stephen A. Larrabee, 'English Poets and Grecian Marbles', New York, 1943, pp. 223ff.; and Kenneth Muir, Keats and Hazlitt in 'John Keats: A Reassessment', ed Muir, Liverpool, 1958, pp. 139ff.
63 Jack, op. cit., p. 72.
64 Hazlitt, On Poetry in General in 'Lectures on the English Poets'.
65 Hazlitt, 'Complete Works', vol. 6, p. 49.
66 Hazlitt, On Criticism in 'Complete Works', vol. 8, p. 217.
67 Lamb, 'Specimens of English Dramatic Poets', London, n.d., p. 158n.
68 Coleridge, To the Author of 'The Robbers', in 'Coleridge's Verse: A Selection', ed. William Empson and David Pirie, London, 1972, p. 101. The poem was probably written in 1795.
69 Hazlitt, 'Complete Works', vol. 6, p. 301.

CHAPTER 4 VICTORIAN CRITICISM: THE REPUBLIC OF LETTERS

1 Present System of Education, in 'Westminster Review' 4, 1825, p. 166. See also 2, 1824, pp. 334ff.
2 Belles Lettres, in 'Westminster Review' 34, 1868, p. 259.
3 Carlyle, Voltaire, in 'Critical and Miscellaneous Essays', London, 1899, vol. 2.
4 Carlyle, Goethe, in ibid., vol. 1.
5 Quoted in 'Mill's Essays on Literature and Society', ed J.B. Schneewind, New York, 1965, pp. 351-2.
6 Ibid., p. 407.

7   Newman, 'On the Scope and Nature of University Education',
    Everyman edn, London, 1915, p. 82.
8   Carlyle, The Hero as Man of Letters, in 'Sartor Resartus and
    on Heroes', Everyman edn, London, 1908, p. 384.
9   Carlyle, Burns, in 'Critical and Miscellaneous Essays',
    vol. 2.
10 Hallam, review in the 'Englishman's Magazine' (1831),
    reprinted in 'Tennyson: The Critical Heritage', ed John D.
    Jump, London, 1967, p. 41.
11 Mill, What is Poetry? in 'Essays on Literature and Society',
    ed. cit., p. 109.
12 Ibid., p. 122.
13 I.A. Richards, 'Science and Poetry', London, 1926, p. 59.
14 Saintsbury, 'A History of English Criticism', Edinburgh, 1936,
    p. 452.
15 On Dallas, see Alba H. Warren, Jr, 'English Poetic Theory
    1825-1865', Princeton, 1950, pp. 129ff.
16 Ruskin, Of the received Opinions touching the 'Grand Style',
    in 'Modern Painters', vol. 3.
17 Harold Bloom, 'The Ringers in the Tower', Chicago, 1971, p. 174.
18 Marx and Engels, 'The German Ideology', quoted in 'On
    Literature and Art', ed Lee Baxandall and Stefan Morawski,
    New York, 1974, p. 71.
19 Morris, 'Collected Works', ed May Morris, London, 1914, vol. 22,
    p. 132.
20 Cf. E.P. Thompson, 'William Morris: From Romantic to
    Revolutionary', London, 1955, p. 768.
21 See the discussions by Patrick Brantlinger, 'News from
    Nowhere': Morris's Socialist Anti-Novel, in 'Victorian
    Studies', 19, 1975, pp. 35ff., and in my article, 'News from
    Nowhere', 'The Time Machine' and the Break-Up of Classical
    Realism, in 'Science-Fiction Studies', 10, 1976.
22 Reprinted in 'Essays, Letters and Reviews by Matthew Arnold',
    ed Fraser Neiman, Cambridge, Mass., 1960, p. 199.
23 On this question see Lionel Trilling, 'Matthew Arnold', London,
    1949, pp. 158 and 160.
24 Quoted in John Holloway, 'The Victorian Sage', New York,
    1965, p. 202.
25 For a discussion of this link see B.C. Southam, 'A Student's
    Guide to the Selected Poems of T.S. Eliot', London, 1968, p. 37.
26 On 'Middlemarch', see my article The Look of Sympathy, in
    'Novel', 5, 1972, pp. 146-7.
27 Tillotson, 'Criticism and the Nineteenth Century', London,
    1951, p. 52.
28 Quoted in Trilling, op. cit., p. 157.
29 'The Poems of Matthew Arnold 1840-1867', London, 1913, p. 9.
30 Holloway, op. cit., p. 222.
31 Trilling, op. cit., p. 161.
32 'Literary Criticism of George Henry Lewes', ed Alice R.
    Kaminsky, Lincoln, Nebraska, 1964, p. 62.
33 Francis W. Newman, Homeric Translation in Theory and Practice,
    in Matthew Arnold, 'Essays Literary and Critical', Everyman
    edn, London, 1906, p. 312.
34 Saintsbury, 'Matthew Arnold', Edinburgh, 1911, p. 67.

35 From the first section of 'On Translating Homer': '"The poet", says Mr Ruskin, "has to speak of the earth in sadness; but he will not let that sadness affect or change his thought of it. No; though Castor and Pollux be dead, yet the earth is our mother still, - fruitful, life-giving." This is a just specimen of that sort of application of modern sentiment to the ancients, against which a student, who wishes to feel the ancients truly, cannot too resolutely defend himself. It reminds one, as alas! so much of Mr Ruskin's writing reminds one, of those words of the most delicate of living critics: "Comme tout genre de composition a son écueil particulier, celui du genre romanesque, c'est le faux."' When one considers this in its context, it is Arnold, not Ruskin, who is per-petuating a fraud.
36 See Ruskin, 'Modern Painters', vol. 3, chapter 8.
37 T.S. Eliot, The Perfect Critic, in 'The Sacred Wood'.
38 Marx and Engels, op. cit., p. 117.
39 Arnold, 'Complete Prose Works', ed R.H. Super, Ann Arbor, 1960- , vol. 3, pp. 40ff.
40 Arnold, Joubert, in 'Essays in Criticism', London, 1865.
41 On Arnold and the Sainte-Beuve circle, see Christophe Campos, 'The View of France: From Arnold to Bloomsbury', London, 1965, p. 16.
42 Frederic Harrison, 'Tennyson, Ruskin, Mill and Other Literary Estimates', London, 1899, pp. 132-2. Harrison's Culture: A Dialogue was reprinted in 'The Choice of Books', London, 1917, pp. 97ff.
43 The first part was, in fact, originally called 'Culture and Its Enemies'.
44 Trilling, op. cit., pp. 277ff.
45 Quoted by Trilling, op. cit., p. 278.
46 On this point see Trilling, op. cit., pp. 259ff.
47 E.g. Arnold's denunciation of 'the hideous anarchy which is modern English literature' in Tractatus Theologico-Politicus, 'Complete Prose Works', vol. 3, p. 64.
48 Trilling, op. cit., p. 375.
49 A.C. Bradley, 'Oxford Lectures on Poetry', London, 1909, p. 127; Bloom, op. cit., pp. 19-20.
50 T.S. Eliot, The Function of Criticism, in 'Selected Essays'.
51 Quotations from Pater's essay Coleridge's Writings are from the text reprinted in 'English Critical Essays: Nineteenth Century', ed Edmund D. Jones, London, 1971, pp. 421ff.
52 Pater, Preface to 'The Renaissance'.
53 On this point see Anthony Ward, 'Walter Pater: The Idea in Nature', London, 1966, p. 194.
54 Poems by William Morris, in 'Westminster Review', 34, 1868, pp. 300-1.
55 On Pater and the Hegelians see Ward, op. cit., pp. 43ff.
56 Cf. Ian Fletcher, 'Walter Pater', London, 1971, p. 29.
57 Cf. Bernard Bergonzi, 'The Turn of a Century', London, 1973, p. 21.
58 Clyde K. Hyder, 'Swinburne as Critic', London, 1972, p. xi.
59 Ibid., p. 115.
60 Ibid., p. 75.

61 Reprinted in 'Pre-Raphaelite Writing', ed Derek Stanford, London, 1973, p. 163.
62 Swinburne, John Webster, in Hyder, op. cit., pp. 286ff.
63 Ibid., p. 308.
64 Wilde, The Critic as Artist, in 'Intentions', London, 1945, p. 111.
65 Ibid., p. 160.
66 Pater, Postscript to 'Appreciations', London, 1927, p. 271.
67 Harrison, 'The Choice of Books', London, 1917, p. 6.
68 Ibid., p. 212.
69 Saintsbury, 'Dryden', London, 1912, p. 31.
70 James, 'Letters', ed Leon Edel, London, 1975, vol. 1, p. 76.
71 James, 'Hawthorne', ed Tony Tanner, London, 1967, p. 23.
72 'Henry James and H.G. Wells', ed Leon Edel and Gordon N. Ray, London, 1958, p. 267.
73 James, 'Selected Literary Criticism', ed Morris Shapira, London, 1963, p. 10.
74 James, Emile Zola, 1903, in ibid., p. 258.
75 James, Honoré de Balzac, 1902, in ibid., p. 211.
76 Stephen, Sterne, in 'Hours in a Library', London, 1892, vol. 3, p. 139.
77 Stephen, Sir Thomas Browne, in ibid., vol. 1, pp. 297-8.
78 Q.D. Leavis, Leslie Stephen: Cambridge Critic, 1939, reprinted in 'A Selection from Scrutiny', ed F.R. Leavis, Cambridge, 1968, vol. 1, pp. 22ff.
79 Thoughts on Criticism by a Critic, 1876, reprinted in Stephen, 'Men, Books and Mountains', ed S.O.A. Ullmann, London, 1956, p. 68.
80 Noel Annan, 'Leslie Stephen', London, 1951, p. 276.
81 Ibid., p. 271.
82 Bradley, 'Oxford Lectures on Poetry', p. 395.
83 Bradley, 'Shakespearean Tragedy', London, 1974, p. 421. For a recent view of the Knights-Bradley controversy see J.M. Newton, 'Scrutiny''s Failure with Shakespeare, in 'Cambridge Quarterly', 1, 1966, pp. 144ff.
84 Yeats, 'Essays and Introductions', London, 1961, p. 197.
85 Symons, 'The Symbolist Movement in Literature', London, 1908, pp. 8-9.
86 Morris, 'Collected Works', ed May Morris, London, 1914, vol. 23, p. 167.
87 Yeats, op. cit., p. 289.
88 Ibid., p. 128.
89 Ibid., p. 162.
90 Ibid., p. 245.

POSTSCRIPT

1 T.S. Eliot, Tradition and the Individual Talent in 'Selected Essays'.
2 Ibid.
3 Empson, 'Seven Types of Ambiguity', Harmondsworth, 1961, p. 247.
4 Quoted by C.H. Page, Professor Empson's 'Sanitary Efforts': Part I, in 'Delta', 49, 1971, p. 28.

SELECT BIBLIOGRAPHY

1 GENERAL HISTORIES OF CRITICISM AND LITERARY CULTURE

ALTICK, RICHARD D., 'The English Common Reader', Chicago
University Press, 1957.
GROSS, JOHN, 'The Rise and Fall of the Man of Letters', Harmonds-
worth, Penguin, 1973.
SAINTSBURY, GEORGE, 'A History of Criticism and Literary Taste
in Europe', 3 vols, Edinburgh, Blackwood, 1900-4. The English
chapters of this were later published separately as 'A History of
English Criticism', Edinburgh, Blackwood, 1936.
WATSON, GEORGE, 'The Literary Critics', Harmondsworth, Penguin,
1962.
WELLEK, RENÉ, 'A History of Modern Criticism 1750-1950', 4 vols,
London, Cape, 1955-66.
WILLIAMS, RAYMOND, 'Culture and Society 1780-1950', Harmondsworth,
Penguin, 1961.
WIMSATT, W.K. and BROOKS, CLEANTH, 'Literary Criticism: A Short
History', New York, Knopf, 1957.

2 THE EIGHTEENTH CENTURY

(a) General Studies

ANDERSON, HOWARD and SHEA, JOHN S. (eds), 'Studies in Criticism
and Aesthetics 1660-1800', Minneapolis, Minnesota University
Press, 1967.
ATKINS, J.W.H., 'English Literary Criticism: Seventeenth and
Eighteenth Centuries', London, Methuen, 1966.
BATE, WALTER JACKSON, 'From Classic to Romantic', New York,
Harper, 1961.
BATE, WALTER JACKSON, 'The Burden of the Past and the English
Poet', London, Chatto & Windus, 1971.
BELJAME, ALEXANDRE, 'Men of Letters and the English Public in the
Eighteenth Century', ed Bonamy Dobrée, London, Kegan Paul, 1948.
CLIFFORD, JAMES (ed), 'Eighteenth-Century English Literature: Modern
Essays in Criticism', London, Oxford University Press, 1959.

CRANE, R.S., English Neoclassical Criticism: An Outline Sketch,
in 'Critics and Criticism Ancient and Modern', ed R.S. Crane,
University of Chicago Press, 1952, pp. 372ff.
CRANE, R.S., On Writing the History of Criticism in England 1650-
1800, in 'The Idea of the Humanities', University of Chicago
Press, 1967, pp. 157ff.
GAY, PETER, 'The Enlightenment: An Interpretation', 2 vols,
London, Weidenfeld & Nicolson, 1967-70.
JACK, IAN, 'Augustan Satire', Oxford, Clarendon Press, 1966.
LIPKING, LAWRENCE, 'The Ordering of the Arts in Eighteenth-Century
England', Princeton University Press, 1970.
PITTOCK, JOAN, 'The Ascendancy of Taste', London, Routledge &
Kegan Paul, 1973.
ROGERS, PAT, 'Grub Street', London, Methuen, 1972.
WELLEK, RENE, 'The Rise of English Literary History', New York,
McGraw-Hill, 1966.

(b)   Anthologies

JONES, EDMUND D. (ed), 'English Critical Essays: Sixteenth,
Seventeenth and Eighteenth Centuries', London, Oxford University
Press, 1922.
NICHOL SMITH, D. (ed), 'Shakespeare Criticism: A Selection',
London, Oxford University Press, 1916.

(c)   Individual critics: modern editions and commentaries

ADDISON, JOSEPH, 'Critical Essays from the Spectator', ed Donald
    F. Bond, Oxford, Clarendon Press, 1970.
    'The Spectator', ed G. Gregory Smith, 4 vols, London, Dent,
    1907.
BLAKE, WILLIAM, 'Complete Writings', ed Geoffrey Keynes, London,
    Oxford University Press, 1966.
DRYDEN, JOHN, 'Of Dramatic Poesy and Other Critical Essays', ed
    George Watson, 2 vols, London, Dent, 1962.
    'Selected Criticism', ed James Kinsley and George Parfitt,
    Oxford, Clarendon Press, 1970.
JOHNSON, SAMUEL, 'Yale Edition of the Works of Samuel Johnson',
    New Haven, Yale University Press, 1958- (in progress).
    'Johnsonian Miscellanies', ed G. Birkbeck Hill, 2 vols, Oxford,
    Clarendon Press, 1897.
    'Lives of the English Poets', ed G. Birkbeck Hill, 2 vols,
    Oxford, Clarendon Press, 1905.
    'Johnson as Critic', ed John Wain, London, Routledge & Kegan
    Paul, 1973.
    BOSWELL, JAMES, 'Life of Johnson', London, Oxford University
    Press, 1953.
    BRONSON, BERTRAND H., 'Johnson Agonistes and Other Essays',
    Berkeley and Los Angeles, California University Press, 1965.
    FUSSELL, PAUL, 'Samuel Johnson and the Life of Writing', London,
    Chatto & Windus, 1972.

HAGSTRUM, JEAN H., 'Samuel Johnson's Literary Criticism',
    University of Chicago Press, 1967.
HODGART, M.J.C., 'Samuel Johnson and his Times', London,
    Batsford, 1962.
KEAST, W.R., The Theoretical Foundations of Johnson's Criticism,
    in 'Critics and Criticism Ancient and Modern', ed R.S. Crane,
    University of Chicago Press, 1952.
LEAVIS, F.R., Johnson as Critic, in 'Anna Karenina and Other
    Essays', London, Chatto & Windus, 1967.
STOCKDALE, PERCIVAL, 'Lectures on the Truly Eminent English
    Poets', 2 vols, London, 1807.
'Memoirs of the Extraordinary Life, Works and Discoveries of
    Martinus Scriblerus', ed Charles Kerby-Miller, New York, Russell
    & Russell, 1966.
REYNOLDS, Sir Joshua, 'Discourses on Art', ed Robert R. Wark, San
    Marino, Calif., Huntington Library, 1959.
RYMER, THOMAS, 'Critical Works', ed Curt A. Zimansky, New Haven,
    Yale University Press, 1956.
YOUNG, EDWARD, 'Conjectures on Original Composition', ed Edith
    J. Morley, Manchester University Press, 1918.

3   THE ROMANTIC PERIOD

(a)   General Studies

ABRAMS, M.H. 'The Mirror and the Lamp: Romantic Theory and the
Critical Tradition', New York, Norton, 1958.
ABRAMS, M.H., 'Natural Supernaturalism', London, Oxford University
Press, 1971.
BRONOWSKI, J. 'The Poet's Defence', Cambridge University Press,
1939.
FRYE, NORTHROP (ed.), 'Romanticism Reconsidered', New York and
London, Columbia University Press, 1963.
HILLES, FREDERICK and BLOOM, HAROLD (eds), 'From Sensibility to
Romanticism', New York, Oxford University Press, 1965.
HOBSBAWM, E.J., 'The Age of Revolution', London, Weidenfeld &
Nicolson, 1962.
HOUGH, GRAHAM, 'The Romantic Poets', London, Hutchinson, 1953.
LARRABEE, STEPHEN A., 'English Bards and Grecian Marbles', New
York, Columbia University Press, 1943.
READ, HERBERT, 'The True Voice of Feeling', London, Faber, 1968.
THOMPSON, E.P., 'The Making of the English Working Class',
Harmondsworth, Penguin, 1968.

(b)   Anthologies

BRETT-SMITH, H.F.B. (ed.), 'Peacock's "Four Ages of Poetry",
Shelley's "Defence of Poetry", Browning's Essay on Shelley',
Oxford, Blackwell, 1921.
HAYDEN, JOHN O. (ed.), 'Romantic Bards and British Reviewers',
London, Routledge & Kegan Paul, 1971.

JONES, EDMUND D. (ed.), 'English Critical Essays: Nineteenth
Century', London, Oxford University Press, 1971.
STEVENSON, E. (ed), 'Early Reviews of Great Writers', London,
Walter Scott, n.d.

(c) Individual critics: modern editions and commentaries

COLERIDGE, S.T., 'Collected Works', London, Routledge & Kegan Paul,
    1971- (in progress).
    'Biographia Literaria', ed J. Shawcross, 2 vols, London, Oxford
    University Press, 1907.
    'Biographia Literaria', ed George Watson, London, Dent, 1956.
    'Coleridge's Miscellaneous Criticism', ed T.M. Raysor, London,
    Constable, 1936.
    'Coleridge's Shakespearean Criticism', ed T.M. Raysor, 2 vols,
    London, Constable, 1930.
    'Coleridge on Shakespeare', ed R.A. Foakes, London, Routledge
    & Kegan Paul, 1971.
    'On the Constitution of the Church and State', ed John Barrell,
    London, Dent, 1972.
    'Coleridge's Verse: A Selection', ed William Empson and
    David Pirie, London, Faber, 1972.
    'Inquiring Spirit', ed Kathleen Coburn, London, Routledge &
    Kegan Paul, 1951.
    'Select Poetry and Prose', ed Stephen Potter, London, Nonesuch,
    1962.
    'Miscellanies, Aesthetic and Literary', ed T. Ashe, London,
    Bell, 1892.
APPLEYARD, J.A., 'Coleridge's Philosophy of Literature',
Cambridge, Mass., Harvard University Press, 1965.
BADAWI, M.M., 'Coleridge: Critic of Shakespeare', Cambridge
University Press, 1973.
BRETT, R.L. (ed.), 'S.T. Coleridge', London, Bell, 1971.
COLMER, JOHN, 'Coleridge: Critic of Society', Oxford, Clarendon
Press, 1959.
FRUMAN, NORMAN, 'Coleridge: The Damaged Archangel', London,
Allen & Unwin, 1972.
HARTMAN, GEOFFREY H. (ed.), 'New Perspectives on Coleridge and
Wordsworth', New York and London, Columbia University Press,
1972.
HOUSE, HUMPHRY, 'Coleridge', London, Hart-Davis, 1953.
JACKSON, J.R. de J., 'Method and Imagination in Coleridge's
Criticism', London, Routledge & Kegan Paul, 1969.
LEAVIS, F.R., Coleridge in Criticism, in 'A Selection from
Scrutiny', ed F.R. Leavis, Cambridge University Press, 1968,
vol. 1, pp. 268ff.
McFARLAND, THOMAS, 'Coleridge and the Pantheist Tradition',
Oxford, Clarendon Press, 1969.
McFARLAND, THOMAS, Coleridge's Plagiarisms Once More, 'Yale
Review' 63, 1972, pp. 252ff.
RICHARDS, I.A., 'Coleridge on Imagination', London, Kegan Paul,
1934.

WHALLEY, GEORGE, The Integrity of 'Biographia Literaria', in
'Essays and Studies', 6 n.s., 1953, pp. 87ff.
HAZLITT, WILLIAM, 'Complete Works', ed P.P. Howe, 21 vols,
London, Dent, 1920-4.
'Lectures on the English Poets and The Spirit of the Age',
London, Dent, 1910.
'Selected Essays', ed Geoffrey Keynes, London, Nonesuch, 1930.
'Selected Writings', ed Christopher Salvesen, New York, Signet,
1972.
'Winterslow: Essays and Characters Written There', collected
by his son, London, David Bogue, 1850.
PARK, ROY, 'Hazlitt and the Spirit of the Age', Oxford, Clarendon
Press, 1971.
JEFFREY, FRANCIS, 'Jeffrey's Literary Criticism', ed D. Nichol
Smith, London, Henry Froude, 1910.
KEATS, JOHN, 'Letters', ed M. Buxton Forman, London, Oxford
University Press, 1935.
JACK, IAN, 'Keats and the Mirror of Art', Oxford, Clarendon
Press, 1967.
MUIR, Kenneth (ed.), 'John Keats: A Reassessment', Liverpool
University Press, 1958.
LAMB, CHARLES, 'Lamb's Criticism', ed E.M.W. Tillyard, Cambridge
University Press, 1923.
DE QUINCEY, THOMAS, 'De Quincey as Critic', ed John E. Jordan,
London, Routledge & Kegan Paul, 1973.
'De Quincey's Literary Criticism', ed H. Darbishire, London,
Henry Froude, 1909.
'Reminiscences of the English Lake Poets', ed John E. Jordan,
London, Dent, 1961.
JORDAN, JOHN E., 'Thomas de Quincey, Literary Critic',
Berkeley and Los Angeles, California University Press, 1952.
WORDSWORTH, WILLIAM, 'Prose Works', ed W.J.B. Owen and Jane
Worthington Smyser, 3 vols, Oxford, Clarendon Press, 1973.
'Literary Criticism', ed Paul M. Zall, Lincoln, Nebraska
University Press, 1966.
'Lyrical Ballads', ed H. Littledale, London, Oxford University
Press, 1911.
'Lyrical Ballads', ed R.L. Brett and A.R. Jones, London,
Methuen, 1968.
JONES, ALUN R. and TYDEMAN, WILLIAM (eds), 'Lyrical Ballads:
A Casebook', London, Macmillan, 1972.
KIERNAN, V.G., Wordsworth and the People, in 'Democracy and
the Labour Movement', ed John Saville, London, Lawrence &
Wishart, 1954.
MAYO, R., The Contemporaneity of 'Lyrical Ballads', 'PMLA',
69, 1954, pp. 486ff.
OWEN, W.J.B., 'Wordsworth as Critic', Toronto and London,
Toronto University Press, 1969.
PARRISH, S.M., The Wordsworth-Coleridge Controversy, 'PMLA',
73, 1958, pp. 367ff.
STEMPEL, DANIEL, Revelation on Mount Snowdon, in 'Journal of
Aesthetics', 29, 1971, pp. 371ff.
THOMPSON, E.P., Disenchantment or Default? A Lay Sermon, in
'Power and Consciousness', ed Conor Cruise O'Brien and William
Dean Vanech, London University Press, 1969, pp. 149ff.

WORDSWORTH, Jonathan (ed.), 'Bicentenary Wordsworth Studies',
Ithaca, New York, Cornell University Press, 1970.

4   THE VICTORIAN PERIOD

(a)   Bibliography

DELAURA, DAVID J. (ed.), 'Victorian Prose: A Guide to Research',
New York, MLA, 1973.

(b)   General Studies

BERGONZI, BERNARD, 'The Turn of a Century', London, Macmillan, 1973.
BUCKLEY, JEROME HAMILTON, 'The Victorian Temper: A Study in
Literary Culture', London, Cass, 1966.
CAMPOS, CHRISTOPHE, 'The View of France: From Arnold to Bloomsbury',
London, Oxford University Press, 1965.
DELAURA, DAVID J., 'Hebrew and Hellene in Victorian England', Austin
and London, Texas University Press, 1969.
EVERETT, EDWIN MALLARD, 'The Party of Humanity: The "Fortnightly
Review" and Its Contributors', New York, Russell & Russell, 1971.
GRAHAM, KENNETH, 'English Criticism of the Novel 1865-1900', Oxford,
Clarendon Press, 1965.
HOLLOWAY, JOHN, 'The Victorian Sage', New York, Norton, 1965.
HOUGH, GRAHAM, 'The Last Romantics', London, Duckworth, 1949.
HOUGHTON, WALTER E., 'The Victorian Frame of Mind 1830-1870', New
Haven and London, Yale University Press, 1957.
KERMODE, FRANK, 'Romantic Image', London, Collins, 1971.
LEVINE, GEORGE and MADDEN, WILLIAM (eds), 'The Art of Victorian
Prose', New York, Oxford University Press, 1968.
NESBITT, GEORGE L., 'Benthamite Reviewing', New York, Columbia
University Press, 1934.
PALMER, D.J., 'The Rise of English Studies', London, Oxford
University Press, 1965.
POTTER, STEPHEN, 'The Muse in Chains', London, Cape, 1937.
SCHOENBAUM, S., 'Shakespeare's Lives', Oxford, Clarendon Press,
1970.
TILLOTSON, GEOFFREY, 'Criticism and the Nineteenth Century', London,
Athlone Press, 1951.
WARREN, ALBA H., JR, 'English Poetic Theory 1825-1865', Princeton
University Press, 1950.
WATSON, GEORGE, 'The English Ideology', London, Allen Lane, 1973.

(c)   Anthologies

JONES, EDMUND D. (ed.), 'English Critical Essays: Nineteenth
Century', London, Oxford University Press, 1971.
STANFORD, DEREK (ed.), 'Writing of the Nineties', London, Dent,
1971.
STANFORD, DEREK (ed.), 'Pre-Raphaelite Writing', London, Dent,
1973.

(d) Individual critics: modern editions and commentaries

ARNOLD, MATTHEW, 'Complete Prose Works', ed R.H. Super, Ann
    Arbor, Michigan University Press, 1962- (in progress).
    'Essays in Criticism', London, Dent, 1964.
    'Essays Literary and Critical', London, Dent, 1906.
    'Essays, Letters and Reviews', ed Fraser Neiman, Cambridge,
    Mass., Harvard University Press, 1960.
    'Poetry and Prose', ed John Bryson, London, Hart-Davis, 1954.
    'Selected Criticism', ed Christopher Ricks, New York, Signet,
    1972.
    ALEXANDER, EDWARD, 'Matthew Arnold and John Stuart Mill',
    London, Routledge & Kegan Paul, 1965.
    ELIOT, T.S., Arnold and Pater, in 'Selected Essays', London,
    Faber, 1951, pp. 431ff.
    HARRISON, FREDERIC, Culture: A Dialogue, in 'The Choice of
    Books', London, 1886.
    LEAVIS, F.R., Arnold as Critic, in 'A Selection from Scrutiny',
    ed F.R. Leavis, Cambridge University Press, 1968, vol. 1,
    pp. 268ff.
    SAINTSBURY, GEORGE, 'Matthew Arnold', Edinburgh, Blackwood,
    1911.
    TRILLING, LIONEL, 'Matthew Arnold', London, Allen & Unwin,
    1955.
BAGEHOT, WALTER, 'Selected Essays', London, Nelson, n.d.
BRADLEY, A.C., 'Shakespearean Tragedy', London, Macmillan, 1974.
    COOKE, KATHARINE, 'A.C. Bradley and his influence on Twentieth-
    Century Shakespeare Criticism', Oxford, Clarendon Press, 1972.
CARLYLE, THOMAS, 'Critical and Miscellaneous Essays', 5 vols,
    London, Chapman & Hall, 1899.
    'Sartor Resartus and On Heroes', London, Dent, 1908.
HALLAM, A.H., Review of Tennyson's 'Poems, Chiefly Lyrical', in
    'Tennyson: The Critical Heritage', ed John D. Jump, London,
    Routledge & Kegan Paul, 1967, pp. 34ff.
HUXLEY, T.H., 'Collected Essays', 9 vols, London, Macmillan,
    1893-5.
JAMES, HENRY, 'The Art of the Novel', ed R.P. Blackmur, New York,
    Scribner, 1950.
    'Hawthorne', ed Tony Tanner, London, Macmillan, 1967.
    'Henry James and H.G. Wells', ed Leon Edel and Gordon N. Ray,
    London, Hart-Davis, 1958.
    'Literary Reviews and Essays', ed Albert Mordell, New York,
    Grove Press, 1957.
    'Selected Literary Criticism', ed Morris Shapira, London,
    Heinemann, 1963.
    GOODE, JOHN, The art of fiction: Walter Besant and Henry James,
    in 'Tradition and Tolerance in Nineteenth-Century Fiction',
    ed John Goode, David Howard and John Lucas, London, Routledge
    & Kegan Paul, 1966, pp. 243ff.
    ROBERTS, MORRIS, 'Henry James's Criticism', New York, Haskell
    House, 1965.
JOHNSON, LIONEL, 'Post Liminium: Essays and Critical Papers',
    ed Thomas Whittemore, London, Elkin Mathews, 1911.

LEWES, G.H., 'Literary Criticism of George Henry Lewes', ed
    Alice R. Kaminsky, Lincoln, Nebraska University Press, 1964.
    KAMINSKY, ALICE R., 'George Henry Lewes as Literary Critic',
    New York, Syracuse University Press, 1968.
MACAULAY, T.B., 'Critical and Historical Essays', ed A.J. Grieve,
    2 vols, London, Dent, 1963.
MARX, Karl and ENGELS, FREDERICK, 'On Literature and Art', ed
    Lee Baxandall and Stefan Morawski, New York, International
    General, 1974.
    DEMETZ, PETER, 'Marx, Engels and the Poets', University of
    Chicago Press, 1967.
MILL, J.S., 'Mill on Bentham and Coleridge', ed F.R. Leavis,
    London, Chatto, 1950.
    'Mill's Essays on Literature and Society', ed J.B. Schneewind,
    New York, Collier, 1965.
    ROBSON, JOHN M., J.S. Mill's Theory of Poetry, in 'Mill: A
    Collection of Critical Essays', ed J.B. Schneewind, Garden
    City, N.Y., Anchor Books, 1968.
MORRIS, WILLIAM, 'Collected Works', ed May Morris, 24 vols,
    London, Longmans, 1910-15.
    THOMPSON, E.P., 'William Morris: From Romantic to Revolu-
    tionary', London, Lawrence & Wishart, 1955.
NEWMAN, J.H., 'On the Scope and Nature of University Education',
    London, Dent, 1965.
    Poetry with reference to Aristotle's Poetics, in 'English
    Critical Essays: Nineteenth Century', ed Edmund D. Jones,
    London, Oxford University Press, 1971.
PATER, WALTER, 'Works', 9 vols, London, Macmillan, 1900-1.
    Coleridge's Writings, in 'English Critical Essays: Nineteenth
    Century', ed Edmund D. Jones, London, Oxford University Press,
    1971.
    'Essays on Literature and Art', ed Jennifer Uglow, London,
    Dent, 1974.
    'The Renaissance', intro. by Louis Kronenberger, New York,
    Mentor, 1959.
    FLETCHER, IAN, 'Walter Pater', London, Longmans for the British
    Council, 1971.
    WARD, ANTHONY, 'Walter Pater: The Idea in Nature', London,
    MacGibbon & Kee, 1966.
PUGIN, A.W.N., 'Contrasts', ed H.-R. Hitchcock, Leicester University
    Press, 1969.
RUSKIN, John, 'Complete Works', ed Sir E.T. Cook and A.D.O.
    Wedderburn, 39 vols, London, George Allen, 1902-12.
    'The Genius of John Ruskin', ed John D. Rosenberg, London,
    Allen & Unwin, 1964.
    'Literary Criticism of John Ruskin', ed Harold Bloom, Garden
    City, New York, Anchor Books, 1965.
    'Selected Prose', ed Matthew Hodgart, New York, Signet, 1972.
STEPHEN, SIR LESLIE, 'Collected Essays', 10 vols, London,
    Duckworth, 1907.
    'English Literature and Society in the Eighteenth Century',
    London, Duckworth, 1955.
    'Men, Books and Mountains: Essays', ed S.O.A. Ullmann, London,
    Hogarth Press, 1956.

ANNAN, Noel Gilroy, 'Leslie Stephen', London, MacGibbon & Kee, 1951.
LEAVIS, Q.D., Leslie Stephen: Cambridge Critic, in 'A Selection from Scrutiny', ed F.R. Leavis, Cambridge University Press, 1968, vol. 1, pp. 22ff.
MACCARTHY, DESMOND, 'Leslie Stephen', Cambridge University Press, 1937.
ZINK, David D., 'Leslie Stephen', New York, Twayne, 1972.
SWINBURNE, A.C., 'Complete Works', ed Sir E. Gosse and T.J. Wise, 20 vols, London, Heinemann, 1925-7.
'Swinburne as Critic', ed Clyde K. Hyder, London, Routledge & Kegan Paul, 1972.
PETERS, ROBERT L., 'The Crowns of Apollo: Swinburne's Principles of Literature and Art', Detroit, Wayne State University Press, 1965.
SYMONS, ARTHUR, 'The Symbolist Movement in Literature', intro. by Richard Ellmann, New York, Dutton, 1958.
WILDE, OSCAR, 'The Artist as Critic', ed Richard Ellmann, London, W.H. Allen, 1970.
'A Critic in Pall Mall', ed E.V. Lucas, London, Methuen, 1919.
'Intentions', London, Unicorn Press, 1945.
YEATS, W.B., 'Autobiographies', London, Macmillan, 1955.
'Essays and Introductions', London, Macmillan, 1961.

5 CONTEMPORARY CRITICISM AND CULTURE

(The following selection of books and articles in this area has been made for its bearing on the problem of seeing criticism in historical perspective.)

ANDERSON, PERRY, Components of the National Culture, in 'Student Power', ed Alexander Cockburn and Robin Blackburn, Harmondsworth, Penguin, 1969, pp. 214ff.
BARTHES, ROLAND, 'Writing Degree Zero', London, Cape, 1967.
CASEY, JOHN, 'The Language of Criticism', London, Methuen, 1966.
CAUDWELL, Christopher, 'Illusion and Reality', London, Lawrence & Wishart, 1973.
'Contemporary Criticism', Stratford-upon-Avon Studies no 12, London, Edward Arnold, 1970.
CRANE, R.S. (ed), 'Critics and Criticism Ancient and Modern', University of Chicago Press, 1952.
CREWS, FREDERICK, Do Literary Studies have an Ideology? in 'PMLA', 85, 1970, pp. 423ff.
ELIOT, T.S., 'The Sacred Wood', London, Methuen, 1920.
ELIOT, T.S., 'Selected Essays', London, Faber, 1951.
FOUCAULT, MICHEL, 'The Order of Things', London, Tavistock, 1970.
FRYE, NORTHROP, 'The Stubborn Structure', London, Methuen, 1970.
HOUGH, GRAHAM, 'The Dream and the Task', London, Duckworth, 1963.
JAMESON, FREDRIC, 'Marxism and Form', Princeton University Press, 1971.
JAMESON, FREDRIC, Metacommentary, in 'PMLA', 86, 1971, pp. 9ff.
KUHN, THOMAS S., 'The Structure of Scientific Revolutions', University of Chicago Press, 1962.

LAKATOS, IMRE and MUSGRAVE, ALAN (eds), 'Criticism and the Growth of Knowledge', Cambridge University Press, 1970.
LEAVIS, F.R., 'Education and the University', London, Chatto & Windus, 1948.
LERNER, LAWRENCE, 'The Truest Poetry', London, Hamish Hamilton, 1960.
MANNHEIM, KARL, 'Ideology and Utopia', London, Routledge & Kegan Paul, 1954.
MARCUSE, HERBERT, 'Negations', London, Allen Lane, 1968.
SONTAG, SUSAN, 'Against Interpretation', New York, Noonday Press, 1966.
SPENDER, STEPHEN, 'The Struggle of the Modern', London, Methuen, 1965.
WELLEK, RENÉ and WARREN, AUSTIN, 'Theory of Literature', London, Cape, 1949.
WILLIAMS, RAYMOND, 'The Long Revolution', London, Chatto & Windus, 1961.

INDEX OF AUTHORS
AND CRITICS CITED